PHILOSOPHERS AND KINGS:
EDUCATION FOR LEADERSHIP
IN MODERN ENGLAND

καὶ δεῖ δὴ τὴν παιδείαν μηδαμοῦ ἀτιμάζειν, ὡς
πρῶτον τῶν καλλίστων τοῖς ἀρίστοις ἀνδράσι
παραγιγνόμενον· καὶ εἴ ποτε ἐξέρχεται
δυνατὸν δ' ἐστὶν ἐπανορθοῦσθαι, τοῦτ' ἀεὶ
δραστέον διὰ βίου παντὶ κατὰ δύναμιν.

Plato, *Laws*, 644.

Nowhere must we hold education in dishonour, for with the
noblest of men it ranks foremost among blessings. If ever
it leaves its proper path and can be restored to it again,
to this end everyone should always labour throughout life
with all his powers.

The Norwood report (1943), title-page: Platonic sentiments in the original Greek

PHILOSOPHERS AND KINGS:
EDUCATION FOR LEADERSHIP
IN MODERN ENGLAND

GARY McCULLOCH

*Senior Lecturer in Education at the
University of Auckland*

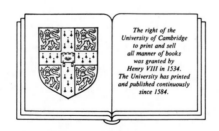

The right of the
University of Cambridge
to print and sell
all manner of books
was granted by
Henry VIII in 1534.
The University has printed
and published continuously
since 1584.

CAMBRIDGE UNIVERSITY PRESS

CAMBRIDGE

NEW YORK   PORT CHESTER   MELBOURNE   SYDNEY

Published by the Press Syndicate of the University of Cambridge
The Pitt Building, Trumpington Street, Cambridge CB2 IRP
40 West 20th Street, New York, NY 10011, USA
10 Stamford Road, Oakleigh, Melbourne 3166, Australia

First published 1991

Printed in Great Britain at the University Press, Cambridge

British Library cataloguing in publication data
McCulloch, Gary
Philosophers and kings: education for leadership in modern England.
1. England. Education, history. Social aspects
1. Title
370.190942

Library of Congress cataloguing in publication data
McCulloch, Gary.
Philosophers and kings: education for leadership in modern
England / Gary McCulloch.
p.   cm.
Includes bibliographical references.
ISBN 0 521 39175 X
1. Education, Secondary – Social aspects – Great Britain – History.
I. Title.
LA634.M29   1990
370.19'0942 – dc20   89-78220 CIP

ISBN 0 521 39175 X

FOR MY PARENTS

CONTENTS

ILLUSTRATIONS

PREFACE AND ACKNOWLEDGEMENTS

Of all books relating to education, the most frequently discussed must surely be Plato's *Republic*. Of all educational institutions, the nineteenth-century English public school has a strong claim to be considered the most widely known, admired and attacked. This book examines the impact and influence of these two great sources of darkness and light in twentieth-century England. It does so by focusing upon the theme that was central to both: education for leadership. It shows how the classic 'English tradition' of the nineteenth century has been revised and adapted in various ways in twentieth-century secondary education. And it argues that the decline of this tradition especially in the last thirty years has given way not to social equality, but to an individualistic, competitive materialism – a trend that is the antithesis of what the public schools and indeed the modern comprehensives were meant to stand for.

This book is essentially a study in the social history of education. As should be the case with all educational history, it is about the relationships between education and the many other dimensions of social change; ideas, ideology, culture, religion, science, technology, industry, labour. It stresses continuity, but seeks to illuminate change, novelty, and decay. The book is designed to be suitable for students of education, history and contemporary society, and also offers new research perspectives for advanced students and researchers.

The current work is the second in what I like to see as a trilogy of books concerned with the 'tripartite' dimensions of English secondary education in the twentieth century. The first (*The Secondary Technical School: A Usable Past?*, Falmer Press, 1989) focuses on the technical tradition with special reference to the secondary technical schools of the postwar period. I hope eventually to complete the set with a book on working-class secondary schooling, especially as provided in the secondary modern schools.

Many debts have been incurred in the writing of this book. In particular, I should like to thank the University of Auckland, New Zealand, for granting me research leave in England to complete the research and preparation for the book. My colleagues and students in the Education Department have helped in their various ways to stimulate new insights and shape my interests and aims. I must also thank the School of Education at the University of Leeds for its hospitality during my stay in England. Staff at the Brotherton Library at the University of Leeds, the Modern Records Centre at the University of Warwick, the University of Auckland Library and several other academic institutions have been unfailingly helpful and courteous in helping my research. This is also my opportunity to thank Mr John Bosanko, Miss Sarah Canning, Sir Christopher Hartley, Mrs Celia Strachey and the Confederation of British Industry for permission to consult archives in their care, and Lord James for his hospitality and assistance (details in footnotes and bibliography). Thanks also to Peter Cunningham, Donald Leinster-Mackay and the members of several seminars in which I have taken part for their help in discussing aspects of my research that have come together in this book. The editors of *History of Education*, *History of Education Review*, *Social Studies of Science* and *Journal of Educational Administration and History* have kindly given permission to use material first published in their journals. Any errors and shortcomings that remain in the following pages are, of course, my own responsibility.

I

INTRODUCTION

'Therefore we must elect as ruler and guardian of the city him who as boy and youth and man has been tested and has come out without strain, and render him honours in life and after death, giving him the highest rewards of public burial and other memorials. The others we must reject.'[1] In this way Plato began to elaborate his thesis of 'education for leadership' in the fourth century BC. It was to become a key theme in the humanist scholarship of the sixteenth century, and later, in the nineteenth century, assumed the status and trappings of an English tradition. To a large extent it has fallen from favour in twentieth-century Britain. Nevertheless, there have been several attempts during the present century to adapt the notion to meet changing social, political and cultural demands and opportunities. This book is chiefly concerned with the character-istics, implications and ultimate fate of these more recent efforts.

The historiography of nineteenth-century English education has rightly emphasised the theme of leadership and its social and political implications, especially in relation to the public schools. Historians such as Rupert Wilkinson, J.A. Mangan and Mark Girouard have vividly depicted an ideology that asserted the necessity to train a cohesive, enlightened elite to rule nation and Empire.[2] By contrast, little attention has been paid to the development of the ideal since 1914. In most accounts it is replaced by a preoccupation with attempts to achieve 'equality of opportunity', variously defined; what had been celebrated in the late nineteenth century as a quintessentially English tradition is doomed to steady decline. To be sure, there has been continued fascination with the 'old school tie', with the influence and prestige of the public schools. But such influence has tended to be seen either as quaintly irrelevant or as anachronistic, leading it to be interpreted most commonly as a static and fading ideal, rooted irrevocably in the nineteenth century, marooned and out of place in a modern democracy. Critiques of the public school in the twentieth century have reinforced this image.[3] Attempts to reinvigorate and adapt 'education for leadership' in the changing context of the twentieth century have been all but ignored.

A closer inspection begins to reveal not only continuing attention to this general theme as an educational, social and political priority, but also important changes in its presentation and focus. Once firmly rooted in the public schools attended by a small elite minority, it came to be applied to schools attended by the mass of the people. Originally associated with the classical curriculum, it underwent a metamorphosis that allowed it eventually to support the claims of industry and science. Its elitist connotations most readily supported conservative thought and the retention of established hierarchies, yet it could prove equally attractive to radical and even socialist initiatives in education. This book attempts to outline and explain these adaptations. It seeks also to address what appears to be a most troubling puzzle: why it was that, despite the overall decline of the Platonic vision and of the classic ideology of the public schools during the twentieth century, educational and social inequalities have remained almost impervious to reform. It seems that competitive individualism has largely replaced explicitly hierarchical notions of social relationships in twentieth-century education, leaving established inequalities relatively unscathed. The aspirations of egalitarian reformers have been effectively frustrated throughout. If we are fully to comprehend the reasons for this, it is necessary to reconstruct the various forces that have been involved. This book seeks to help restore a significant piece of the puzzle to the overall picture.

Several educational historians have explored and sought to explain the persistence of educational inequalities in twentieth-century England, usually emphasising the role of academic selection and examinations in legitimising 'success' and 'failure'. One of the best and most influential treatments, Brian Simon's *The Politics of Educational Reform, 1920–1940* notes that in the interwar years education was regarded as a race in which the fittest won through to the finish and the unfit dropped out, a situation that reflected the realities of a selective and competitive system. Simon continues: 'Once incorporated in the school system, in terms of classification for purposes of selection, this doctrine justified that system and the society that gave it birth by stratifying children ever more distinctly.'[4] This view helps to explain the importance of devices such as intelligence testing, and the continuing resilience even after the second world war of 'the doctrine that secondary education is not for all, that only the selected qualify for a complete form of it, that the requirements of the few will define provision for the many at whatever cost to that majority, that differentiation will prevail, even if it negates education, in terms of streaming and classification for the purposes of selection'.[5] The present work argues that there was a further factor involved in patterns of educational inequality, another *type* of inequality, that has tended to be neglected: the survival, extension and adaptation of an ideology that had hitherto been centred on the public schools. That is to say, inequalities were structured and reinforced not only through the apparatus of selection and classification, not only through the imperatives of the academic curriculum in what R.H. Tawney called the 'tadpole society', but also through the *moral* curriculum of English secondary education. The preparation of pupils for the society to which they belonged, which has reflected a strong and enduring Platonic influence in English secondary education, has been just as important as the academic curriculum of examination-centred school subjects in reproducing and constructing inequality. This book seeks to reassert the vital contribution of the Platonic influence in fashioning the values and structures of English secondary education in the twentieth century.

If we focus on secondary education, it is easy to discern three general phases of development since the turn of the century. First would be the period from the Education Act of 1902 until the second world war, when state secondary (grammar) schools were restricted to a small minority of the population. The grammar schools charged fees, but also had a system of 'free places' of scholarships for pupils from the elementary schools who passed an examination at the age of eleven. The majority of children went only to elementary school; a small number went on to junior technical schools at the age of thirteen. The School Certificate examination, introduced in 1917, offered grammar school pupils the credentials to proceed to university and into respectable, secure and well-paid professional careers.[6] During this period, the key issues with respect to 'education for leadership' were, first, to what extent the established public schools would be able to retain their predominance in this field and, second, how far the grammar schools would be able to share in or even take over this role.

The second phase comprises the period from the Education Act of 1944 to the educational reorganisations of the 1960s. This was the era of the so-called 'tripartite system' of secondary education. Under the 1944 Act, secondary education was to be free and provided for all from the age of eleven, and a minimum leaving age was soon set at fifteen. But local education authorities were encouraged to provide three different types of secondary school, each intended for different types of pupil. The grammar schools were to remain, for the top 20 per cent or so of the age-range as judged in academic competition at 11-plus. Secondary technical schools, at least in theory of an equal stature to the grammar schools, were to be oriented towards industry and commerce rather than to the professions. Meanwhile, secondary modern schools were supposed to cater for the majority of the age-range. In practice, grammar schools retained their supremacy in terms of popular appeal and resources and as the key route to university and the professions. Secondary technical schools failed to develop in most areas as was envisaged, and modern schools only rarely managed to find a coherent and integrated approach to their ill-considered role.[7] In this situation, then, the grammar schools still tended to be the chief focus in discussions of how to promote education for leadership. And yet although the 'tripartite system' resembled nothing more than a working model of Plato's classic typology of gold, silver and copper, the social and political context of postwar England led to a strong challenge to notions of education for leadership, and to a sharp decline in their currency. Grammar schools in this period came in fact to depend less on any claims for social and political leadership than on their academic record as a justification for their continued existence.

The third phase takes us from the spread of comprehensive schools in the 1960s up to the present day. Intended for all abilities and aptitudes, these schools have not in general produced the kind of equality that was often anticipated at their inception but have tended rather to incorporate the structures of the grammar schools. Stephen Ball has reported that the 'vast majority' of comprehensive schools have effectively maintained policies that reflect earlier notions of 'meritocracy and separate provision'.[8] According to Ball, then, the 'noise' of educational reform has generally not been matched by 'real' changes in educational practices.[9] Ivor Goodson makes a similar point to explain the lack of change in curriculum patterns: 'As in the tripartite system so in the comprehensive system, academic subjects for able pupils are accorded the highest status and resources. The triple alliance between academic subjects, academic examinations and able pupils ensures that comprehensive schools provide similar patterns of success and failure to previous school systems.'[10] Thus well-established forms of curriculum and assessment have survived the outward shift to comprehensive education, with the result that the criteria for success are substantially the same as in the heyday of the grammar schools.

Again, however, it is important here to distinguish between the academic curriculum and the moral curriculum. There seems in general to have been a lack of attention to the cultivation of social and political leadership in the comprehensive schools that is chiefly attributable to the emergence of a what David Hargreaves has called a 'culture of individualism', and a loss of earlier concerns with the social functions of education.[11] Hargreaves argues forcefully that 'Our present obsession with individuals has led teachers to deny and fear the social functions of education, and sociological critics to point out that some of those nineteenth-century functions are still operative within our society and must be rooted out.'[12] And yet he too seems content to explain this simply in terms of the incorporation within the comprehensive schools of the academic 'grammar school curriculum', the 'heavy emphasis on the cognitive-intellectual skills and abilities of the traditional school subjects'.[13] This notion tends to neglect the partial way in which comprehensives tended to interpret what the grammar school curriculum involved. It also implies that the grammar school curriculum was a simple, static, even ahistorical construct that could easily be applied to new institutions regardless of changes in society and culture. Surely, however, there was much more to the grammar school curriculum than such a view would suggest. We should give more scrutiny to the changing fortunes and composition of the moral curriculum in twentieth-century secondary education. In such a project the social and educational role of 'education for leadership' must be central. More specifically, what still needs attention is the historical decline of the kind of moral curriculum originally associated with the public schools and largely transferred to the state grammar schools in the early part of the twentieth century. In fact over the last quarter of a century the ideal of 'education for leadership' has been consigned to the outer margins of English educational debate. This situation has not significantly altered in the late 1980s despite renewed interest in 'Victorian values', heated discussions over the character and aims of secondary schooling and the introduction in 1988 of the Education Reform Act.

While the actual idea of education for leadership has fallen into disrepute since the second world war, then, the social divisions that underpinned the provision of schooling in the Victorian era have proven in practice to be remarkably resilient. The late Raymond Williams, writing in the early 1960s at a time when it could be hoped that comprehensive schools might radically transform established patterns, noted a basic continuity in twentieth-century secondary education of a framework drawn from the rigid class society of nineteenth-century England.[14] This framework was essentially tripartite in character, consisting of a 'liberal' education for the dominant social group, technical instruction for those intended to be skilled workers and a rudimentary schooling in the expected codes of behaviour and work for the majority of the population. Through economic and social changes and a large increase in the scale of provision of schooling this has been a familiar and recurring pattern in twentieth-century secondary education. These distinctions and gradations were at their most explicit, institutionalised as they were in the three types of school, in the 1940s and 1950s, but they remained pervasive in the comprehensive schools and may well re-emerge with renewed strength following the educational reforms of the 1980s. Although distinctively Platonic in its overall form, however, there was an important ingredient that seemed increasingly to be missing. The tripartite structure was maintained and reinforced by the ingrained assumptions and realities of social class, but the guiding vision of 'education for leadership' struggled to survive.

In order to come to terms with the waning fortunes of education for leadership, and with the successive patterns of secondary education in twentieth-century England, we must understand them in their changing social and historical context. The decline and eventual disappearance of the British Empire in itself implied important changes in the role of schooling, for the social elite as for the rest of the population. Less and less could it be claimed that education for leadership was necessary in order to groom a select few to govern the natives of a global empire, as the public schools had done in the Victorian era. If the idea of education for leadership was to survive the retreat from Empire, therefore, it required fresh justifications to support it. At the same time the demands of the English people themselves, the clamour of democracy, extended and improved the provision of schooling for all: a 'silent social revolution' that challenged among other things the previously unquestioned preeminence of the public schools. This in turn raised the issue of how far the kind of preparation that had once been attached exclusively to the public schools should be extended to a wider group of pupils – first to those in state grammar schools, then to secondary schools designed to cater for the whole age-range.

Education for leadership, as a basic principle underpinning education, was also directly affected by other major developments in twentieth-century society and politics. The two world wars raised different kinds of issues impinging on education for leadership. The first helped at least for a time to bolster claims of a moral kind on behalf of this ideal. The second excited discussions of how to produce citizens who would lead the struggle against fascism, but also encouraged stronger notions of equality and democracy that were eventually to discredit the whole idea of education for leadership. The existence of sharp social divisions and differences in the early part of the century, reflected in the growth of class politics and industrial conflict, led some educators to try to create more flexible, imaginative or subtle leadership through changes in the kind of training imparted to the future rulers. But there was also resistance to the connotations of social control inherent in this approach that in the longer term probably helped to make education for leadership a tainted proposition. The rise of the welfare state and growing aspirations for social equality at mid-century combined to render older notions of education for leadership increasingly anachronistic. On the other hand it was by no means clear what kind of education *would* be appropriate to encourage the right kind of 'leadership' for what was hoped would be a classless and more equal society.

As a result of such developments, many institutions and ideas that had previously gone unquestioned underwent searching and often hostile reassessment. The changing reception of Plato is a good example of this kind of process. It could be said that the twentieth century has remodelled Plato in its own image. From the liberal reformer familiar to Victorian audiences,[15] Plato has become identified and most often reviled as the source of modern totalitarianism. The social and political implications of his *Republic* have increasingly outweighed appreciation of his ideas on aesthetics, or even of the details of his educational proposals. The public schools that were so authoritative in the late nineteenth century have similarly fallen from grace, often coming under attack for being in some way responsible for many of the problems and failures that Britain has experienced during the present century. Thus for example Wilkinson and more recently Peter Parker have related the sacrifices and disasters of the Great War to the shortcomings of the 'public school ethos'.[16] At the same time such historians as Correlli Barnett have suggested that the cultural values encouraged by the public schools have been at least partly responsible for Britain's 'industrial decline', and therefore also for the nation's relative economic decline.[17] It is in this inauspicious climate of opinion that we must appraise the changing fortunes during the twentieth century of what was probably the key principle not only of Plato but also of the public schools: education for leadership.

It seems appropriate for the purposes of the present study to concentrate mainly on the sphere of *secondary* education. It is this level of schooling that has been most directly comparable to that of the public schools of the nineteenth century. It is also here that we can see most clearly the character and effects of the overall shift from an elite form to a mass basis of schooling. Wider implications for higher education and adult education should not, however, be ignored; indeed, the role of higher education, and the dissemination and reception of the ideal of education for leadership in other countries, are important themes that are each worthy of substantial studies in their own right.[18] The present work will discuss some of the most direct ways in which these spheres interrelated with secondary education, and it is hoped that further research will focus on these other areas to explore in greater detail their distinctive and comparable characteristics. It is also most suitable to limit the present work to a discussion of the *English* experience in secondary education, in due recognition that, in so many respects, the traditions and practices of Scotland, Wales, and the two Irelands have been substantially different. It is the adaptation, indeed at some points the reconstitution, of what has often been regarded as a distinctively 'English tradition' with which this book is principally concerned.

In the following chapters, therefore, the twentieth-century career of this idea will be examined as it has been reflected in English secondary education, paying special attention to chosen educators who have emphasised the notion and to key episodes in its development and demise. This will help to illuminate the educational work of such figures as Cyril Norwood, Eric James and Victor Gollancz, the significance of which has been unjustly neglected. It will also be possible to relate the concerns of the Norwood report on the secondary school curriculum and examinations, published in 1943, and of the Fleming report on public schools of the following year, to their long-term historical context. And it will help us more fully to understand the contributions of critics of education for leadership such as T.C. Worsley, Richard Crossman and Michael Young. Further, this book bears witness not only to the general decline, even disintegration, of the ideal but also to a number of startling mutations that have occurred as its sympathisers sought to adapt it to the changing concerns and priorities of the twentieth century. In this situation there have been diehards who have defended the classic ideal to their final breath, but also revisionists and radicals who have tried to compromise on selected aspects while adhering to the faith. A number of versions of education for leadership, including the moral, the military, the meritocratic, the scientific, the industrial and the socialist, have resulted from these efforts.

The sources employed to explore this theme comprise a wide range of evidence that reveals the extent to which education for leadership, in its various guises, has been a significant topic for debate in English secondary education during the present century. Texts such as Norwood's *English Tradition of Education* (1929) and James's *Education and Leadership* (1951) may readily be used to assess changes in the presentation and orientation of the ideal. Their reception and the kinds of debates that surrounded them also help us to gauge the influence that education for leadership exerted on secondary education and also the relationship of the ideal to wider social and political configurations, although these aspects are bound to be more contentious and problematic. The ideals of leading educators and the policy formulations of the Board and Ministry of Education did not permeate educational practice in any automatic, immediate or predictable way. Very often, too, the efforts of individual pupils, teachers and schools have succeeded in resisting or transcending the ideals and structures that have been imposed upon them. Moreover, educational change has not had anything like the kind of simple or linear relationship to political, social or economic change that is often assumed. The present work focuses more upon an important discourse on the value and role of education for leadership that sought to justify, sustain and develop an educational ideal. Chapter 2 discusses the 'English tradition' at its height in the nineteenth century, and the needs and opportunities that combined to make it appear no less important in the early decades of the twentieth century. In chapter 3, we focus on the changing rationale of the public school in the twentieth century, with special reference to the key debates of the second world war that culminated in the Fleming report. We then turn to the career and ideology of an influential educator whose reputation has declined in recent years, Sir Cyril Norwood. His hopes for the state education system, expressed finally in the Norwood report of 1943, encouraged him to attempt to build upon the classic public school ethos and adapt it to a changing society. Similarly in the postwar years, the energetic attempts of Eric James of Manchester Grammar School to revitalise and update the idea of education for leadership form the focus of chapter 5. The aims of the 'technocrats' of the 1950s and their relationship to earlier notions of enlightened social and political leadership are studied in chapter 6. We then examine the radical attempts of some in the labour movement during the twentieth century to develop education designed to promote socialist leadership. Lastly, in chapter 8, some lessons for our contemporary education and for the future of our society will be suggested in the light of historical change. The changing discourse surrounding education for leadership in the twentieth century does not provide us with a 'usable past' in the strong sense that has been claimed for other dimensions of our recent educational history, such as secondary technical education.[19] Many would see it as simply unusable for contemporary policy purposes. It raises implications and is associated with themes that in many ways are very hard to reconcile with current aspirations and assumptions. On the other hand, the explanatory leverage that it offers is of significant value towards a greater understanding of the changing roles and aims of secondary education in particular. To assert the importance of education for leadership in twentieth-century England is not to indulge in a nostalgic lament. Still less is it to call for the revival of arguments that owed their currency to particular contexts and needs in any simple, wholesale or unreconstructed manner. The chief aim of the study is to help explain, through recourse to aspects that have been unfairly neglected, important characteristics and problems of English education both in the past and in the present.

2

AN ENGLISH TRADITION

To what extent was education for leadership really an 'English tradition'? Although it was appropriated, indeed colonised in the nineteenth century and was often to be celebrated as quintessentially English, many aspects of this ideal had of course originated and developed elsewhere. Chivalry had attained its zenith in medieval France, and it was Renaissance Italy that was largely responsible for giving sixteenth-century England its idea of the proper manners and training of a gentleman.[1] The English manifestation of education for leadership was an instance of a tradition being, if not exactly invented, then certainly shaped to suit a particular configuration of social and political interests.

There were many other examples of societies in which a variant of the Platonic vision of leadership exerted potent influence. The common Greek heritage and Renaissance ideal stimulated in the American colonies, just as in England, grammar schools which sought to promote civic character and leadership qualities. In the new Republic educational institutions were often regarded as a means of selecting and educating future leaders, a perception that gave education a central place in politics and society.[2] Thomas Jefferson was especially concerned with the education of the future leaders of the United States, seeking to identify a 'natural aristocracy'. The galaxy of strong political leaders in eighteenth-century America has been attributed in part to the quality and character of education, with its emphasis on the classics and on history intended to inspire a sense of duty and of civic virtue.[3] And it is possible to discern a strong elite tradition in American education over the past century too, especially in the form of the private boarding school movement.[4] Such institutions and the aspirations that they represent have survived and even prospered into the late twentieth century, alongside the egalitarian myth of 'log cabin to White House'.[5]

In France also, education has often been used to prepare the offspring of the affluent and successful for their almost predestined roles in exercising power, as in the case of the *grandes écoles*.[6] The *lycée* was explicitly intended to educate the future elite, as Alexandre Ribot made clear through his committee's inquiry in

1902: 'To form a leadership elite [*élite dirigeante*], such is the role of secondary education.'[7] The demands of imperial administration also encouraged elite training, for example through the *Ecole Coloniale*, established in 1887, which was intended to prepare colonial administrators and officials for their duties.[8] Again this kind of leadership preparation for a relatively small elite was held to be justified in spite of contrary pressures favouring greater equality of opportunity for all. The fascist and authoritarian regimes of the twentieth century have had their own reasons for using education as a means of training the future elite. Such regimes, like Nazi Germany in the 1930s, have often attempted to differentiate between the 'leaders' and the 'led' by cultivating suitable differences from early childhood.[9] And yet it has not always required such a total rejection of the tenets of democracy and equality for other modern societies to incorporate at least a limited role for leadership training within their educational structures.

Although ideas and practices involving education for leadership had a wider currency, however, they attained peculiar strength, character and influence in nineteenth-century England. The uniquely 'English tradition' may be associated with a strain of thought dating from Thomas Elyot in the sixteenth century. Equally significant was its role as a social, cultural and political artefact, employed for particular ends in a changing context. In this classic phase, we may identify the English tradition of education for leadership with certain key characteristics. First, it was based on a *classical* curriculum. Second, it placed emphasis on training for *character*, in a strong moral sense. Third, it stressed the value of *communal living* and shared experiences, well removed from the influences of family. Fourth, it was geared towards the received ideal of the 'English gentleman', involving self-restraint and *public service*. Fifth, it was *class-based*, allowing little role for social mobility except in a highly restricted way. Sixth, it was essentially *gender-specific*: women were excluded from this ideal, as they were from the leading public schools and from 'public life' in general. Let us examine the historical development of the ideal, before proceeding to investigate the Victorian 'tradition' and attempts during the twentieth century both to maintain and revise it.

PHILOSOPHERS AND KINGS

Plato's *Republic* provided the touchstone for the idea of education for leadership, to which all later theorists and practitioners were consciously endebted. According to Plato, the best and wisest leadership for a community could be gained only by selecting those members with ability at a young age, and training them to bring out their qualities of leadership. He saw the existence of three distinct classes in society, to each of which a different preparation or education was due. The first class, associated with gold, was that of the philosophers. The second, made of silver, embraced the 'auxiliaries', or skilled merchants and tradesmen. Last came the artisans and farmers, made of iron and copper. Future 'guardians' or rulers should be taken only from those made of gold, and these 'must have the right kind of education, whatever that may be, if they are to have what will do more than anything else to make them gentle to one another and to those they guard'.[10] This education would involve training in music and gymnastics, and then, for those most promising, tests of courage and particularly of self-control. Those emerging from such training would be not only 'philosophers' but 'rulers' also, spending most of their time in philosophic pursuits,

but when their time comes, they will endure the toil of directing politics and being rulers for the sake of their city, regarding such action not as anything noble but as a compulsion laid upon them; and so each generation, having trained up others like to themselves whom they can leave to be the city's guardians, will depart to the islands of the blest and dwell there.[11]

Two aspects of this general view may be noted here. First, and most obviously, it encouraged a different kind of education for different classes in the community. Second, it stressed the importance of bringing 'political power' and 'philosophy' together, so that 'philosophers bear kingly rule in cities, or those who are now called kings and princes become genuine and adequate philosophers'.[12] Both sympathisers and opponents of Plato's philosophy later recognised these aspects as central. According to R.C. Lodge, discussing Plato's theory of education in 1947, Plato's view that education for leadership can be given wisely only to students who have demonstrated that they possess the capacity for leadership was still 'recognised as true in our time'. Furthermore, Lodge claimed, Plato's ideas were still ours, and 'his inspiration is still vital and useful to us in our task of creating a humanly worthwhile educational system'.[13] On the other hand, Plato's argument on this was widely criticised during the twentieth century for being 'socially divisive' and 'elitist'.[14] The notion of the 'philosopher-king' also had lasting influence, and in its various formulations remained a potent ideal and prescription.

In the work of John of Salisbury, for example, the moral, social and spiritual values of the properly educated cleric were preferred to the corruption of the courtier. *Policraticus*, completed in 1159 and presented to the king's chancellor, Thomas Becket, anticipated the kind of humanism later fashionable in Renaissance Italy. According to James Bowen,

The ideal type of creative leader he considered to be the educated man, the man of Latin scholarship whose vision links the historical past with the present, and so is best equipped to grapple with the problems of the future . . . The aim of genuine education, in his view, is to produce the cleric whose central trait is expressed in those qualities known collectively as *civilitas*.[15]

During the Renaissance, attention to the authors of classical Rome and Greece was elevated to new heights in the search for the qualities of *virtù* that could preserve social and political unity. In Italy, Niccolò Machiavelli and Desiderius Erasmus put forward very different versions of the attributes required. Whereas Machiavelli emphasised the realities of power and opportunism, Erasmus was squarely in the tradition of political idealism and stressed the importance of the education of the prince. In England, Thomas More's *Utopia* strongly echoed the line taken by Erasmus. Equally significant, though, was Thomas Elyot's *The Boke Named The Governour*, published in 1531, the first book to be published in English on the subject of education. The basic theme of Elyot's work was the education of civil governors to advise the prince, to the extent that it was basically 'a handbook of education and ethics for the English ruling class'.[16] Such governors, Elyot argued, should be well-born, and their education should emphasise moral conduct and self-restraint. As Geoffrey Bantock notes, the effect of this was 'to marry knowledge to action after the Platonic model of an elite of guardians', trained through a rigorous education in relevant intellectual disciplines as preconditions of virtuous behaviour.[17] In theory at least, the education of the 'knight' was thus united with that of the 'cleric' to allow the possibility of producing philosopher-rulers. Quentin Skinner suggests that

It was the humanists who first introduced into northern Europe the immensely influential belief that a training in the *litterae humaniores* represents an indispensable requirement for public life. And it was they who first succeeded in consequence in breaking down the age-old distinctions – already abolished in Italy – between the education of the ruling classes and the education of 'clerks'.[18]

Indeed, it seems to have been this that motivated the aristocracy to educate their children in a form of learning hitherto almost monopolised by clerics: that is to say, in order to preserve their authority and power.[19]

Elyot continued to emphasise the importance of good birth as a prerequisite for being educated for governorship. Even so, an insistence upon 'virtue', to be developed through education, for political leadership was potentially a radical doctrine implying that an hereditary ruling class based on lineage and wealth might be less worthy to act as leaders than the most virtuous members of society from whatever ranks or backgrounds.[20] It could thus be used to promote social mobility and even, in some circumstances, revolution. In seventeenth-century England the relative merits of birth and virtue were much debated, and a large number of grammar schools intended for children of all social classes were established. Despite this, an emphasis on the role of education in establishing 'public spirit', and to equip the gentleman to serve society both as a politician and as a private citizen, was maintained.[21] Whether this could best be achieved through education at home or at school was again a matter of some dispute.

By the eighteenth century it seemed clear that, in England at least, the radical implications of 'education for leadership' had been effectively contained. Many of the grammar schools created before 1660 had been allowed to decline.[22] John Cannon has noted four aspects of the education of the English aristocracy at this time that helped to maintain its political supremacy. First, their education was intended to fit them for their leading role in society and for their responsibilities in government. Second, an increasingly standardised curriculum encouraged a common attitude and sense of purpose. The classical curriculum fostered a code of values that emphasised 'the duty of service and a conviction of the rightness of patrician rule'. Third, school and university created a network of acquaintances that reinforced close family ties. And fourth,

the virtual monopoly of higher education which the upper classes possessed – and safeguarded – gave apparent validity to their rule. To the claims of blue blood, they could add superior education: it was, in the eighteenth century, a formidable combination. They were right to mistrust Dissenting Academies as threats to their position, and their determination to exclude Dissenters from Oxford and Cambridge suggests a recognition of the important part which educational privilege played in maintaining aristocratic supremacy.[23]

In the English context the notion of education for leadership was henceforth closely associated with the cultivation of an existing social elite rather than with support for social mobility.

FOUNTAINS OF CIVILITY

During the nineteenth century not only was this tendency confirmed and hardened, but it became elevated to the status of a distinctively English tradition. In this process the role of the great 'public schools', usually long established but newly invigorated, was central. Thomas Arnold, headmaster of Rugby from 1828 until his death in 1842, personified this strengthened ideal, insisting on the development of public spirit and character in his young gentlemen. The classics were used once again to emphasise the values of leadership. Prefects were selected to maintain discipline, promote uniformity and help to foster a moral and spiritual *esprit de corps*. Such developments were both vitally important in their time and of lasting significance. Nineteenth-century public schools bestowed the sixth form with distinctive characteristics that it has been associated with to this day.[24] The headmaster himself was invested with a charismatic quality that has been influential in notions of the school even in the twentieth century.[25] The Clarendon Commission of 1861–4 recognised only nine 'public schools' in England, 'the chief nurseries of our statesmen': Charterhouse, Eton, Harrow, Merchant Taylors', Rugby, St Paul's, Shrewsbury, Westminster, and Winchester. According to Clarendon,

in them, and in schools modelled after them, men of all the various classes that make up English society, destined for every profession and career, have been brought up on a footing of social equality, and have contracted the most enduring friendships, and some of the ruling habits of their lives; and they have had perhaps the biggest share in moulding the character of an English gentleman.[26]

Certainly, scores of newly founded schools also sought the respectability and prestige of public school status. Grammar schools and private institutions reorganised themselves to conform with the values and mission projected by the leading public schools. According to Sheldon Rothblatt, 'Throughout the century headmasters who went from the older to the newer public schools brought with them typical public school symbols and institutions: prefects in mortar-boards, school songs, caps, hats, foundation day ceremonies and speeches.'[27] Preparatory schools increasingly became an 'infrastructure' for the public school 'system'.[28] The public schools created an identifiable elite, a community of men with shared outlooks, values and codes of honour imbued in them through their shared boyhood experience, a breed of 'philosopher-rulers' fit for public service and the running of an Empire.[29] This was 'Dr Moberly's mint-mark': as Rev. George Moberly, Headmaster of Winchester College, informed the Parliamentary Commission in 1862, 'Every school of this size has a definite character, and gives a peculiar stamp to its pupils; and I could, with more or less distinctness, characterise the pupils of the public schools of England by the particular stamp or mint-mark they bear.'[30]

This social and political function of the Victorian public school has been well studied by Rupert Wilkinson, who stresses the role of Thomas Arnold's formula for creating the 'Christian gentlemen', consciously or unconsciously, in developing a public school elite.[31] As Wilkinson points out, the products of Victorian and Edwardian public schools dominated public affairs until the second world war, with a common tendency 'to treat community service as the price of material privilege and the hallmark of social prestige'.[32] They also increasingly embodied conservative attitudes and values:

During the late nineteenth century the schools undoubtedly formed a citadel against the materialism and selfishness generated by the new capitalism of the Industrial Revolution. But when they performed their offsetting function, they did so by stressing tradition rather than supporting intellectual criticism and imagination. They chose to make themselves an anchor of stability, a guardian of conservatism, in such a way that they were unable also to serve the cause of intellectual enlightenment. As a result, they produced leaders whose good sense was too often not accompanied by vision, and whose insularity and complacence matched too perfectly the insularity and complacence of their island people.[33]

Martin Wiener has emphasised another aspect of Victorian public schools: their 'detachment from the modern world', allegedly exemplified by the lack of science education in their curricula.[34] Thus, Wiener argues, 'Public school boys made excellent administrators of a far-flung empire, but the training so admirably suited for that task ill fitted them for economic leadership.'[35] The public schools thus carried within themselves, according to this kind of view, the seeds of Britain's later relative economic and industrial decline.[36]

By the end of the nineteenth century, 'education for leadership' as practised by the public schools could be widely portrayed as a specifically English tradition. As Eric Hobsbawm has observed, 'traditions' despite all appearances are often invented or constructed to meet particular and changing needs.[37] This particular 'tradition' legitimised status and authority relations in a rapidly changing social context following the industrial revolution. John Roach makes this point very effectively in his history of nineteenth-century secondary education. Public schools, he notes, 'combined stability and tradition with adaptability and change'. This was an attractive combination, increasing the 'drawing power' of the public schools over that of their competitors.[38] Such 'myth-making' contributed to the identification of public schools and the ancient universities of Oxford and Cambridge as the custodians and trans-mitters of English culture.[39] Thus the production of 'English gentlemen' who would rule nation and Empire, through the devices of the public school, came to be celebrated as the culmination of an historical process which had promoted and safeguarded authentically English ideals and interests. It was possible to look back at the 'scholar-gentlemen' of Thomas Elyot and to see in them the source of contemporary glory. Sir Ernest Barker recalled in 1948 that

The public schools of the Victorian age were the late but abundant harvest of ideas which had already been sown in the sixteenth century. 'Fountains of civility and politic rule', they issued in a type of 'governor' who might have satified Elyot, and in a type of disciplined servant of 'the very and true commonweal' who might have comforted Starkey.[40]

Harold Laski was more critical of this 'type of disciplined servant', but certainly agreed that 'gentlemen' had ruled the country unchallenged until the 1914–18 War: 'His genius for compromise and his capacity for absorption have given him control for two hundred years of English destiny.'[41]

Notions of the 'clerisy' helped to reinforce the importance of education for leadership in nineteenth-century England. According to this kind of view, intellectuals formed a distinct and socially beneficial group, guarding culture and morality at a time of threatening changes and instability. Members of this philosophic class comprised the 'arbiters of value' in society without seeking coercive power, hoping to influence society in various and often hidden ways, even through agencies that they themselves distrusted such as the press.[42] Plato's ideal of the 'philosopher-ruler' was a common theme for such theorists as Samuel Coleridge, and there were also strong echoes of Renaissance humanism. But the notion of the clerisy was novel in that its members were opposed to many of the dominant ideas and trends of social leaders and actually sought to refine and reform society: Coleridge and his clerisy were defined as much in terms of what they would be against as what they stood for.[43] Equally as it affirmed the importance of maintaining an elite for the health and progress of society, it buttressed the view that such an elite should be 'enlightened' through the right kind of education. John Stuart Mill supported Coleridge's notion of a clerisy, especially for the hope that it offered for an intellectual and cultural leadership that would promote improvement and defend against mediocrity.[44] Such was also the view of Matthew Arnold, son of the late Headmaster of Rugby, who sought to defend the finer values of British civilisation against the vulgarities of Americanism and the rising tide of democracy through 'the highly instructed few', rather than 'the scantily instructed many', as 'the organ to the human race of knowledge and truth'.[45] The younger Arnold was particularly interested in the problems of middle-class education because he saw the creation of a middle class fit to lead, filling the vacuum left by the gradual decay of the old aristocratic leadership, as the key to future progress.[46] While dominant ideals of education for leadership harked back to Platonic and Renaissance notions, they were strongly influenced by responses to contemporary change and predictions of future need.

The cogency of the ideal in nineteenth-century England also reflected the emergence of two separate educational systems, and helped to ensure their maintenance. On the one hand the public schools and a large number of local grammar schools catered for the needs of the social elite. On the other, elementary schools were established for 'the scantily instructed many', the industrial working class. Albeit with some reluctance, it was gradually accepted by the majority of middle-class educators that greater provision of education for the working class would be necessary.[47] Generally this was rationalised as an important device for maintaining social order and promoting economic productivity.[48] Thus Robert Lowe, a highly influential official and MP, and a former vice-president of the Committee of Council on Education, argued against the 1867 Reform Bill and suggested that in general,

The lower classes ought to be educated to discharge the duties cast upon them. They should also be educated that they may appreciate and defer to a higher cultivation when they meet it; and the higher classes ought to be educated in a very different manner, in order that they may exhibit to the lower classes that higher education to which, if it were shown to them, they would bow down and defer.[49]

The Elementary Education Act of 1870 helped to consolidate the creation of a state system of education for the working class, while the 'higher classes' continued to be educated 'in a very different manner' in public and grammar schools. Hence the strengthened barriers of social class relationships in nineteenth-century England both helped to condition the emergence of a mass educational system and provided a new meaning and context for 'education for leadership'.

THE NEW STATESMAN

Several factors combined in the late nineteenth and early twentieth centuries not only to emphasise the social and political importance of 'education for leadership', but also to suggest new methods of promoting this tradition. First among these was the growing role of the State in the education system, as in other areas of social policy. The Elementary Education Act of 1870 provided the foundation for mass elementary education under the auspices of the State; in 1899 the Board of Education was consolidated; in 1902 state control over both elementary and secondary education was affirmed. As Lowe and Matthew Arnold, among others, had anticipated, the State provided a potential means of control over the character, direction and aims of education at different levels. Public schools in the nineteenth century had been highly effective in promoting their ideals among a selected few; a state education system, with all the resources at its disposal, might be able to further the same cause on a national scale. This was clearly the view of Sir Robert Morant, permanent secretary at the Board of Education from 1903 until 1911, and an important influence in the passage and implementation of the 1902 Education Act. Educated at Winchester, he conceived the new state secondary schools as being in the image of the public schools of the nineteenth century.[50] The Regulations for secondary schools adopted in 1904 also helped to ensure that the secondary school curriculum resembled that of the public schools much more than that of the higher grade schools of the late nineteenth century.[51] At this crucial formative time, state secondary education potentially represented a key means of maintaining and regenerating the 'English tradition'.

Morant was, of course, far from alone in his views on the future of secondary education. He was also one of many influential officials with a public school background. Indeed, the continued dominance of products of the leading public schools in educational policy well into the twentieth century presented a further opportunity to maintain the key precepts of education for leadership. Half of the civil servants at the Board of Education between 1919 and 1939 had attended a Headmasters' Conference school, and half of these had attended one of the nine Clarendon schools. Gail Savage suggests that 'The aspects of secondary education that Board officials were most anxious to preserve were those that the state-aided grammar schools had in common with public schools . . . The training of an elite, previously the exclusive province of the public schools, became the mission of the grammar schools.'[52] This general factor is well known in the sense that it was a powerful legacy from the past. Much less recognised have been the efforts to make use of such influence and power in order to reconstitute and reformulate the public school ethos of the nineteenth century in ways that would be acceptable in an age of mass democracy.

The growth, diversification and general 'transformation' of higher education in the late nineteenth and early twentieth centuries also offered a novel means of promoting 'education for leadership'. On the one hand the universities, and especially the new university colleges in the north of England, began to broaden social recruitment to higher learning, to such an extent, indeed, that Harold Perkin discerns a 'revolution' in English higher education between 1850 and 1930, 'nothing less than the transformation of the university from a marginal institution . . . into the central power house of modern industrial society'.[53] On the other hand, this general process opened the way for the creation of what has been described in the rather different context of the German academic community as a 'mandarin' elite:

a social and cultural elite which owes its status primarily to educational qualifications, rather than to hereditary rights or wealth . . . made up of doctors, lawyers, ministers, government officials, secondary school teachers, and university professors, all of them men with advanced academic degrees based on the completion of a certain minimum curriculum and the passing of a conventional group of examinations.[54]

Controversy over the kind of education suitable for a 'modern' elite began to affect the curriculum and expectations even of the two longest established universities in England, Oxford and Cambridge. It appears that the conflict between 'liberal' and 'professional' education celebrated by John Stuart Mill in his inaugural address at St Andrews in 1867 had come to be reconciled in the minds of Cambridge academics by the end of the century, leading them to seek a combination of expert knowledge and general qualities.[55] Such fresh demands raised new questions about how best to educate the future leaders of a rapidly changing society. At Oxford, for example, the adequacy of the School of *Literae Humaniores*, or 'Greats', for the preparation of twentieth-century statesmen came under increasing scrutiny. The role of science and technology in the 'mandarin' culture, and how to incorporate them within the curriculum of schools and universities, were also to become matters of debate, particularly after the second world war. University reformers were not necessarily intending to manipulate the new mass democracy through their reforms.[56] Even so, the increasing importance of higher education was bound to be significant in both maintaining and developing the tradition of 'education for leadership'.

At the same time, more informal channels of education also appeared to suggest a new form and substance for this established tradition. Organisations such as the Boys' Brigade and Robert Baden-Powell's scout movement sought to extend the values of manly character to working-class youth.[57] The National Association of Boys' Clubs, formed in 1924, was an attempt to consolidate the efforts of such clubs to promote social responsibility. Lord Aberdare, supporting this initiative, argued that the clubs could help more than schools in promoting the 'idea of leadership' among working-class boys.[58] The notion of 'leaders for social service' attracted patrons such as the Duke of York with his camp school at New Romsey and his Playing Field Movement.[59] These latter initiatives, it was suggested, were about recruiting and preparing voluntary leaders in all areas of society with 'personality, sympathy, and, above all, idealism'.[60]

In the dissemination of such ideals to a wider population, the new proliferation of newspapers and books was potentially crucial. The reading public grew markedly during the nineteenth century as the railway system helped to distribute newspapers, magazines and books. Private circulating libraries began to come within the price range of working people. Public libraries expanded their services following the Public Libraries Act of 1850, to become available to 62.5 per cent of the population by 1911, and to 96.3 per cent by 1926. Popular newspapers found a mass audience by the 1890s, and the general organisation of the modern reading public was in place by the turn of the century.[61] This new development, together with the system of state elementary education, had major potential for social control. Gary D. Stark has shown how neo-conservative publishers in Germany, for instance, sought to impose their own views upon a mass readership.[62] This must have seemed especially attractive because of the political implications that the new media appeared to hold. It was widely assumed that books and newspapers, actively promoted on a mass market, would act as a 'magic bullet', exerting an immediate, direct, predictable and uniform impact upon their readership.[63] During the first world war, newspaper 'atrocity stories' played an important role in strengthening anti-German feeling in Britain. In the interwar years, widespread concern was expressed over the sinister uses to which the power of the media might be put. The evidence of the 'Red Letter' scare which was believed to have damaged the Labour Party cause in the general election of 1924, the apparent influence of Philip Snowden's denunciation of Labour in his election broadcast of 1931, and above all the propaganda techniques of the Nazi Party in its rise to power in Germany, helped to fuel such concern. Thus the publisher and the newspaper magnate appeared to be figures of immense potential influence, both educationally and politically. By the 1950s, it was generally accepted that the influence of the new mass media was much less strong and predictable than had been anticipated. In the interwar years, though, the orthodox view was that their future significance was profound, and attitudes towards their educational, political and social importance were based on this assumption.

This new situation invited differing responses. For some it emphasised a need to promote 'enlightened' leadership dedicated to social and political progress, a twentieth-century version of the clerisy. For others it spelled out the importance of fostering independent working-class leadership. J.A. Hobson called in 1909 for 'equality of access to knowledge and culture' as a central aspect of equality of opportunity: 'What is needed is not an educational ladder, narrowing as it rises, to be climbed with difficulty by a chosen energetic few, who as they rise enter a new social stratum, breathe the atmosphere of another class, and are absorbed in official and professional occupations which dissociate them from the common life of the people.'[64] Authentic working-class leadership was especially urgent, Hobson insisted, because the success of popular demands depended on 'the intelligent use of the franchise and the instruments of government, so as to form sound judgments, to express them in valid legal forms, to press these demands through the legislative machinery, and to secure accurate, even-handed administration of the laws'. Without such leaders, 'an ignorant, dull, capricious people, more interested in drink, sport, and gambling than in anything else, easily diverted from pressing their "rights" by some artful appeal to military or commercial Jingoism, and broken into contentious forms by any specious promises of present gain, is incapable of a sustained, energetic, and well-directed effort to realise Democracy'. In this situation, Hobson continued,

Skilled sophists of the law, the Press, the party, aye of the pulpit and the lecture-room, become the conscious or unconscious tools of reaction and obstruction, denouncing the illegality, the immorality, the unreason, and the futility of the popular demands. The greatest of immediate needs, therefore, is the training of popular leaders with the intelligence, the knowledge, the discretion and the confidence required to break down these sophisticated defences, together with that broader general intelligence which will enable the people to choose able leaders, to resist scares and bribes, and to form sober judgments on the broad issues of public policy submitted to them.[65]

Alongside the ideals of the mandarin and the clerisy we may place that of the *tribune*.

New threats emerging in the early twentieth century helped to sharpen the demand for 'new statesmen'. The social and political tensions that ultimately contributed to the 'strange death' of Liberal England seemed to require a new kind of leader. After 1914, international confrontations and crises equally gave rise to new attention to the qualities of statesmanship. David Lloyd George, a beneficiary of both of these tendencies in rapid succession, was cast down from power when his qualities of leadership seemed no longer adequate for future challenges. A novel complexity, interdependence and enlarged scale in international affairs, combined with an increase in the pace of events, were noted by Alfred Zimmern, who stressed the need for a 'collaboration between Learning and Leadership'[66] to 'adjust the available resources of goodwill, expert knowledge, and intellectual and moral leadership to the needs of the post-war world, and to set them to work together according to the rhythm of the age'.[67] The rapidly changing world scene could be interpreted as a threat to British dominance and culture; the rise of fascist regimes in the 1920s and 1930s, and the drift towards a second world war, appeared to threaten 'civilisation' itself. Leonard Woolf, in a book completed only just before the Nazi–Soviet pact of 1939, reflected that since 1918, 'The forces of civilisation have been hopelessly divided and in their internecine quarrel they have frequently forgotten or abandoned the principles and standards of civilisation.' Now, he warned, the 'barbarians' were 'at the gate', and had to be resisted by means of rational and enlightened leadership.[68] Meanwhile Lord Lloyd of Dolobran, from a different background and political perspective, sounded a similar note: 'For lack of courage and candour we have been brought to the edge of catastrophe. We can be saved only by leadership. In saving ourselves we can surely save the world.'[69] Such idealism and commitment could be based on a variety of sources. For some, it was principally a matter of finding fresh moral guidance at a time when the political and even the social influence of the Churches was waning.[70] Others stressed the importance of science and social planning, often in the 1930s pointing to the example that the Soviet Union appeared to represent.[71] This kind of 'technocratic' vision coexisted with liberal hopes of cooperation among 'progressives' of all parties.[72]

At the same time, the continuing appeal of Plato's typology remained explicit and important. At least until the second world war, it was commonly employed to support arguments in favour of 'enlightened leadership'. To some, indeed, the contemporary crisis and drift into war made Plato's ideas more relevant than ever. Thus Sir Walter Moberly, chairman of the University Grants Committee and president of the Classical Association, claimed that Plato's world was similar to that of the 1930s and 1940s: shaken, shattered and with accepted standards called into question: 'Thus I have come to feel, with a new intensity, that Plato speaks to *our* condition.'[73] Unlike in Nazi Germany, he continued, the guardians of the British Empire should be trained as a 'watchdog' rather than as a 'wolf'.[74] Appeals to Plato, as Moberly also showed, were a useful way of legitimising inequality: 'To reproaches on the score of the two ladders and denial of equality, he would urge that, in education at least, equality is an impossible ideal. You cannot attain it by levelling up, for differences of human capacity will always defeat you.'[75] Similarly Sir Richard Livingstone, a classics specialist at Oxford and prominent publicist, argued persistently that the most appropriate education for a 'world adrift' was one that would emphasise 'character': 'Character means for us courage, truthfulness, trustworthiness, a sense of honour, independence, fair play, public spirit and leadership. These are national ideals and on the whole national virtues, and in developing them the English race and the English school compare favourably with any other.'[76] Clearly there was still a strong awareness of the 'English tradition' and its continuing value.

Yet alongside this continuity and renewed relevance the twentieth century brought with it new challenges to Victorian orthodoxy. The opportunities, demands, threats and perceived needs of the time helped to refashion the established tradition of 'education for leadership' in fresh and often radically different directions. Among the clearest challenges of the new century was mounting criticism of the public school as the hallowed repository of leadership and character, the 'fountain of civility'. In a rapidly changing social and political order the public schools were obliged to confront and rationalise their functions anew.

3

THE END OF
THE OLD SCHOOL TIE?

In the darkest days of the second world war, the public schools faced a crisis of their own. Declining enrolments and growing financial problems were not the sole source of anxiety: even more perturbing were strong criticisms of their general social purposes that threatened to lead to their destruction or emasculation. That they survived to prosper once again was due in no small measure to the Fleming report on public schools and the general educational system, published in 1944. The 'old school tie' continued to exert a strong influence on English society. Even so, the public schools of the postwar period were in some respects significantly different from those of the classic phase half a century earlier, and this adaptation to changing circumstances affected their role and rationale as the main producers of future leaders.

DEMOCRACY AND THE PUBLIC SCHOOLS

It has become conventional wisdom that the first world war marked a decisive period in the decline of the public schools and the values associated with them. According to Mark Girouard, for instance, the Great War 'both brought Victorian chivalry to its climax and helped to destroy it'.[1] He explains: 'As a dominant code of conduct it never recovered from the Great War partly because the war itself was such a shatterer of illusions, partly because it helped produce a world in which the necessary conditions for chivalry were increasingly absent.'[2] J.A. Mangan, in his fascinating study of athleticism in the public schools, concurs with this analysis, claiming that 'The Great War may be conveniently taken as a divide – political, social, economic and educational: new political principles, creeping embourgeoisement, declining national prosperity and a reformulation of educational ideals increasingly characterised the next fifty years.'[3] Yet the public schools, unreformed, continued to be the recognised major source of social and political leadership in the interwar period, even if this did give rise to increasing criticism. In some ways of greater significance was the second world war of 1939 to 1945. This latter period was a time of strong political tension and ideological conflict, despite the appearance of national unity, during which a thorough 'audit' of social priorities took place.[4] The role and future of the public schools were to be a matter of intense debate in these circumstances, with important consequences for the postwar era.

The experience of the first world war was in fact widely taken to be a triumphant vindication of the public schools' contribution to society. The sacrifice and heroism shown by a generation of leaders that the public schools had produced seemed to demonstrate the qualities of character and public service so long associated with such schools. The military connotations of such service, and its potential value in helping to preserve the society and Empire against any further attacks, were strongly emphasised during the 1920s. One sympathiser of the public schools, Bernard Darwin, chose to single out 'a readiness to be an officer' as the 'essential quality produced by the public schools'. This, he made clear, carried with it responsibilities for social and political leadership in peace as in war:

As regards the years between 1914 and 1918 it possesses a special application, but it was meant in a more general sense. It means, I take it, a willingness to shoulder responsibility and to set an example. It can, to some extent, be more grandiloquently expressed by *noblesse oblige*. The public school impresses on its boys that there are a number of things that are not to be done . . . But it is important to remember that the discipline of a public school is not only negative. If it teaches obedience by prohibition it also teaches command by encouraging leadership.[5]

The Officers' Training Corps, a feature of most leading schools, provided a lasting reminder of this kind of public service. It was employed to help legitimise the aspirations and purposes of the public schools into and beyond the second world war, as a training in 'unselfish public service, ready submission to intelligible discipline and an instinctive rising to the challenge of responsibility'[6] that could spell the difference between victory and defeat. Military academies such as Wellington College and Sandhurst could take special advantage from such sentiments, but other public schools were also able to exploit memories of the Great War when it suited them.

In the interwar years, too, new independent schools developed, often styling themselves as 'progressive' but modelled in many cases upon the forms and ideals of the Victorian public school. These new institutions suggested the continuing appeal of such ideals and some determination to protect them beyond the influence of the modern State or of a wider populace. Perhaps, however, they also reflected an awareness that the 'classic' or unreconstructed public schools would be too conservative and hidebound to respond effectively to new educational and social challenges. Even in the late nineteenth century, Cecil Reddie's Abbotsholme, and Bedales under J.H. Badley, signalled the emergence of an alternative, radical style of independent education. They also represented attempts to reinvigorate what they took to be the basic purposes of the public schools, to restore their mission of fitting the social elite for political leadership. Reddie in particular, a strong Platonist, sought to renew the vigour and commitment to service of the 'directing classes' while expecting the masses to be obedient and productive.[7]

A later initiative in a similar spirit was Kurt Hahn's Gordonstoun. Hahn, a German Jew, was strongly influenced by the example of Abbotsholme and was also inspired by the educational and political precepts that he drew from Plato. His ambitious plans to cultivate a moral leadership that would not give way to corruption or to popular demands were forged first in Germany's military defeat in the Great War and, no less importantly, in the social uprising that followed. He opened Salem School in 1919, overlooking Lake Constance in Germany but redolent of English boarding schools in general and of Eton and Abbotsholme in particular. His prefect system was both a revival of Thomas Arnold and self-consciously Platonic, with titles awarded of 'Guardians' and 'Helpers'. Hahn was especially concerned to cultivate 'character' and community service, emphasising the importance of physical health and the environment. Hitler's rise to power in Germany forced him into exile in Scotland, where he re-established his school under the name of Gordonstoun in April 1934. This new situation, combined with his own personal example, enabled him to emphasise the difference between a Platonic elite and the Nazi or fascist ideal of leadership. After the second world war Hahn founded the Outward Bound Movement, another initiative in youth service and character training, and strongly influenced new ventures such as Atlantic College in Wales.[8]

Thus the public schools remained powerful symbols of elite leadership in the interwar years. They could point to international turbulence and social instability at home as important reasons to maintain a firm and stabilising, but at the same time a wise and disinterested, authority. And yet by the 1930s the social and political role of the public schools was a matter of keen controversy. The heroic image of the public schools largely faded to give way to a less flattering view of a self-perpetuating clique, not easing but actually responsible for exacerbating the domestic and international difficulties in which the country was increasingly embroiled. The ostentatious flaunting of privilege in the midst of social conflict, unemployment and depression no doubt had much to do with the growing unpopularity of the public schools at this time. Richard Ollard tells us that the tone of Eton College in the 1920s and 1930s, when he was a pupil, was perhaps even more assertive than before 1914, with 'the emergence of a self-satisfaction and a self-advertisement that an earlier generation might have found vulgar'.[9] The exclusive character of the club of gentlemen–rulers equally gave rise to adverse comment and resentment. Ollard suggests in retrospect that in the 1920s and 1930s 'the school dress, tail-coats, top hats, or for the smallest boys, Eton jackets topped by the starched slopes of an Eton collar, seemed an ostentatious and arrogant defiance of contemporary society'. Indeed, he affirms, 'To those who had suffered the futilities and frustrations of the old boy network it was hardly necessary to look further for its complete embodiment.'[10] The connection between public schools and power appeared all too obvious, as too were the conservative – and Conservative – characteristics of such leadership. Stanley Baldwin openly rejoiced in the influence of the products of Harrow in his Conservative cabinet of 1924. The new Parliament elected in 1931 included no fewer than 104 Old Etonians, all Conservatives. The 'old school tie' linking the public schools not only to the Conservative Party but also to all of the key institutions of society and state symbolised the political dominance of an established ruling class. Its appearance as the passport to elite status provoked growing criticism on the part of those excluded from the charmed circle; that is, it became increasingly prominent in the class politics and warfare of the 1930s.

The socialist intellectual Harold Laski expressed something of this discontent when he argued in 1932 that the undisputed rule of the 'English gentleman' was coming to an end. According to Laski, the leadership offered by such gentlemen had itself created or worsened many of the problems that now afflicted the nation: 'The gentleman's characteristics are a public danger in all matters where quantitative knowledge, unremitting effort, vivid imagination, organised planning are concerned.' They were, he alleged, out of place in a rapidly changing world, a costly and decorative anachronism: 'The gentleman in the presence of modern democracy is as bewildered as Pilate before the spectacle of Christianity.'[11] In the context of acute industrial difficulties, social divisions and renewed threats of international conflict, it became increasingly attractive to perceive the exclusive club of 'gentlemen' as part of the problem rather than as the key to salvation. On this view the public schools and the Platonic values that underlay them were ultimately responsible for Britain's failure to adapt itself to the advent of mass democracy and the decline of the Empire, and to rise to the challenge of international competition whether military, scientific or industrial.

To the cartoonist David Low, newly arrived in London from the antipodean colonies, this ruling group was frustratingly inaccessible. He rapidly came to understand the basis for inclusion as being something which he could never attain: the breeding and confidence of a distinct and identifiable social elite, whose members had known each other since childhood and who relied on such contacts to maintain their advantages in later life. As he later recalled, there seemed to be 'almost a standard type', the 'uniform product of a system'. The core of British public life were 'the public school–university men who had "gone in" for politics as a career'. The ruling elite was 'confident of its mission to rule, its members all understanding one another perfectly, laying down the conditions, setting the standards and in general making politics fit for gentlemen and Westminster "the finest club in Europe"'. Outsiders from a different background seemed almost excluded from this 'club'.[12] But such a group was also vulnerable to satire and ridicule, as Low tellingly demonstrated in his political cartoons lampooning the conservatism and class mentality of characters such as 'Colonel Blimp'.

This notion of the 'old school tie' probably exaggerated the cohesion and unity of the social and political elite. Doubtless, too, most of its critics failed to acknowledge its often unpredictable effects. In January 1957, for example, after Sir Edward Boyle had resigned as a junior minister from Anthony Eden's cabinet over the Suez crisis, the headmaster of his old school, Eton, wrote to congratulate him on his stand:

The other day I had to talk about Eton at a Working-Men's Club in the East End of London. I pointed out to them that while people thought of the Suez policy of the Government as an 'Eton' policy, because of the number of Etonians in the Cabinet, they had not recognised that both the junior Members of the Government who resigned and the majority of the 'dissident' Conservatives were Old Etonians. I said that what we wanted to do at Eton was to produce men who would hold independent views and be prepared to stick up for them, not men who would take an 'Etonian' line and that I thought that that was the essential political tradition of Eton.[13]

Even so, despite such rationalisations and the complex relationships they imply, there is no doubt that the idea of a monolithic elite sharing a common vocabulary and outlook was a potent myth that had important political effects. Above all it sharpened social class antagonism already evident in the political and industrial confrontations of the interwar years.

If hostility to this established elite began to tarnish the image of leadership of the old school, the growing fascist threat on the Continent in the 1930s gave rise to new grounds for suspicion. Antipathy to the *Fuehrerschaft* shown by the fascist dictators also harmed the credibility of the public schools, especially when Adolf Hitler created his own schools designed for leadership training supposedly on the English model. This association was acutely damaging after the outbreak of the second world war: not only had the products of the public schools failed to prevent Britain's drift into the second major war in a generation, but they had also inspired a dangerous new breed of leaders in their quest for world domination. Some observers, like J.B. Firth, tried to emphasise a distinction between older schemes intended 'to educate the best youths drawn from every class . . . in the noblest arts of government directed to the good of the governed and the advancement of mankind', and the Nazi design for

the creation of a Junker class of Nazi leaders, Herrenfolk, lords of mankind, jack-booted, intolerant of all criticism, imperious in command, exacting an instant obedience, responsible only to the Fuehrer of the day, leaders intoxicated with the corrupting poison of race consciousness, despots without a touch of benevolence to those under their rule, who have learnt their notions of truth at the feet of Goebbels and their conceptions of justice and mercy from the pitiless despoiler of Czechoslovakia and Poland.[14]

But this did not prove greatly convincing. Preferable both to the nineteenth-century model and to the modern fascist creed appeared the prospect of achieving social and political equality. The war years were notable for the attention widely given to hopes, plans and blueprints of a 'New Jerusalem' that might emerge if only the Nazi threat could be overcome. The public schools, it was generally assumed, would have little role in this new society.

David Low, cartoon, 'New pupils at Dr. Göbbel's academy', 11 July 1940

Especially virulent in his condemnation of the public schools at this time was the critic T.C. Worsley, himself a former assistant master at a public school. He argued in 1940, in his book *Barbarians and Philistines: Democracy and the Public Schools*, that the public schools were central to the issues of democracy facing the country. Worsley fiercely attacked the 'Fuehrerprinzip' upon which he alleged English education was founded: 'It is primarily concerned, that is to say, with the selection and special training of "leaders". And in this task the Public Schools have not only been the pioneers and the example; they have also been the monopolists.'[15] He went on to blame the public schools for Britain's parlous position in the war, on the grounds that 80 to 90 per cent of ruling positions in the Church, State and Armed Forces were held by public school men. More than this, he suggested, the kind of training which these leaders had gone through gave them little qualification to fight for a democratic world: 'How can their products be expected to fight convincingly, or to work enthusiastically, on behalf of a democracy of which they have, in their most formative years, no experience?'[16] The classical curriculum of the public schools was also dangerously out of date, with the result that the nation was now saddled 'with a body of leaders whose understanding of the world they live in is hopelessly inadequate'.[17] The strong influence of Thomas Arnold in reforming the public schools in the nineteenth century, he continued, had given them a distinct ethos that was now irrelevant yet which stubbornly resisted change. In the new democracy, they would be hopelessly out of place, even if they were taken over by the State. Reliance upon such schools for the 'leadership' of the nation would, according to Worsley, become unnecessary in a 'more equitably based society' in which 'the whole six million of the school population were the potential reserve, instead of the fifty or sixty thousand of the Public Schools plus an odd forty thousand of scholarship Secondary School boys'. In such a society, 'natural leaders' would 'emerge' from among the mass of the people.[18] Indeed, he concluded stirringly, the education of the future should concentrate on followers rather than leaders: 'Educate the followers to understand themselves and their world, so that they may control both, and there will be no need to worry about leaders.'[19]

Worsley gained a widespread and sympathetic response, and returned to the attack the following year with the aptly named The End of the 'Old School Tie'. Again he blamed an incompetent and anachronistic ruling elite produced by the public schools for Britain's recent misfortunes:

For the second time in twenty years Britain and the British Empire are plunged into the catastrophe of war; and the men who led the British people in the period between the two wars have all one thing in common – they have received the same kind of education. The ruling class of England for the last twenty or thirty years has been drawn from the Public Schools . . . All these people consider themselves Britain's ruling class and they make sure that as many of themselves and their kind as possible get the leading positions. Four out of five of them were educated at the Public Schools, and the Public Schools claim to give a special training in leadership. It is by this claim that they justify their existence and on the strength of it demand continued support . . . They were trained to lead, and they have led us up the garden.[20]

They had, he complained, failed to understand the character of Nazism 'because their gentlemanly education had not equipped them to understand'. And this in turn was because 'They were still living in a world which had long since vanished . . . A new world of mechanical power, a new industrial and technical civilisation, found the wealthy rulers of Britain living still in the casual and spacious ease of the day before yesterday.'[21] Few public schools were exempt from his claims that they represented not only anachronism and privilege but also the kind of Fuehrerprinzip against which the nation was supposed to be fighting. Even Kurt Hahn, who had fled from Hitler's Germany, found it impossible to explain to Worsley the differences between a Platonic elite and a fascist master race.[22] The only way to end these divisions and the conflicts to which they led, Worsley declared, was to abolish the public schools and to develop a common educational background for all.

Worsley was unusually forthright in his comments. Even so, his expectations of radical change for the education system in general and the public schools in particular were widely shared. The American historian Edward C. Mack concluded a thorough and well-researched history of the public schools, published in 1941, with equally trenchant verdicts and a radical prediction. The financial problems of the public schools, he suggested, put them in 'a very precarious position'. Drastic change seemed likely: 'Even should England win the war, it is hard to believe that her social, economic, political, and social systems will not experience revolutionary changes. It appears, indeed, to a casual observer in this year of 1941 that the long development in terms of original structure, which England's institutions have undergone, is on the verge of being rudely shattered.'[23] Mack also agreed with the view that the public school educated leadership of the interwar years was partly responsible for the failure either to usher in a new order, or to protect the old. But he sought what he called a 'compromise', to reform rather than abolish the public schools: 'The most likely solution − if there is to be one at all − would be one in which the public schools would take state money and accept state interference in order to bring into their ranks the best elements of the working class, would reform in the direction of liberal and working-class aims, and would yet remain at least semi-independent boarding schools, emphasizing training for leadership.'[24] Just a few years earlier such a 'solution' would have been regarded as revolution rather than compromise; now it was a serious proposition. This rapid shift in opinion was vividly reflected in the columns of the *Times Educational Supplement*. In March 1940, while allowing that the public schools did face new difficulties and that they were open to the 'serious charges' of class segregation and exclusivity, the *TES* nevertheless accused the Labour Party spokesman of 'exaggerated prophecy and some inconsistency of argument' in his criticisms, and played down the notion of the 'old school tie'.[25] By May, in the midst of national crisis, the journal was more cautious in its opinions, and gave some support to the idea of a Royal Commission on the public schools.[26] A year later, under new editorial direction, it was calling for the public schools to be incorporated into the state education system. Indeed, it now urged, 'the schools would never be more true to their tradition than if they came voluntarily and willingly to the nation and placed themselves unreservedly in its hands, to take and to use as it thought best'.[27] The Dunkirk experience had wrought another miracle.

Another measure of the new situation was the response of Sir Cyril Norwood, a distinguished former Head of Harrow School and Master of Marlborough College, and now President of St John's College, Oxford. Throughout the interwar period Norwood had been a staunch though not uncritical supporter of the public schools. The essential truth about Harrow, he had observed in 1928, was 'that it is the creation of its own pupils, and inspired at its best by a living tradition of public service, proved in the past, fruitful in the present, full of hope for the future'. He noted that the public schools tended to attract criticism, 'Yet next term Harrow will welcome visitors from Germany and the United States, from the Dominions, India, and Japan, who will all come thinking that there is something worth their examination, some secret worth the catching, if it can be surprised. It is the secret of the English Public School.' The curriculum of such schools had begun to change, but 'the principles which govern their inner life' had not changed and should not be allowed so to do:

They can be stated in brief compass – that you must show yourself capable of obedience if you are ever to be fit to rule, capable of loyalty if you are to be trusted, that in every responsibility you must think of others before yourself, and that in every position of trust the one unforgivable sin is to fail in the task which has been given you to do. This code of conduct still finds the proper field for its exercise in the life of the Houses and the team-contests of the playing-fields.[28]

In general terms, he was emphatic that 'The claim made for the public schools . . ., that, whatever their shortcomings may be, they are at any rate successful in producing sound character and public spirit was put to a severe test on the outbreak of War in 1914 and triumphantly sustained.' That the schools were 'filled to overflowing' seemed to Norwood to attest to 'the success in leadership of boys trained in the schools, to an increased sense in the nation at large of the value of education, and particularly this form of education, and to a wider diffusion of wealth, which made possible a public school course for the sons of many who would not have been able to afford it before'.[29] He was aware of their problems and dangers – 'but the attacks that are commonly made on them I believe to be either exaggerated or ignorant, sometimes, indeed not infrequently, malicious'.[30] Norwood, then, was convinced of the continuing mission of the public schools in society, that of providing leadership and a spirit of service.

By the late 1930s, though, Norwood had become more pessimistic about their future prospects. In October 1938 he wrote to the senior chief inspector at the Board of Education, F.R.G. Duckworth, telling him of his increasing concern at 'the progressive lowering of professional standards which is going on through the growing decline in the numbers of entrants for the Preparatory and Public Schools'. Headmasters, he alleged, were 'literally spending half their time in commercial travelling and touting on Prep School doorsteps'. The situation demanded a Royal Commission on the public schools: 'I have my own ideas about what might be done, which do not matter: what does matter is that the Public Schools cannot save themselves. They cannot do more than pass pious resolutions which all the unscrupulous break.'[31] An interview with Norwood at the Board served to underline his message. He emphasised to Board officials that the growing problems of the public schools might even lead to 'something approaching a collapse' unless 'outside assistance' was forthcoming.[32]

The outbreak of war in September 1939 deepened Norwood's forebodings, as he commented privately: 'I do not see how as a system they are to survive the war. They have had their hundred years, and have rendered very great service with certain limitations. But the order of society to which they belong is at an end, or near it, however we may regret the fact.' Scholarships would be unable to 'stop the rot', 'unless you made it obligatory on all Boarding Schools, and that means taking full control'. But he did have a constructive proposal for the Board of Education to consider:

Start after the war a National system of boarding schools, age range 12–18 +, take the boys from the elementary schools and sons of clergy and ministers and from other classes on a small payment, and run the public school system yourselves through Boards of Governors as now. Do not let it fall into the hands of L.E.A.s who would not understand it. It may be expensive, but not more expensive than such a system of scholarships as would really save the public schools. And you would really democratise it without destroying its values.[33]

By February 1940 he felt prepared to make a public declaration of his position on 'The crisis in education'. In two strong and influential articles he freely acknowledged that 'the problem of the class-division created by the existence of the public-schools and the State-aided schools side by side, and the inequality of opportunity which it thereby created', had led to strong attacks on the public schools. He referred to a 'growing hostility' to the public schools, and even conceded that

It is hard to resist the argument that a State which draws its leaders in overwhelming proportion from a class as limited as this is not a democracy, but a demo-plutocracy, and it is impossible to hope that the classes of this country will ever be united in spirit unless their members cease to be educated in two separate systems of schools, one of which is counted as definitely superior to the other.

Even so, he insisted, the public schools were too valuable to lose. In particular,

They have shown that they can produce leaders, and for this reason they are one of the few features of our country's life which Hitler has attempted to copy. It is certain that a democracy which does not possess an innate sense of discipline, and which does not know how to train leaders, will not endure. There is no better school for either than the good boarding-school of the public-school tradition.[34]

Norwood concluded that the public schools should now become a 'vital part' of the education system by changing their age of admission from thirteen to eleven and organising a four- or six-year course on the same basis as the secondary school. They should accept from elementary schools an entry of not less than 10 per cent every year chosen on the basis of their record, an interview and a qualifying examination. Financial responsibilities, he avowed, should be taken over by Whitehall; but the schools should not be handed over to the LEAs, and their individuality and tradition should be preserved. The aim, according to

Norwood, was to open the doors of the public schools without respect of class, while maintaining their essential mission of 'education for leadership'.[36] It was another revolutionary compromise, again inspired by the new situation created by war.

There seemed little prospect of rapid or peaceful agreement, however. T.C. Worsley was hostile to these suggestions, which he claimed would 'introduce an even more favoured and reserved clique than the present State Secondary Schools'. According to Worsley, 'if, as I suspect is intended, these State schools are to be leadership colleges (like the Hitler colleges, only not called so), they will be open to exactly the same objections as are raised against the present system which isolates the ruling class from contact with the rest of the nation'.[36] Nor was there any apparent readiness for change among the public schools themselves, despite Norwood's own professed optimism on this score. Lord Hugh Cecil, Provost of Eton College, was so vexed by Norwood's public utterances that he wrote to the Minister of Education, Lord de la Warr, to protest. He was, he declared, against any Royal Commission; in fact, he was opposed to any state policy on the matter at all. His Governing Body had already unanimously expressed its 'sense of the extreme danger of any appeal to, or any interference by, the State'. Apparently unaware of any contradiction in his own position, or perhaps just confiding in an Old Boy of the school, he complained to the Minister that Norwood's articles 'seem to me pure Totalitarianism'.[37] The Minister contrived to be both reassuring and olympian in manner in his reply to the affronted Provost: 'I don't think we need attach too much importance to some of the matter which has appeared in the press, and, so far as Sir Cyril Norwood's articles are concerned, I gather that he speaks for no one but himself.'[38] The role of the public schools remained bitterly contentious, with no clear solution in sight.

THE FLEMING REPORT

By 1942, circumstances had changed sufficiently to allow a possible comprom- ise. At the Board of Education, Lord de la Warr was removed in April 1940. His successor, Herbert Ramsbotham, was replaced in July 1941 by a President of the Board, R.A. Butler, determined to introduce large-scale reforms throughout the education system. Butler himself seems to have been receptive to argument about the character of the changes needed. One idea that he floated within the Board was that all children might go into the same kind of school at the preparatory stage and then 'branch off into the various types of education provided, namely, Senior (Modern), Secondary, Technical or Boarding'. On the other hand, 'in framing educational policy I am continually inspired by relics of the belief that we are a free country'. Even if common schools were established, he observed, 'there is the risk that the law would be got round and people would start up a series of private schools, less satisfactory than those existing at present'. He was conscious of the need for advice but no less so of the urgency of reform:

I do not think that we should underestimate the extent of the social revolution through which England is now passing . . . I feel convinced that any educational measure will have to make it clear that we in the Education Department are not afraid of change; that we wish to preserve quality; that we have not in this country two absolutely separate types of education; and that they converge at various points.[39]

Sir Maurice Holmes, his senior official, was also hesitant in his estimate as to the probable amount of change, pointing to basic differences in political views of the issues involved. On the one hand, it seemed important to preserve the rights of parents who chose to send their children at their own expense to schools outside the public system. On the other, 'it will be argued that national unity depends on a national system of education for all and that the smaller classes of the preparatory schools give an unfair advantage to the child who attends them'.[40] The war itself had strengthened demands for social equality and unity. In this situation the Board of Education was able to play a key role in channelling aspirations towards a postwar settlement, though not necessarily in the 'Conservative' and concerted manner recently depicted by the historian Brian Simon.[41]

So far as the public schools were concerned a realistic measure of reform meant, as Cyril Norwood among others had predicted, setting up an official committee to investigate all aspects of the problem. The new President felt that 'Neither the Government nor the country were ready for a solution of the public schools question', and that 'the solution would be bound to be many headed'.[42] It is clear that Butler was aware of the historical dimensions, and the philosophical roots, of the public school dilemma. In a fascinating discussion with the Labour Party intellectual G.D.H. Cole in May 1942, the President of the Board considered 'in an amiable manner what Plato had attempted to discuss before us, namely, the best method of training the leaders of a community'. According to Butler's account of this conversation, Cole 'thought that the Public Schools should renounce their proud claim to constitute the method of training our leaders and should simply regard themselves as the boarding element in a national system of education. He thought they would have a happy future provided they assimilated themselves in some way to the State system.'[43] This was a useful indication of possible agreement, and indeed Cole was included in the Board of Education committee on 'The public schools and the general educational system' that Butler subsequently announced.

The terms of reference of the committee appointed in July 1942 were

To consider means whereby the association between the Public Schools (by which term is meant schools which are in membership of the Governing Bodies' Association or Headmasters' Conference) and the general educational system of the country could be developed and extended; also to consider how far any measures recommended in the case of boys' Public Schools could be applied to comparable schools for girls.

The sensitive task of choosing suitable members for the committee to represent different shades of opinion demanded considerable attention, as did the question of who should chair the committee. With regard to the latter, Butler eventually chose Lord Fleming, Senator of the College of Justice in Scotland. Fleming provided an authoritative and independent image for the committee, demonstrating to outsiders that the Board had not predetermined the report's conclusions. An experienced judge with no personal stake or 'old school tie' in the English scene, he was a reliable choice for a difficult assignment. The Fleming committee was appointed almost exactly one hundred years after the death of Thomas Arnold, committed to the reform of the schools identified with his name.

Evidence submitted to the Fleming committee by a large number of interested organisations gave clear expression to both sides of the debate. On the side of the established role and character of the public schools were groups such as the Association of Governing Bodies of Public Schools (GBA). This Association emphasised the special value of public schools for boys. It conceded that they should be made more accessible, but insisted that they should retain the freedom and independence necessary to preserve their character. The key qualities promoted by the public schools, according to the GBA, were '*Service, Responsibility and Leadership*'. They were uniquely qualified to cultivate these properties because

In Public Schools there are greater facilities for boys to enjoy a measure of self-government which gives to all the habits of service and responsibility, and to many a training in leadership; and it is particularly in Boarding Schools with their characteristic 'out-of-school' life that self-government and leadership can be fully exercised. Such leadership involves the readiness to take responsibility, the exercise of initiative, the power to give orders and to choose between persons without offence being given or taken, and the habit of settling issues, large or small, on the principle of the good of the community.

It accepted that the schools had once been nurseries of class privilege, but argued strongly that this was no longer the case. On the other hand, it suggested that 'to assist in diminishing social cleavage' the public schools should now be opened 'to boys in all social positions, so that the schools may in fact represent the community as a whole'. It concluded:

Experiments already tried have shown that boys coming from poorer homes very soon become amalgamated with the rest of the community, and we believe that the result will be not that the boys will be 'declassed' and become assimilated to alien social circles, but that they will bring back into their own circles the powers of leadership and the 'public spirit' which the Public Schools tend to develop.[44]

The Independent Schools Association similarly defended the established character and role of the public schools: 'The value of the Public Schools as a national asset lies firstly in the opportunity which they afford as a training in community life and as a milieu in which qualities of leadership and responsibility may develop. In this respect they are unique and are the envy of other peoples.'[45]

Little compromise was to be found here; nor was there any among the critics of the public schools, who often singled out the supposed leadership qualities of the schools for special attention. The Workers' Educational Association, for example, sought to refute such claims once and for all:

> The function of the Public Schools is often expressed briefly as to provide a training for 'leadership' in the State. The word has unhappy connotations; but what is meant is apparently, that these schools have developed a technique which produces the qualities which are needed for positions of higher responsibility in the public service and in professional and political life. If this claim is pressed, the answer is twofold: 'The qualities of leadership are not confined to a single privileged class; yet the overwhelming majority of positions of responsibility in the Church, State and the armed forces of the Crown have gone to Public School men.'

The WEA stressed the undemocratic nature of the schools' exclusive role as training grounds for leadership, and also opposed any schemes to throw them open more widely. It disliked 'not only the restricted scope of the schools for leadership, but their very existence as such'.[46] The Standing Joint Committee of Working Women's Organisations, similarly, saw 'no educational justification for the continuance of the Public School System'. It was merely a social institution, based on exclusivity. According to the Standing Joint Committee, this fact alone was sufficient to dispose of their leadership pretensions:

> Even if it were established that its characteristic educational methods provide the best training for leadership, it would still be true that it does not and cannot provide the best leaders, since it has no means of selecting for training those young people who by their intellectual equipment are best fitted to lead in any sphere of public life. What in fact the Public School System does is to preserve leadership in the State and entry to the higher ranks of many professions, in the main for a small privileged class.

Instead of retaining this system, it concluded, there should be a single, state system of education for all children up to sixteen years of age. Secondary education would comprise a variety of courses but with a large 'common core' of subjects for all pupils in the first two years.[47] These arguments were echoed by the Trades Union Congress, which also attacked the public schools' distinctive leadership role. The community, it urged, should not consist of 'two pre-determined groups of leaders and led'. In fact, 'The result of practising this system in the past is that our rulers have been largely drawn from a class apart from the general community, and have for that very reason been less well-fitted to occupy their positions than they might have been. It should be the aim of the state to abolish this caste system.' According to the TUC, in conclusion, the proper alternative would be very different:

> The aim of our national system of education should be to give every individual full and free opportunity of developing his capacities to the fullest extent, and of becoming a

conscious and responsible citizen. It need not be feared that a society based on such educational ideals will fail to throw up its own leaders – leaders who have shared a common experience with the people they are to lead, and who achieve their position of leadership through their own outstanding ability, their understanding of their fellows and their capacity to interpret common aspirations in terms of government.[49]

Thus the unequal and undemocratic character of the public schools was held to discredit their tradition and aspiration of leadership.

The Fleming committee steered a careful path between these widely varying recommendations. It did not submit its report until July 1944, by which time the headier hopes of 1940–1 had begun to subside and the probable contours of the postwar world were becoming visible. As the *TES* noted on its publication, the report rejected both 'the viewpoint of those who see no justification for the continued existence of the schools, and would completely abolish them', and 'that of those who find no imperfections in them as they are, and so would have them unaltered and unchanged'.[49] It opposed the abolition of the public schools, and also the idea of bringing them under the control of the LEAs, but declared the need to take advantage of 'a unique opportunity for incorporating the Public Schools with their distinctive characteristics into the general system, and of helping to close, in the world of schools, a social breach that follows and aggravates, if it does not actually cause, the much more serious divisions in society at large'.[50] Its avowed aim was to mitigate the social exclusiveness associated with the schools, 'making possible the voluntary association with the general educational system of all Public Schools, whatever their financial position, without any sacrifice of educational standards or of reasonable freedom in such matters as school government, curriculum, religion, and general educational principle'.[51]

The report examined in detail the historical roots of the contemporary problem, describing the revival of the public schools in the nineteenth century and their dominant characteristics since that time. Their established role in producing leaders of society was particularly mentioned. It saw the prefect system as highly important towards this end: 'When a school is able to train boys to accept responsibility, and to regard it as a responsibility for the welfare and good discipline of others, rather than as a means of securing advantages for themselves, it is making a valuable contribution to society.'[52] In the previous century, too much emphasis had perhaps been placed upon the disciplinary aspect. 'But we believe that this tradition, which allows so large a degree of responsibility to the boys themselves, is one of great educational value.' Other secondary schools might also be able to promote this, 'but it has of necessity even greater opportunities of development in boarding schools'.[53]

The Fleming committee also endorsed the essential sense of purpose of the public schools: 'During the last hundred years they have preserved for English education a belief in the value of humane studies, in the need for a training in responsibility, and in the essential part to be played by religion in education.'[54] It sought to retain this tradition while remedying their main weakness, 'derived from the fact that at present they too often concern themselves with children coming from only a limited section of society'.[55] Boarding schools had vital advantages over other kinds of school, especially in allowing 'a training in community life which enables the boys and girls to work in and for a society composed of very different types, to sacrifice their personal wishes to the general good, to find their place in the community and be ready, if called upon, to take responsibility'.[56] Even so, it added, as if in direct response to the TUC's argument,

It must not be supposed that, when the common life of either a Boarding or a Day School is said to produce qualities which fit the young for responsibility, the object or the effect of the school's training is to produce a superior class of leaders whom the rest of the world are to follow, or that the community consists of two predetermined groups of leaders and led. What is meant is that the common life of the school prepares boys and girls to take responsibility if it comes to them, giving them scope and initiative and developing self-reliance, but prepares them no less to follow the lead of others in the school, and afterwards, if that should be their duty.[57]

This view led Fleming to recommend an extension of opportunities for boarding to all, first through the admission of pupils from grant-earning primary schools to boarding schools already in existence, and also by providing more boarding schools. Two schemes of association were proposed: Scheme A, for the schools to be fully accessible to all pupils, either by abolishing tuition fees or by grading fees according to the means of the parent; and Scheme B, in which a number of places in public boarding schools would be filled by pupils who would have their fees made up either by means of state bursaries or through assistance from the LEAs. In brief, Fleming was attempting to reconcile the tradition of education for leadership, which he saw as admirable, with the demands of democracy and equality.

Whether or not the Fleming report achieved this objective is debatable. Critics of the public schools continued to complain of their essentially elitist and undemocratic character. G.D.H. Cole, obliged to resign from the Fleming committee due to illness, distanced himself from the final report:

I do not believe the 'snob' boarding schools can be democratised, as the Fleming committee suggests, by admitting to them a proportion of entrants from the State primary schools. There are not enough of them for such a process to be effective: it would more probably lead, in view of their expensive standards, to the assimilation of the new entrants into the middle class.[58]

These fears proved to be justified, as a later Public Schools Commission reporting in 1968 confirmed. Indeed, according to this later report, 'as an instrument of national policy, the Fleming report rapidly became a dead letter'.[59]

It seemed true also that the products of the public schools remained dominant in the leading positions of society and State. Analyses by W.L. Guttsman and David Boyd, among others, continued to emphasise the role of key educational institutions in maintaining the exclusivity of the elite.[60] On the other hand, W.D. Rubinstein and Harold Perkin have argued more recently that avenues of elite recruitment have widened considerably.[61] Still, it has been calculated that in 1970–1, a generation after the Fleming report, 62 per cent of top rank civil servants, 83 per cent of foreign ambassadors, 67 per cent of top rank clergy in the Church of England, and 83 per cent of directors of clearing banks had been educated at public schools. In 1982, at least 42 per cent of Members of Parliament had been educated in public schools, and 20 per cent of these at one particular school – Eton.[62] In many ways it appeared that the hold of former public school boys on 'top jobs' was undiminished in its strength.[63] In 1983 the foreign secretary and the lord president, the chairman of Lloyds Bank and the director-general of the BBC were all Wykehamists. Eton – in Anthony Sampson's words 'not only an educational establishment but a political training-ground, a charm school and a unique national network' – could boast the governor of the Bank of England, the chief of the Defence Staff, the editor of the *Times* and the heads of both the home civil and the foreign service.[64] According to Shirley Williams, formerly secretary of state for education, 'Public school alumni move on into the better jobs society has to offer, exercising influence as managers, MPs, bankers and professionals – the officer class of the country; yet nothing in their lives will have made them familiar with the majority of those they seek to lead, to supervise or to govern.'[65]

Yet there were also signs of change. In particular, the public schools themselves seemed to learn a great deal from the debates of the early 1940s. As will be seen in chapter 6, the curriculum of many public schools began to make more allowance for science education. The supporters of the public schools also became much less prepared than they had been before to announce publicly their role as 'leadership' colleges. According to John Dancy, Master of Marlborough College, in 1963,

anyone who knows anything about public schools since the war knows that the most important change that has occurred in them during that time is the change in personal relations generally and in ideas of leadership in particular. One might sum the point up by saying that the word leadership is hardly ever mentioned: it has been replaced by the key-concept of responsibility, and this replacement is not merely verbal but actual.[66]

Certainly by comparison with evidence to the Fleming committee, there was very little mention of 'leadership' from defenders of independent education in their evidence to the Public Schools Commission of the late 1960s.[67] The real or underlying purpose of the schools may have changed little. Jonathan Gathorne-Hardy concludes that 'The premise behind a public school education – although a great deal more subtle and humane – is the same as it has always been: it is to train the leaders of society.'[68] But by contrast with the proud claims made before the second world war, since that time their adherents have been very reticent about declaring this in public. As late as 1938, Annesley Somerville, formerly a master at Eton, could tell the House of Commons in a debate on education: 'Let us face the facts. A great majority of the rank and file in this country have to be manual workers. What we want in the secondary schools is to develop leaders. We ought to acknowledge that.'[69] Since 1945 this has been acknowledged only *sotto voce*. We may regard this as both the limited achievement of critics of the 'old school tie', and a judicious retreat on the part of the public schools themselves. But if the critics had won the argument, they had lost the wider battle. The established structures and institutions survived relatively unscathed, as did the social inequalities that they encouraged and nurtured. What was to a large extent lost was the Platonic vision of enlightened moral, social and political leadership that the public schools had represented before the second world war. In its day this education for leadership had been frankly elitist, notoriously inflexible, often complacent and hypocritical. And yet there was little to replace it in terms of a social or community mission more appropriate for the postwar era. Perhaps the public schools adapted too well to the demands of a secular, atomistic society that valued individual achievement above public service. Above all, though, there is no mistaking the fact that equality – certainly the social equality that T.C. Worsley and others had anticipated during the second world war – was as far distant as ever.

The defenders of the public schools in the 1930s and 1940s saw their values and ideals as more important than ever, but often recognised that new forces and pressures challenged their future. The key issue for such educators was to discover how to maintain the essential mission of the public schools in this time of change. They had not given up hope of rehabilitating the public schools, nor of converting a new public to their enduring tradition. But another attractive strategy was also to hand: to infuse the values of the new state system of secondary education towards the same ends. It was this that engaged much of the attention of at least one prominent adherent of the 'English tradition', Sir Cyril Norwood.

4

THE IDEOLOGY OF
SIR CYRIL NORWOOD

The efforts of Sir Cyril Norwood on behalf of the public schools were only one aspect of his endeavour to develop an approach to 'education for leadership' that might be successful in a changing society. The key problem as he saw it was to infuse the values of the public schools, which he associated with a long-established 'English tradition' in education, into the new state secondary schools. It was this aim that above all informed his major report to the Board of Education in 1943, on the curriculum and examinations in secondary schools.

NORWOOD AND THE ENGLISH TRADITION

Cyril Norwood, born in 1875, was educated at Merchant Taylors' School and St John's College, Oxford. An outstanding student, he gained a first class degree in classical moderations and *literae humaniores*, before heading the list for entry to the civil service and being posted to the Admiralty in 1899. Within two years he resigned from this post to become sixth form classics master at Leeds Grammar School. This major shift in his prospective career was apparently made because of the scant scope for initiative that the Admiralty allowed; the new opportunities offered by the imminent introduction of state secondary education were probably another important factor in his decision. Such was his impact that in 1906 he was appointed Headmaster of Bristol Grammar School, whose academic fortunes he quickly helped to restore.[1] In 1916 he left the state sector to become Master of Marlborough College in Wiltshire, and then in 1926 took over as Head of Harrow School. After eight often difficult years at Harrow he accepted an invitation to become President of his old college in Oxford, where he remained until his retirement in 1946. It has been suggested that 'More than any of his contemporaries, Norwood was in the tradition of the great Victorian headmasters, and the rapid spread of English education gave him a wider stage than theirs on which to play his part.'[2] More particularly, it enabled him to encourage what he saw as the finest features of the public school to spread throughout the new state system of education. Norwood held that the

'English tradition of education', with which he associated the public schools of the nineteenth century, should now be adapted to meet the changing circumstances of the twentieth-century world. The best qualities of such schools were, he argued, as relevant and important as ever. Chief among these were the 'public spirit' and moral values involved in their approach to education for leadership.

This theme was central to Norwood's educational thought. The new municipal secondary school, he argued in 1909, 'should aim at developing more of the public spirit of the older schools both among masters and boys, since its best success depends upon the hearty co-operation of Head and staff and pupils in building up, by personal devotion, that tradition of intense corporate life which has been denied it by its history'. He felt that the grammar school would increasingly come to dominate 'English higher education' due to 'its combination of liberal study and contact with life'. The public school should therefore 'be brought into line and given the leading place it merits in a national system'. Even at this early date, while emphasising above all the unique contribution of the public schools and the need for their retention, he suggested that

As a residential school and as a school endowed for learning it is in equal need of inspection, and public control alone can improve the standard of its average intellectual work and break down its caste spirit, without impairing its individuality or that keen spirit of loyalty and that athletic energy which have made its contribution to international education of unique and lasting value.[3]

Like Sir Robert Morant at the Board of Education he defended the public school tradition and sought to apply it to the new state secondary schools, but he was willing to introduce a measure of state control for the public schools also in order to develop a fully national system. In this way, he hoped, '*The Value of Secondary Education*, already dimly recognised, will under expert State control become as patent to English, as to foreign, parents and employers', especially in 'bringing different classes together when they are young and generous, and thereby introducing a spirit of union and mutual sympathy into a nation so split today by fraction that it is risking both its internal prosperity and its outward strength.'[4] Thus the growth of political and social tension in the first decade of the century heightened Norwood's awareness of the need to augment through fresh channels the public school tradition of the past. This ethos, he suggested, could help to preserve social cohesion and prevent conflict between different groups. But it would at the same time maintain a recognisable social hierarchy, with a renewed mission for the governing elite as for the mass of the population.

Thus Norwood may be taken to represent for our purposes an elitist tradition of education, reflecting the extent to which education for leadership remained a key issue for state secondary education as for the public schools in the first part of this century. Not that he can be taken as precisely representative of educators in this tradition. On the one hand, he was surely the most prominent and influential of educators expounding this kind of approach during his active career, which stretched over four decades. On the other, his own personal experiences undoubtedly led him to interpret what he took to be the 'English tradition' in a distinctive, often idiosyncratic manner. His schooling at Merchant Taylors', a leading 'great' day school, seems to have ensured that he was never as suspicious of day schooling, as distinct from the boarding element usually seen as crucial to the public school ethos, as were other public school headmasters of his generation. His struggle to re-establish Bristol Grammar School before the Great War reflected a pursuit of acceptability and respectability in relation to the public schools, giving him first-hand experience of the problems that such a process would involve.[5]

The experience of the Great War confirmed Norwood in this faith in the importance of education for leadership, rather than undermining it. He treated it as a unique opportunity for his pupils to display 'sound character and public spirit'. One ex-pupil from Bristol Grammar School, Stanley Booker, wrote to him at the outbreak of war in August 1914 to ask for his advice on his entitlement to a scholarship which he had won at St John's College, Oxford, if he took up a commission in the Army. Norwood replied: 'I am sure that your scholarship will not be affected, and I think it is your duty. Please God this country will not know invasion, but apart from that there is much to do. So please go on, and all good be with you.'[6] Booker did not let him down. He applied for the commission and was awarded a Military Cross in France. His attitude to the sacrifice and hardship of the war was all that his old headmaster could have expected. He wrote to Norwood from the trenches in 1916:

I am sorry to see the school casualty list mounting up so quickly but it is all in a good cause and one cannot help being proud of the friends who have laid down their lives: and for oneself one feels almost glad to be in the danger of it. War does bring out the qualities that count: and it is a great moulder of things great and good. I feel now that life is more worth living than ever it was before, though at the same time one feels ready to lay it down if one must.

He was now Lewis Gun Officer of his battalion, the 2/7th Worcesters:

It gives me more work in many ways but I like it as it is a fairly responsible and independent command. I have a horse to ride and live at the Battalion HQ out here. Of course when in the line I have a lot to do and whatever happens never have to leave the front line trench. So it requires a good man and I trust I shall prove equal to it if ever we are really tried.[7]

Stanley Booker was indeed the personification of the values that Norwood cherished: public spirit, character, leadership. Almost inevitably, he was killed in action soon after writing the above letter. Norwood wrote to console his brother:

He died like a hero, and he was not afraid to die: he wrote to me about it when he won the Military Cross, a letter of fine simplicity accepting the risks and their probable result without any flinching. I am proud and shall always be proud of having had him as a pupil and counted him as a friend . . . 'Greater love has no man than this, than that he should lay down his life for his friends', and you can always be very proud of him and know that his short life was not lived in vain.[8]

Stanley Booker, like the many others who fought and died in the Great War, continued to inspire Norwood's teaching in later years.[9]

In the 1920s, at the peak of his career at Marlborough and then at Harrow, Norwood developed a distinctive and potent outlook on the traditions and potential contribution of English secondary education. He told the Educational Science section of the British Association for the Advancement of Science, in 1928, that 'every part and parcel of our educational system' should foster 'the highest and truest English tradition',

that education is more than instruction, that character counts for more than brains and lives more than learning, that the true basis of life is religious, and the only real values spiritual. I would say that the main end and aim is to train boys and girls for service to the community, and to make clear that their lives can be lived in this spirit, whether they are tradesmen or merchants, engineers or manufacturers, clergymen or doctors, or followers of any career whatever, and that the only life deserving of contempt is the life that contributes nothing, or contributes evil, to the common stock. We have a fine traditional method to follow, which has been handed down to us from the best of our predecessors; we can build our school lives on fellowship and the sense of honour, on the team-spirit and not on individualism.[10]

It was this view that underpinned the most detailed and complete statement of Norwood's philosophy, published in 1929 under the title *The English Tradition of Education*. This 'tradition', he claimed, 'was not in its origin based on a logical theory, nor is it the creation of any inspired educational reformer. It has merely grown out of the life of the nation, and therefore to those who are born within that nation it seems commonplace. It is taken to be something which everybody knows.' As such, it was often taken for granted, but 'it stood the strain of the War, and emerged very much the stronger from the ordeal, as a system which had been tried in the furnace, and had not been found wanting'.[11] He was pleased to see, too, that the Germans were now turning to English schools to learn a secret that had eluded them:

That English tradition not only carried the country through the War, but to it we owe our acquisition, maintenance, and development of our present Empire, to it we owe the fact that is of vital import for the future of humanity, that in essence it is not an Empire of conquest and exploitation, but of trusteeship, development, and growth. It is free to change, to cast off the old, and to seek the new.[12]

The English tradition of education, he continued, should not be regarded as the monopoly of a class, but on the contrary was the common inheritance of all English schools, which could save the nation from both 'international war' and 'social war'. And he looked forward to the creation of an 'educated democracy'

Dr Norwood at Harrow

based on this tradition – 'a democracy so educated in every type of school that it will answer to the call of the same ideals, and accept the same standards of conduct and service'.[13]

Norwood argued that this 'English tradition' had remained important but essentially stable through centuries of gradual evolution: 'English education is like the English political system. Its institutions change, and adapt themselves, but maintain their identity from century to century.'[14] It was, he declared, grounded firmly upon the ideal of knighthood, chivalry and the English gentleman, originated in the Middle Ages and revived by Arnold of Rugby. Thus, he concluded, 'the ideal which the public schools are seeking, however imperfectly, is the true ideal, that it answers to our national needs, and has its roots far back in our national history'.[15] According to Norwood, the central aspects of this ideal were discipline, the Chapel, culture, athletics and the ideal of service. Each of these was intended to assist in the training of character and the implanting of values that emphasised public spirit and leadership. The advantage of athletics, for example, was that it could be used to reinforce the message

that a game is to be played for the game's sake, and that it matters not a button whether it is won or lost, so long as both sides play their best: that no unfair advantage of any sort can ever be taken, and that within these rules no mercy is to be expected, or accepted, or shown by either side: that the lesson to be learned by each individual is the subordination of self in order that he may render his best service as the member of a team in which he relies on all the rest, and all the rest rely upon him: that finally, never on any account must he show the white feather.[16]

According to his ideal of service, moreover, boys were 'ranged in a hierarchy, where the youngest are bound merely to obey, but may look to rise through a series of offices and honours, responsibilities, privileges, and duties to positions of real honour'.[17] This was the tradition of education that he hoped now to encourage in the new and growing state system of education: 'I put forward the ideal of the highest English education, of that education which trains a generation through religion and discipline, through culture of the mind and perfection of the body, to a conscious end of service to the community, as an ideal which shall inspire the whole of our education in every type of school, and create the democracy of the future.'[18]

These views attracted wide and generally favourable attention. The strongly conservative message that they contained appealed to many observers, especially those complacent of the virtues of the public schools and seeking to defend them against renewed criticisms. The *Morning Post* celebrated Norwood's 'great book' for its demonstration of the merits of a 'great national tradition of education' that was in growing danger of neglect or even ruin.[19] Norwood's approach also tended to legitimise social and political conservatism. He reasserted and confirmed the unique responsibilities of the dominant group in society, with all the power and authority that went with these duties. He was also clear that it was the duty of the working class to know their place and to obey those in positions of authority, and he had no time for protest action such as the General Strike of 1926.[20] Thus his educational approach could be interpreted as a classic instance of using the state apparatus of education to maintain control and hegemony. But Norwood's book also suggested radical action to renew this 'English tradition' and ensure its continued relevance and central role in the new state system.

REFORM AND RENEWAL

Norwood's notion of reform was limited by his respect for established practices, especially those sanctified by the leading public schools of the nineteenth century. In some respects his attitudes were little different from what one might expect of a Victorian public school headmaster. Thus he explained to one female journalist, in 1928, that 'girls should be educated quite differently from boys'. He felt that the recent Board of Education report on the differentiation of the curriculum between the sexes had taken too radical a line on this issue because 'the *majority* of girls were not considered':

Individual girls can be found who are capable, intellectually, and even physically, of the same work as boys. But when you consider the 100,000 or so of girls of 12 to 18 who are now being educated in the secondary and public schools – the number has increased two and three times since the war – is it not very short-sighted to suppose that a stereotyped course of learning will suit all of them? The majority will eventually marry. At school they are taught exactly as if they were going on to university.[21]

He noted in the preface of his *English Tradition of Education* that 'No reference is made to the education of girls, and the omission is deliberate', although he did concede that 'the writer is well aware that to both sexes the ideal is common, and that to its contribution women will make increasingly rich contribution'.[22] He was clearly little interested in equality of opportunity for girls. But his was also a strong reforming vision, intent essentially to revise the public school tradition in a new age in order to ensure its renewal and even its extension to the whole population.

One clue to this revisionist approach was his view of the kinds of fields to which the pupils of public schools should aspire in the twentieth century. It was no longer sufficient for them to seek to govern the Empire as their fathers had done, he argued. He pointed out a growing need to ensure that public school boys 'get the posts for which they are best fitted; or, what is much the same thing, those in which they will render their country the best service'. The 'normal and obvious' fields of employment for such boys, especially 'the professions and the national services of defence and administration', still called for their recruitment in large numbers, but there were now also 'new, or, if not entirely new, more urgent and extensive calls form other quarters'. The production of oil and rubber, the 'great commercial houses of the East', the development of South America and the domestic requirements of the municipal services, industry, docks, mines and railways, all needed 'boys of the right type'. Indeed, 'From whatever quarter of the world they come, these demands have at bottom much the same character. The need is not only for men who are reliable and adaptable, but for those who can manage other men with justice and goodwill, who can, in two words, administer and lead.' Norwood suggested that a 'clearing house' should be established on behalf of public schools towards these ends.[23] As unemployment increased during the 1920s and the staple industries of Britain were threatened by depression, he called also for the development of new ideas in industry:

Our future depends upon the application of science to industry, in other words, it depends upon our education. We have also to produce in very considerable numbers every year the type of man who is fitted to administer and to govern, and here too the range is widening and the problem is becoming different. Notably in Africa, but also in Asia and elsewhere, we want not only the cadet of the governing stock of whom in the nineteenth century we produced sufficient, but also scientists, entomologists, directors of agriculture, doctors, and engineers of many types, who are all capable of research, or of applying the results of research, and capable also of governing, teaching and directing native and backward populations.[24]

At the same time, he asserted an urgent need for compulsory education for all up to the age of sixteen. At the North of England Conference in Leeds in

January 1926, Norwood emphasised that 'He could not bear to think of the waste by which the products of elementary education were thrown wholesale on to the scrap-heap at 14, and all the benefit they had gained dissipated for want of control and educative employment in the immediately ensuing years.'[25] On the other hand, few were suited, in his opinion, for the kind of education that the secondary schools had usually supplied, and there was in any case a risk of an over-supply of the black-coated workers that such schools tended to produce. For these reasons, he argued, secondary schools should become more varied in their provision and curricula for the different needs of future society. Thus, as he said,

He would seek to bring this reform about by making elementary education stop at the age of 11 or 12, by making a number of elementary schools into central schools with a range of age up to 15 and eventually 16. He would make those schools more frankly vocational than secondary schools of the old type, and he would encourage free experiment and variation.[26]

He supported the proposals of the Hadow report on the education of the adolescent, anticipating that 'all children would go forward after eleven on parallel lines, following the course best suited to each'.[27] The new kinds of secondary school would, he hoped, 'always seek to develop the hand and the eye, and in their last two years will develop a practical bias'.[28] In this way, Norwood envisaged that the pressures on the existing type of secondary education caused by a rapid growth in the number of secondary school pupils would be lessened, and standards restored. As he explained to the Canadian Club of Montreal during a visit to Canada in 1930,

The plain fact is that the majority of boys and girls who are born are not educationally capable of academic education of the high school type. That does not mean that they cannot profit and won't profit very much indeed by having four years of education which is different from the elementary course, but I think it does mean in our country that we have already provided sufficiently for those who are capable of profiting by an ordinary academic education.[29]

Thus there would be important differences in the types of secondary education available for different pupils. Yet they would all, he hoped, be infused with the same spirit or ideal: that which he characterised as the 'English tradition', or public school ethos. He asked rhetorically why, if the public schools sent out 'products better fitted for some of the purposes of life, notably administration and leadership', the best features of such schools should be retained as 'a monopoly of the well-to-do', with 'the door to it banged and bolted in the face of the ablest children of the poor'.[30] If a similar ethos could be extended through the new secondary education, he maintained, the 'deepening fissure' of the education system would be filled and society might be reunited behind a single purpose.

Such views also led Norwood to propose radical reforms in the school curriculum. First, he called for greater attention to be given to the teaching of English. He had complained in 1909 that 'the average boy, even of eighteen or nineteen, when he leaves school, has seldom attained any mastery of his own language, is ignorant of the beauties of his own literature and indifferent to its history, and can seldom write or speak with credit to himself, or with comfort to his audience'.[31] Just as in the United States and France, he suggested, the mother-tongue should be the most important subject in the school curriculum, with Shakespeare and Scott becoming the staple diet for every boys' school. Such a development would permit a greater awareness of national culture and history, or so he hoped. He continued to argue in favour of this in the 1930s. In 1933, the Board of Education's consultative committee under Sir Will Spens, beginning to collect evidence towards a report on secondary education, received a submission from Norwood emphasising the purpose of the school curriculum as 'training for citizenship'. He continued: 'I believe that the foundation should be English culture. English studies should be devoted to the training of pupils in speech, writing and reading (by which I mean that they should be taught how to read for themselves).' English studies should include History and Geography for all, and only one foreign language should be attempted although 'I regard a foreign language as an essential part of a Secondary Education.' At the same time, physical education and hygiene would become more important, and all should have some training in handicraft, art, and musical appreciation. Indeed, he affirmed, 'I regard all this as of nearly equal importance with English subjects, and as more important than the foreign language, or Mathematics and Science.'[32] He expanded on these themes in his oral evidence to the committee, claiming that 'The primary object of the curriculum in a Secondary School should be to inculcate a measure of English culture. At present pupils tend to leave school with a very slight knowledge of the history and manners of the country in which they live.' Norwood recalled that at Harrow he had introduced a course on these lines for boys in their last year before proceeding to the university. The ultimate aim, he reiterated, was to produce good citizens: 'the pupil must one day become a citizen, and his education should be designed and organised with this end in view'. Such an aim would also require the maintenance of the grammar schools, to the extent that, in his view, 'There is a very great moral significance in maintaining the cultural ideal of the better type of Grammar School.'[33] More broadly, he was anxious to reassert the role of moral education in the schools, insisting that 'the supreme importance of spiritual values' should go 'through all the schools of our country, through and through our national education'.[34]

Many of these objectives relating to the 'cultural ideal' of the secondary school seemed to Norwood to be obstructed by a heavy reliance upon external examinations. From 1917, with the introduction of the School Certificate examination, the university examining boards ensured that the established academic subjects would be maintained, and that the examinations themselves exerted a powerful influence upon the form no less than the content of the secondary school curriculum.[35] Norwood helped to introduce external examinations at Marlborough, and was chairman of the Secondary Schools Examinations Council (SSEC) from 1921. Nevertheless, he felt that in the state secondary schools reliance upon external examinations had become too great, to the extent of constricting the possibilities of the curriculum, and should be reduced. This became apparent in September 1928, with his presidential address to the Educational Science section of the British Association for the Advancement of Science in Glasgow. In this wide-ranging speech, he criticised formal and external examinations for their effects on teachers and on the problems of slow developers: 'I believe, therefore, though the time is not yet, that the right course will be to abolish all external examination for the average boy and girl, though leaving it as the avenue to the universities and the professions.'[36] For 'average' boys and girls, he suggested, schools might issue their own certificates of attendance and performance. Then he ventured to question the role of the common entrance examination to the public schools, alleging that it was based on memory and cramming, and concluding: 'I conceive that there is no method of reform save the abolition of so indefensible a system, and I believe that it is, or ought to be, an educational axiom that there should never be any examination of a child under fifteen save by his own teachers.'[37] Norwood's attack on external examinations for the mass of secondary school pupils went almost unnoticed; his suggestions for abolition of the common entrance examination attracted stern rebuffs. The *Times*, in a leading article, commented acidly that although 'Fireworks are more often used by boys than by their teachers', the Headmaster of Harrow through his remarks had 'let off a series of rockets which are dropping their sticks on his own head'.[38] In vain did Norwood try to explain that he preferred 'not to invent new types of certificate and to pile on more examinations, but to trust the school'. He agreed that his ideas implied 'such a revolution in the public attitude towards schools and examinations that I said at Glasgow that the time for it is not yet, but I do not despair of advance, and I hope that the time will come; it might renew and restore life in a region where soon there will be only mechanism'.[39] His audience remained sceptical and generally unmoved – an ominous warning of failure in store.

Norwood's critical stance on external examinations highlights an important difference between his approach and that of the increasingly influential 'psychometric' school in the 1920s and 1930s. For Norwood and those who thought like him it was the cultivation of a community spirit that was important, rather than the assertion or assessment of individual differences that might actually harm or hamper social cohesion and citizenship. In some ways Norwood's approach was reminiscent of the Idealist school associated with T.H. Green, and indeed this philosophy had been highly influential at Oxford when Norwood had been a student in the 1890s.[40] Both intelligence testing and Norwood's vision of the 'English tradition' tended in practice to justify social inequality, but they did so in different ways: psychometrics through the cult of intelligence, Norwood through an emphasis on moral qualities which he equated with leadership. In a sense the growth of external examinations was the outward and visible sign of the competitive individualism to which Norwood was so vigorously opposed. Thus in explaining the educational inequalities of the interwar years and the 'dominant ideology' of that time it is most important to differentiate between Norwood's moral curriculum and the academic regime that has usually been emphasised.

There were some initiatives developed in the 1930s that bore clear marks of Norwood's influence. One of his assistant masters at Harrow, Thorold Coade, was especially prominent in promoting the kinds of ideas with which Norwood was associated. Coade, educated at Harrow and Sandhurst, had been wounded in action in France in 1916 before returning, completing his education at Christ Church, Oxford, and then going back to Harrow in 1922 as a schoolmaster. Under Norwood's headmastership, he was encouraged to make contacts with other young schoolmasters across the country. He helped to organise the first junior public schoolmasters' conference in January 1930, held at Harrow and attended by about 150 men, and edited its proceedings as *Harrow Lectures on Education*. The conference, as he asserted, was based on two related notions:

(i) That there is an urgent and immediate demand in this country and elsewhere for enlightened leadership. (ii) That in the present stage of British education the public schools are still by tradition, environment and constitution potentially the ideal training-grounds for leadership (though this may not continue to be so indefinitely).[41]

Coade was soon to be given the opportunity to provide 'training-grounds for leadership' in a new environment. In 1932 he was appointed Headmaster of Bryanston School in Blandford, Dorset, which had opened only five years before. As he later recalled, 'I welcomed the chance to put into practice, on a larger and more official scale, those plans that for fifteen years had been fermenting within.'[42] The motto of Bryanston, 'Et nova et vetera', summed up Coade's determination to build on and revitalise what he took to be the key ethos of the established public schools. In May 1933 he began a voluntary organisation at the school, the Pioneers, to provide training in 'leadership, self-reliance and self-control', involving community work on the school estate during term time, and work camps and expeditions during holidays. Coade emphasised the moral and religious basis of education, and the need to promote physical, intellectual, aesthetic, moral and social activities. He was forthright, too, on the social demand of the future: 'I believe the maintenance of a democratic structure of Western civilisation depends on two things – (1) on our training the right kind of leader, and (2) on our developing the ability of the rest of our pupils to recognise true leadership, and on their willingness to follow it.'[43] Coade remained Headmaster of Bryanston until 1959, when he retired. His career exemplifies the kind of infusion of public school values into new institutions and forms of education that Norwood had championed.[44]

Another disciple of Norwood who tried to put similar ideas into practice was Ronald Gurner. Like Norwood a former pupil at Merchant Taylors', Gurner became classics master at Marlborough before the first world war. He served in France for two years during the war, and later recalled this 'Himalaya of experience' as the key to his 'whole outlook on education, and on life itself'.[45] After being badly wounded in 1917, he recovered sufficiently for Norwood to invite him to return to Marlborough. His 'lasting gratitude' to Norwood, as much as his faith in Norwood's educational ideas, are evident throughout his memoirs, published in 1937. Norwood's 'terrific moral strength and power'[46] are repeatedly emphasised, and Gurner concludes by describing him as 'that supreme genius among the modern generation of schoolmasters'.[47] Norwood also helped and encouraged Gurner to apply for the headship of a London County Council secondary school despite the fact that Gurner knew 'to all intents and purposes, next to nothing about State secondary schools or State schools of any sort'.[48] Gurner went on to be Head of Strand School from 1920 to 1926, then of King Edward VII School in Sheffield, and subsequently of Whitgift School in Croydon. Again, here we see the application of the public school ethos to the new state secondary education that was characteristic of Norwood's approach.

Gurner remained faithful to the spirit of the public schools through all his travels and experiences. The 'boarding school product', he affirmed, was 'almost *ipso facto* the right man, in essentials, in any place in which he happens to find that his sphere of work lies'. Even if he was 'stupid, unsympathetic, unreasoning, narrow-minded, obstinate', he had one overriding advantage: 'he will not let the side down'.[49] He was also suspicious of the effects of restrictions on state secondary schools that were imposed by LEAs and the Board of Education. Yet he attempted to overcome such constraints, and he did so by following the kinds of precepts that Norwood had proposed. The year after the publication of *The English Tradition of Education*, Gurner followed in Norwood's footsteps in his own, much less weighty work, *Day Schools of England*. He insisted in this book that the leading independent day schools such as Westminster, St Paul's and Merchant Taylors', and also the grammar schools that were scattered all over the country, should be ranked alongside the public schools. This was in spite of the presence of boys from elementary schools who, he revealingly confessed, 'would lower the tone of any school into which they found a way'.[50] He was frankly sympathetic of the problems to which this could lead, not so much for the free-place scholar as for the sensibilities of the cultivated and affluent: 'It is difficult, if you are a country solicitor or doctor of any standing, to contemplate with equanimity the possibility of your son sitting side by side with the son of your junior clerk or chauffeur – better send him to St Cuthbert's on the south coast'.[51] On the other hand, he argued, 'contamination by board-school [sic] boys of manners and accent' and 'degradation of the school by inspector and educational official'[52] were balanced by 'the greatly increased conception of their function' that such schools were now showing.[53] They now provided academic instruction sufficient to equip pupils for entrance into any career. Equally important, according to Gurner, they permitted the inculcation of Norwood's ideals of 'religion, discipline, culture, the team spirit as taught upon the playing fields, and the spirit of service'.[54] Even free-place scholars, despite their 'poor clothes and cockney accents',[55] could benefit from such principles and aspire ultimately to take a part in serving nation and Empire. Indeed, so far as 'service' was concerned, 'a secondary school in a London slum and Eton may well stand, as those from them stood in the trenches not so many years ago, as equals, side by side'.[56] The product of the secondary day school might even prove to be a less conservative, more adaptable leader, with 'less traditional conservatism to overcome'. He would lead the fighting services, become closely identified with home administration, and 'cooperate' with the public school boy in the higher ranks of business. Overall, Gurner concluded, 'To what extent he will lead it is difficult to say, but the experience which he has gained at school will enable him to assume responsibilities, if called upon, equal to those of the public-school boy, and his greater sympathy with the working-classes may enable him to turn those experiences to greater use.'[57] Thus Gurner sought to overcome snobbery and the prejudices and barriers constructed by the public schools, traits that he himself clearly shared, in order to reconstitute the authentic public school ethos in a changing educational and social context. But it is notable that his argument did not stem from democratic instincts. Rather it arose in spite of his distaste for such 'contamination', from a moral commitment stimulated by his wartime service. A broadened social and political leadership might also have the advantage of helping to mitigate social class conflict while retaining the qualities hitherto associated exclusively with the public schools.

If the work of Coade and Gurner provides evidence of Norwood's influence at the school level, the growth of one organisation in the 1930s shows that he also had some following at the national level. This was the Association for Education in Citizenship, established in 1934. The Association was concerned to encourage the education system 'to fit the pupil for the public duties of citizenship in a democratic state'.[58] It argued that in order to counter the tendency towards authoritarian regimes and a widespread decline in faith in democracy, education needed to be designed actively to prepare for citizenship and participation in the modern world. Leaders of the Association included Sir Ernest Simon, an industrialist and former Liberal MP; Eva Hubback, Principal of Morley College for Working Men and Women; and F. Crossfield Happold, Head of Bishop Wordsworth's School in Salisbury. Happold was particularly explicit about the need to promote 'enlightened leadership' and the social implications of this: 'Actually much of what I advocate is neither new nor

modern; it is inspired by the ideas of Plato.'[59] He acknowledged the similarity
of his message to that of Norwood, and called for educational reconstruction.
The curriculum needed to be overhauled, the examination system reduced in
influence, moral values reasserted. But he detected 'peculiar virtues' in English
education also, especially the 'English tradition' typified by the public schools.
This distinctive ethos, he argued, now needed to be developed in the state
education system: 'Imperfect though it is, the English tradition of education is
truly a rich one, containing elements of proved value. It is our task, conscious
alike of its virtues and shortcomings, to mould and adapt that heritage to the
needs of our own day.'[60] The school curriculum, he continued, should be based
not on subjects, but on the five elements of basic culture: social studies,
aesthetics, science, handwork and language study. He claimed, too, that chapels
should be included in new schools alongside the playing fields and laboratories,
to develop the life of the spirit. Such 'schools for citizens' would instil 'the spirit
of social service and political responsibility, of the acceptance of a duty towards
the community to which he belongs and on which he is dependent', and should
arouse 'a reasoned pride in our own particular national tradition'.[61] Happold
also maintained that they should develop 'an aristocracy sufficiently powerful
and informed to direct general opinion'. In fact, he concluded,

The wider the basis of that aristocracy the firmer the foundations of political life will be.
If they wish, the schools of England can create such an aristocracy, an aristocracy based
not on birth or wealth but on intelligence and character, acting as an inner core of
enlightened thought, able not only to permeate the whole mass but also to produce and
support educated and capable leaders.[62]

The 'new aristocracy' would be composed of those with 'potential capacity to
make the fullest and most varied contribution to the community'.[63] At his own
school Happold introduced in 1936 the rather grandiose 'School Company of
Honour and Service', an elected group intended to be 'an instrument for
training boys to be better citizens and for preparing them for service to the
community'.[64] The uniform of its members was similar to that of the Pioneers
of Bryanston, ' a body with similar aims, blue-grey shirt, shorts and stockings'.
He suggested, indeed, that 'It is surprising that public and state secondary
schools have not given more attention to this sort of specific leader training. A
little practical effort to train the leaders, which everyone maintains are lacking,
would be worth more than much talk about the need of social service.'[65]
Happold's ideas, overblown and pretentious as they were, were closely related
to those of Norwood.

   Attempts on the part of the Association for Education in Citizenship to
encourage the Board of Education to emphasise preparation for citizenship
seem also to have been at least in part inspired by Norwood's ideas. At the
beginning of 1937, Sir Ernest Simon approached Oliver Stanley, President of
the Board, to seek assistance in planning a conference on the contemporary
challenge to democracy.[66] In 1938, Simon and Hubback invited themselves to

the Board to press upon Maurice Holmes the idea of a departmental committee to inquire into education for citizenship.[67] According to his own account of the meeting, Holmes 'threw a good deal of cold water on the proposal', and pointed out that the Spens committee on secondary education had already been established.[68] Not to be treated lightly, Simon then pursued Sir Will Spens to argue his case. He seems to have had some success. Spens suggested privately that 'something would be said about it' in his report, although, 'in the nature of things, the issue was much less real in a remit concerned primarily with children up to 16 than it would be over VIth form work'.[69] In fact, the final report, published in December 1938, made a point of emphasising the need to educate for citizenship. It announced solemnly that 'On the extent to which the youth of this country can be fitted to fulfil later their duties, and to take advantage of their opportunities, as citizens of a democratic State may well turn the whole future of democracy, and that not only in this island.'[70] Study of the issues involved in national and international politics 'must in the main come at a later age and be continued throughout life', but 'we believe that valuable foundations for this can be laid before the age of 16'.[71] On the eve of the second major war in a generation, this was explicit acknowledgement of the force of the arguments put forward by the Association for Education in Citizenship: authoritarian propaganda must be countered with education for citizenship. If it did not go so far as Norwood in asserting the social and cultural implications of this, there were faint echoes of Harrow and Marlborough in its advocacy of social service.

In some senses, Norwood was a radical, even isolated figure in the interwar period. It is not entirely surprising that he could name Lord Shaftesbury as a source of inspiration, whose 'whole attitude of mind was foreign to the prevailing spirit of the age', and who 'disapproved of the whole main stream of the development of his period'.[72] Too advanced for most leading administrators and public school headmasters, he was much too far rooted in the traditions of the public schools for most left-wing critics to follow. Yet he offered a coherent and distinctive path of development for the English state system of education, for it to share in the advantages that had been confined to a few through the unique ethos of the public schools. It was this ethos that lay at the core of his envisaged reforms, and he emphasised that without it any reforms would be meaningless or worse: 'Whatever reforms of administration, whatever changes of curriculum, whatever increase of expenditure are approved, the last word lies with the teachers, and all depends on the spirit which animates them and the ideals which move them.'[73] These views continued to guide his last and most important initiative in reform and renewal during the second world war.

THE NORWOOD REPORT

It was the war that allowed Norwood, at the end of his career, an unexpected opportunity to put his ideas into practice throughout the education system. He had anticipated that leaving Harrow to become President of his old Oxford college would mean withdrawing from the national stage; and in 1938, when he received his knighthood, he was sixty-three years old. As we saw in the last chapter, however, the outbreak of war led him to renew activity on behalf of public school reform. It also inspired him to campaign for more general educational reconstruction. His advocacy of change during the war, a crucial formative period in the creation of the postwar system of secondary education, was central to these reforms, culminating as it did in 1943 in his major report to the Board of Education on the curriculum and examinations in secondary schools. It was informed throughout by the views on the traditions and needs of education that he had developed over the previous forty years.

Norwood was among the first to argue publicly that the war had created a new situation, that 'The old education will not do: it must be lengthened, widened, and deepened.'[74] He was already ambitious enough to contemplate 'a common education leading up to common national service for all at 18–19'.[75] If Britain were to survive the war and then help Europe to recover, he argued in February 1940, immediate attention must be given to the education system: 'The leadership which is needed can only be given by an educated democracy, and that educated democracy will not come into being unless we face the problem anew, and determine how we are to build anew, and why.' He therefore called for a Royal Commission to be established to consider the whole field of education, 'and so soon as possible to shape the system which will fit the conditions which will be present after the war, and are indeed arising already, and which will make the nation ready for its high and difficult task'.[76] But he remained emphatic that 'this or any other system must fail us unless it is so inspired by the ideal of public service that it issues in a practical expression of that ideal, and unless it is built on the supremacy of those spiritual values which are cast into deadly hazard by the present war'. He was already clear, too, on the character of the three types of secondary school that might be developed, conforming basically to the suggestions of the Spens report of 1938. The 'main subjects', with Latin and Greek, French and German, and Mathematics and Science, would be maintained in the existing secondary schools; technical high schools would be developed in parallel; and new secondary schools would be introduced 'which would not attempt to carry the pupils beyond the sixteenth year, and would solve their special problems in their own way without attempting to rival unduly either the secondary school [sic] or the technical high school'.[77] These would permit 'greater variety of type', but 'a more conscious and consistent effort must be made to impart a common stock of ideas and a common knowledge as the basis of citizenship'.[78] History, Geography and Literature should be at the centre of the secondary school curriculum, on the grounds that

Everybody ought to know something both of what Britain stands for in the world and also of the world in which Britain stands. Everybody, whether they work in factory or mine, office or farm, wherever they may be, ought to feel more strongly and more intelligently than they do now the uniting bonds of their common citizenship and their common ideals.[79]

Moreover, the principles of the Christian religion should be the foundation of school education: 'The failure of the secular education developed in the nineteenth century has been obvious: it has fed materialism, produced the careerist in some quantity, and a not very respected "intelligentsia".'[80] He claimed that

The business of the schools is to teach that goodness, truth and beauty are absolute values, and every course of study in the school should be so taught as to illustrate these lessons: the life of the school should be designed and lived as something governed by these standards, a life in which example would always count for more than precept.[81]

These, then, were the ideals that continued to shape Norwood's views on the secondary school.

Norwood's substantive contribution to the postwar settlement in education owed much to the intervention of R.A. Butler, President of the Board from July 1941. At the beginning of January 1941, the then President, Herbert Ramsbotham, had invited Norwood, as chairman of the Secondary Schools Examinations Council (SSEC), to take charge of a small committee on the future of examinations in secondary schools.[82] When Butler took over as President he decided that such an enquiry would be 'incomplete unless the content of education were also considered'.[83] On Norwood's suggestion, the terms of reference of the committee were then altered to read 'to advise on suggested changes in the Secondary School curriculum and the question of school examinations in relation thereto'. On the other hand, there was some pressure on Norwood not to widen the focus of the report still further, either by being tempted to 'replough the whole ground of the curriculum', which the Spens report on secondary education had already examined,[84] or by examining the future prospects of the technical and modern schools, or yet by dealing with the problems of the public schools. G.G. Williams, secretary of the SSEC, warned Norwood that Butler, although he was 'already satisfied that there is no reason to think that we are acting improperly vis-à-vis the Spens Report', might 'wonder whether we are properly constituted to go beyond the range of Grammar Schools'.[85] By the end of 1941 Williams was clear that Norwood 'regards himself as entrusted with the task of charting the scope of Grammar Schools in the wider field of Secondary Education'. He was apparently 'quite prepared to agree that it is not the job of the Committee to examine in detail problems of Modern or Technical or Public Schools', even though 'he feels that something must be said of our approach to them'.[86]

Norwood was highly conscious of the potential importance of his new task. Sir Maurice Holmes, permanent secretary at the Board, sent him a copy of a pamphlet on postwar educational reconstruction, the so-called 'Green Book', prepared by a small group of officials for limited circulation. Holmes told

Norwood: 'You will, I think, find nothing in it that clashes with the views which you expressed in the "Fortnightly" for February, 1941.'[87] Norwood was encouraged by this, but pointed out that it had 'omissions':

It is however a skeleton, and someone must make the dry bones live. I suppose Butler is feeling after that, for if you are to ask Parliament for a hundred millions or more after the war, you must make the young men dream dreams. So this old man will try to see a vision, and cautiously enlarge that reference, if he may. We may be able to make a useful contribution.[88]

There were still many who were suspicious of his ideas and intentions. Sir Will Spens, in an interview with Butler in March 1942, 'expressed great distrust of Dr Norwood'.[89] Sir Walter Citrine, general secretary of the Trades Union Congress, complained strongly that he had not been allowed to see the whole of the questionnaire for interested parties that Norwood's committee drew up.[90] But Norwood seized his opportunity to pursue his long-held ideas on examinations, the curriculum and the purposes of secondary education.

A distinction between three types of post-primary school was evident from the earliest discussions of the Norwood committee. The view that 'Post-primary education in the future will include Modern Schools, Grammar Schools and Technical (including Commercial and Art) Schools' was among the 'provisional assumptions' discussed and accepted by the committee in January 1942.[91] Norwood, like Butler, saw the 'common school' as impracticable, at least for the present. Butler noted that Norwood felt it would take 'twenty years to introduce such a reform satisfactorily'; both preferred to expand and improve secondary education first before embarking on such a course.[92] Thus it was agreed that secondary schools would include grammar, modern and technical schools, with 'entry at 11 + on a rough shake-out according to estimate of type of ability'.[93] The final report of the committee, published soon after the White Paper on educational reconstruction in July 1943, argued that secondary technical schools should recruit pupils from the age of eleven both to 'gain a fair share of able pupils' and to 'develop the general education of a kind suitable for technical pupils'. Such schools should be designed, it continued, 'primarily to give a training for entry into industry and commerce at the age of 16 + to meet the demands of local industrial conditions and, wherever possible and expedient, to offer facilities for advanced work from 16 to 18'.[94] Upon the secondary modern school, meanwhile, 'would fall the task of providing a general education for the majority of the boys and girls in the country up to the age fixed for the limit of compulsory school attendance'. This kind of school would 'fulfil its role in the secondary education of the country if it provided curricula closely related to the immediate interests and environment of its pupils and adopted a method of approach which was practical and concrete'.[95] By contrast, secondary grammar schools would appeal to 'those whose real interests are satisfied by an introduction to the matter and methods of the main departments of knowledge valued primarily for its own sake', and the full grammar school course would continue to the age of 18-plus.[96]

Norwood's determination to reduce the role of examinations is also clearly evident from the surviving records of his committee's deliberations. At the first meeting, he suggested that for entrance to universities, training colleges and the professions an examination at 17-plus might be suitable. The question of whether such an examination 'would cramp the curriculum and the treatment of subjects' was discussed, but agreement was reached that 'An examination at 17 +, so reserved for a specific purpose, would prevent an examination being the final goal of a secondary school pupil's course.'[97] In May 1942 he remained unclear 'what results his Committee would reach about the examination', but stressed in discussion with Butler that he would 'attempt to alter the present system'.[98] On the point of entry into secondary education, the committee decided that

At 11 plus it was difficult or impossible to differentiate pupils into 'types' for which a Modern, Grammar, and Technical education was the most suitable . . . It would be advisable to allocate pupils to types of schools on the basis of (i) parent's choice (ii) teachers' advice (iii) administrative considerations and to rely on a progressive indication of aptitudes during the years 11 plus to 13 plus.[99]

The committee also moved towards approving a system of internal examinations similar to that which Norwood had suggested in his Glasgow address in 1928.

The committee's radical stance on examinations brought it into conflict with entrenched educational interests. At the very last meeting of the committee before the report was to be signed, Dr Terry Thomas, Headmaster of Leeds Grammar School, reserved his position on the issue of internal examinations. Norwood commented: 'As our minds have been running in this direction for the last twelve months, he is somewhat belated in the discovery of his own mind, but I do not doubt that pressure has been put on him by the Association of Headmasters.'[100] The report itself was unaffected by this late defection. It recommended that 'In the interest of the individual child and responsibility of the teaching profession change in the School Certificate Examination should be in the direction of making the examination entirely internal, that is to say, conducted by the teachers at the school on syllabuses and papers framed by themselves.'[101] For a transitional period of seven years, this examination should continue to be carried out by existing university examining bodies, but teachers should be strongly represented in administering it, and it should become a 'subject' examination in which pupils took whatever subjects they wished to take. At the end of these seven years, 'the decision should be made whether conditions make possible a change to a wholly internal examination, or whether there should be a further transitional period in which teachers would take still greater control of the examination, and the Universities still less'.[102] A School

Leaving Examination would be conducted twice each year for pupils of 18-plus in order to meet such needs as University Entrance and entry into the professions. On the other hand, 'The present Higher School Certificate Examination should be abolished and State and Local Education Authority scholarships should be awarded on a different basis.'[103] The 'ultimate objective' of the report was that examinations should have only a 'subordinate part' within the school, and that the reduction in their role would allow greater responsibility for teachers and a more 'child-centred' education: 'These are ideals which in our view should be kept steadily in the forefront of educational movement in the years to come, for it will be increasingly difficult to reconcile an external examination at 16 + with the full realisation of that freedom which will then be held to be a vital necessity.'[104] It would also make it possible to achieve 'parity in secondary education', according to the report, 'For the objective of the School Certificate has become so associated in the public mind with secondary education that the establishment of the Technical School and the Modern School as forms of secondary education will be prejudiced from the outset.'[105] A new form of school certificate would involve 'a record of the share which the pupil had taken in the general life of the school, games and societies and the like', no less than 'the record of the pupils' achievement in the examination taken at the end of the Main school course'.[106] Meanwhile, the secondary technical school and the secondary modern school would be free of external examinations. The 'most important factor' in differentiating between pupils at the age of eleven would be 'the judgement of the teacher'.[107]

Norwood's priorities and key values relating to the secondary school curriculum were also quickly established. At the first meeting of his committee, he argued that 'Freedom was essential; yet the tradition of secondary education, the best in the world, must be preserved.'[108] The precise nature of this 'tradition of secondary education' was clarified for the committee in a memorandum circulated in January 1942, almost certainly by Norwood himself. The 'common element' of grammar school courses, it suggested, consisted 'in an attempt to present each study as a coherent and systematic whole'. This kind of treatment, which 'deals largely in abstractions', meant that 'the Grammar School is best suited to the boy or girl who shows promise of ability to deal with abstract notions – who is quick at seizing the relatedness of related things'. It concluded that the 'grammatical' approach to education revealed the 'differentia' of the grammar school, in that unlike other methods 'it fills in the interstices between the facts or principles with others perhaps less easily applied, in order that the coherent structure or logical development of the subject may be apprehended'. Thus Norwood sought to define and maintain a basic distinction between grammar school education and that of other types of school, and located this in the treatment of subjects across the curriculum. He seems to have disregarded possible criticisms of this view: 'It does not seem necessary to argue the case that the "grammatical" treatment is not only eminently desirable for some minds but is also the only treatment which will satisfy them; nor that it is essential for the community that there should be a number of minds so educated.'[109] It was emphasised also that 'The "Grammar School" course must begin at 11 plus if the tradition, particularly in respect of languages, were to be preserved.'[110]

On the other hand, the committee also developed a strong notion of principles that united the different kinds of secondary school. It was agreed, first, that the curriculum from 11-plus to 13-plus would be 'much the same in any type of school'.[111] This meant that pupils from 11-plus to 13-plus would form a 'lower school' in each type of school, with a 'generally common curriculum', and that 'observation of interest plus ability during these years will form basis of transfer at 13 + '.[112] Also, the committee agreed, at all stages stress should be 'laid on 3 "elements" of education which are not mere "subjects"', namely: '(i) physical education; (ii) training of character with its implications of religious education, except for those with conscientious objections; and (iii) training in the study and practice of the English language'.[113] These 'elements' were consistent with Norwood's earlier views on the infusion of values characteristic of the public schools and of the 'English tradition of education' into all kinds of secondary school. They were intended to encourage service to the community and a sense of civic responsibility and citizenship in all pupils, whether or not they were at grammar school. He sought to go further towards this end by arguing upon his committee the idea of a 'year of national service', but met with some resistance and was obliged to be content with 'the term of words "an educational break"'.[114]

Thus, the final report emphasised both the special character of the grammar school curriculum for a limited number of pupils, and the civic and spiritual values with which all secondary school pupils should be imbued. It suggested, indeed, that while 'in the Grammar School the pupil is offered, because he is capable of reaching towards it, a conception of knowledge which is different from that which can be and should be envisaged in other types of school', in other respects 'the ideals of all types of school are generally similar, though the measures taken to achieve them may vary'.[115] The ethos of the public schools, and a reduction in the role of examinations, would animate the curriculum of all secondary school pupils. According to the report, in fact, individual subjects were less important than 'the attitude of each pupil to his own bodily welfare, to moral and spiritual ideals and to the clear and correct use of his own language', and teachers should concentrate upon these aspects at all times.[116] These proposals were developed in detail in Part III of the report. With regard to 'ideals of character' in particular, it argued, 'it is part of the function of a school to set before its pupils ideals of character and of conduct, individual and social, and to provide through its own manifold activities means of realising in some measure and in varied ways the aspirations which in the last resort constitute the justification of those activities and furnish their motive power'.[117] It was with these ideals and aspirations in view that Norwood prescribed the various subjects to be taken. The 'common curriculum' of the 'lower school' would comprise Physical Education, Religious Instruction, English, History, Geography, Mathematics, Natural Science, Art, Handicrafts, Music, and one or two foreign languages. In the higher forms of the grammar school Physical Education, Religious Instruction, and English would again be emphasised throughout the school; opportunity for Art, Music and Handicraft would be encouraged; foreign languages, Mathematics and Natural Science would be part of the curriculum of all pupils; and History and Geography would generally be maintained at least to the age of fourteen or fifteen.

The work of the committee was completed in an almost euphoric atmosphere, in which Norwood reverted to type and decided 'to assume the part of Head Master, and hold a Prize-Giving, like the last day of term at a Public School'.[118] He himself was presented on behalf of the committee with the Cambridge Ancient History, 'duly acknowledging the contribution of an Oxford man to future history through his leadership and tact'.[119] Butler was highly satisfied: 'This well-written report will serve our book very well – particularly its layout of the Secondary world. Spens will be furious.'[120] The publication of the report marked the crowning achievement of Norwood's long career. It looked forward to a national system of education in which his ideals of leadership, service and public spirit were central purposes for all.

THE NEW SECONDARY EDUCATION

Yet Norwood's hopes were to remain unrealised. Key recommendations in his report, and especially the 'public spirit' and leadership qualities which he intended to be central, found little place in the new secondary education that developed after the war. Norwood's own reputation rapidly declined; indeed, when he died at the age of eighty in March 1956 the *Times Educational Supplement*, in a brief notice of his death, could observe that he had 'outlived his fame'.[121] He has been remembered chiefly for his report's reinforcement of the 'tripartite ideology' of secondary education, but also as a figure of ridicule. Thus according to Jonathan Gathorne-Hardy, he was 'a kindly but distant figure, not really interested either in teaching or in boys, who enjoyed woolly discussions about educational theory (religion and games) and writing hymns', and who made 'many ineffably silly remarks'.[122] In retrospect, it appears that even as the Norwood report was being published, the values and morality for which it spoke were losing their potency and relevance.

Many historians, including most recently Correlli Barnett and Brian Simon, have held Norwood directly responsible for the development of three types of secondary school – grammar, technical and modern – in the 1940s and 1950s. Barnett argues that the report exemplified the educational attitudes that led to 'industrial decline'. It was, he alleges, 'an exercise in hypocrisy, if not actual deception', which created an 'amazing document' that 'publicly affirmed in uncompromising language the prevailing outlook and beliefs of the British educational establishment, and in particular of those who controlled, and would control, the levers of the educational system'.[123] The marxist educational historian Brian Simon, similarly, describes the educational policy of the Board of Education during the war as 'A Case Study in Manipulative Politics', in which 'One action, initiated by the group of officials, can now be seen as a master-stroke: the appointment of the Norwood Committee on Curriculum and Examinations in Secondary Schools.' The politics of the Norwood committee, according to Simon, were 'devious and multifarious'.[124] Its final report 'produced an ideological underpinning for the tripartite system', laying down 'a clear pattern (and rationale) for a divided system of secondary education following whatever reforms were to be brought about by legislation'.[125] Thus, 'The threat of radical change had been held at bay. The "New Order" in English education . . . turned out to be the old order in a new disguise.'[126] Other historians have suggested that the curriculum pattern suggested by the Norwood report has continued to influence the comprehensive schools, supposedly designed to cater for pupils of all abilities and aptitudes, that have become dominant since the 1960s.[127]

It is clearly true that Norwood's report was partly responsible for the 'tripartite ideology', albeit with accomplices both before and after the fact such as the Spens report of 1938, the White Paper on educational reconstruction (1943) and the Ministry of Education's pamphlet no. 9, *The New Secondary Education*, published in 1947. But in other respects its influence was limited. With regard to school examinations, its proposals were blocked and subverted by powerful educational interests. Following the publication of the report, Norwood noted that both the Oxford and the Cambridge Local Examining Boards were 'doing their best to undermine and be-little the Report from pure motives of self-interest'. He insisted that 'we must not for a moment let the University Examining Bodies get away with the idea that they either represent the Universities or the traditional wisdom of centuries, they need to be sharply reminded that they are servants of the public and not masters of the educational house, and above all, they must not be let loose on the SSEC'.[128] Despite his initial optimism that the School Certificate examination would die a natural death, 'of inanition, if it is left to itself',[129] the subsequent processes of negotiation thwarted his plans. By 1947, R.H. Barrow, formerly secretary of the Norwood committee and now secretary of the Secondary Schools Examination Council was complaining privately to Norwood that

The outlook on the educational front is pretty bleak – indeed, I wish it were educational, it seems to be anything but that! You have seen the examination circular. It is being accepted, because everyone thinks they can interpret it as they wish: and that is why the Council accepted it unanimously. Of course, all principle is sacrificed, and the status quo is read into it by those who want to do that, and reform is hoped for by the few who want it. There is a vague recommendation that the best boys [*sic*] should by-pass the 'Ordinary' standard; but, as far as I can see, no H.M. will have the courage to do that, for boys and parents will compel him to let the boy take all he can. A great deal depends on the Univ.; but already the provincial Universities show signs of using O(rdinary) as well as A(dvanced) for purposes of entry.[130]

Norwood tried to encourage Barrow in his efforts, but the latter responded like a defeated man: 'I hasten to say that it is no good comforting yourself that I am still in the Ministry, for I am quite powerless and my own opinion is that the Ministry is powerless. It has yielded in the past so much to the "unions" that it seems unable to resist. The schools seem to be possessed by a blind madness which drives them to resist any change.'[131] It seems more reasonable to interpret the Norwood report as a victim of these interests and tendencies than as a successful conspiracy on the part of a supposedly united 'educational establishment'.

The failure of Norwood's proposals on examinations effectively hardened the divisions between the different types of secondary school. It ensured that the 11-plus, and later the new Ordinary and Advanced level examinations, would become key institutions determining individual success and the character of the school curriculum. It also meant that Norwood's endeavours to renew and extend the public school 'spirit' in the new secondary schools met with little success. His elucidation of the 'ideals' and 'aspirations' of secondary education was almost ignored in the years that followed. There was very little similarity between the ideals put forward by Norwood and the practices developed either in the tripartite system or in the comprehensive schools. His 'grammar school values' were subverted to serve an examination system that he deplored.

English society after 1945 did not in any case provide a cultural context in which Norwood's ideology was likely to flourish. His attitudes were solidly based in the values of the nineteenth-century public schools, with a continued emphasis on classics, games, religion, character and masculinity. He was a revisionist in that he was willing to contemplate public school reform, and sought to apply their values to a changing educational and social milieu. By the 1950s, though, his concessions fell far short of what would be needed to satisfy contemporaries that the notion of 'education for leadership' was important or appropriate for the future. The 'new secondary education' was to be founded upon structural divisions that would ensure the maintenance of educational and social inequalities. But it would find little place for the kind of moral curriculum with which Norwood and the public schools had been associated. The real significance and underlying irony of the Norwood report itself was that it so vividly reflected this general drift: conceived in terms of spiritual values and public service, it was interpreted in terms of individual achievement and economic competition.

Norwood continued to state his beliefs after the war, although now in retirement. In 1948, he identified four separate problems awaiting solution. First was to develop primary education; second was to plan a suitable religious education, especially in modern schools; third was to cater for technical schools. But fourth,

There is finally, what is perhaps the most important problem of all, the education up to the age of 18 of the grammar school children, the academically gifted: I call this the most important, not because I am undemocratic in sympathy, but because from this class must infallibly be drawn the future leaders in thought, and most of the governors and administrators of the country. It is here, in the teaching of sixth forms everywhere, that in my belief Christian Modernism can play its most serviceable part.[132]

He found little sympathy for this latter assertion in a secular, materialistic society, one, moreover, in which the notion of 'leadership' had itself become suspect. Norwood's ideas had always been contentious – too radical for many of his colleagues, too conservative for critics of the public schools. Now his day was suddenly, but irrevocably, yesterday. The idea of infusing the state secondary schools with the ethos of the public schools had become unattractive and dangerous. If 'education for leadership' were to survive in a hostile postwar society it would require a fresh rationale, and a new champion.

5

THE RISE AND FALL OF THE

MERITOCRACY

The failure of the public school dominated Establishment to avoid the drift to global conflict, and the clear risks involved in producing dynamic leaders like the fascist dictators, produced a decisive reaction in the decades after 1945 against both old and new doctrines of 'education for leadership'. Eric James's vision of the grammar schools, dubbed 'meritocratic' by Michael Young at the end of the 1950s, represented an important but ultimately unsuccessful attempt to adapt to this new situation while retaining key elements of the classic public school purpose.

THE NEW SCHOOL TIE

The dangers of education for leadership, associated on the one hand with Nazism and on the other hand with the 'old school tie', appeared one of the most important lessons to be learned from the experience of the second world war. It was symptomatic of this that the educational theories of Plato came under increasing attack in the immediate postwar years as being at least in part responsible for Hitler's notions of the 'master race'. Even before the beginning of the war there had been important indications of this new mood – Richard Crossman's *Plato Today*, in 1937, was an uncompromising assault upon the social implications of Plato's thought. After 1945, this kind of rejection of Plato became much more common although, naturally enough, such denunciations remained fiercely contested. Articles by Otto Neurath and J.A. Lauwerys on the resemblance between Plato's *Republic* and Nazi propaganda met with a mixed reception that included ripostes from philosophers including G.C. Field and C.E.M. Joad.[1] Even so, it was a significant measure of the prevailing reaction against education for leadership that the oracle, Plato himself, seemed at last to be crumbling.

The postwar orthodoxy was well anticipated and beautifully expressed by the philosopher Karl Popper in his major work *The Open Society and its Enemies*, published in 1945. In the first volume of this treatise, Popper launched a strongly worded attack upon the implications and effects of Plato's thought – 'The Spell of Plato', as he described it. He claimed that there was a strong similarity 'between the Platonic theory of justice and the theory and practice of modern totalitarianism'.[2] According to Popper, Plato despised the world's state of flux, and in attempting to unveil the secret of its decay and the historical laws of political change 'aimed at discovering the secret of the royal knowledge of politics, of the art of ruling men'.[3] The Theory of Forms or Ideas, Popper continued, allowed Plato to inquire into the problems of a changing society but also opened the way to social engineering. Plato's educational agenda was 'the purely political aim of stabilizing the state by blending a fierce and a gentle element in the character of the rulers'.[4] This development, involving a basic connection between the theory and practice of education and the principle of leadership, had in Popper's view wrought great damage: 'Plato's assumption that it should be the task of education (or more precisely, of the educational institutions) to select the future leaders, and to train them for leadership, is still largely taken for granted. By burdening these institutions with a task which must go beyond the scope of any institution, Plato is partly responsible for their deplorable state.'[5] Popper urged that modern society should break free from Plato's 'spell' and cease to burden educational institutions 'with the impossible task of selecting the best', concluding:

This tendency transforms our educational system into a race-course, and turns a course of studies into a hurdle-race. Instead of encouraging the student to devote himself to his studies for the sake of studying, instead of encouraging in him a real love for his subject and for enquiry, he is encouraged to study for the sake of his personal career; he is led to acquire only such knowledge as is serviceable in getting over the hurdles which he must clear for the sake of his advancement . . . The impossible demand for an institutional selection of intellectual leaders endangers the very life not only of science, but of intelligence.[6]

Popper's criticisms helped to undermine the idea of the 'philosopher-king', and indeed the view that a particular group within society should be chosen for a distinctive kind of education to train them for social and political leadership. Henceforth Plato's liberal friends were to be on the defensive, very unlike the situation in the late nineteenth century when Plato had attracted broad support.[7] At a less rarified level, English secondary education strongly reflected this reaction against 'education for leadership', in favour of growing concern for the implications of equality of opportunity.

The three different kinds of state secondary school that emerged after the war were soon under challenge. Secondary technical schools attracted little tangible support.[8] Meanwhile the secondary modern schools, intended to cater for the majority of secondary school pupils, never became popular.[9] As the sociologist Olive Banks pointed out, 'In its confidence in the future of the secondary modern school the Ministry [of Education], in fact, seems to have underestimated the hold of the grammar school on popular esteem.'[10] On the face of it, then, state grammar schools remained unchallenged as the schools for the academic elite. Harry Judge has recalled that the grammar schools of the 1950s 'cultivated the virtues of hard work, celebrated the advantages of competition and the accessibility of success for any able and determined pupil, and efficiently pursued victory in the examination system'.[11] The Spens report of 1938 had found that about two-thirds of grammar school pupils entered higher education, became teachers or took up professional, commercial or clerical posts.[12] Charles Tennyson, chairman of the education committee of the Federation of British Industries, predicted with considerable accuracy that the products of grammar schools would continue to enter the professions while those educated at technical and modern schools would tend to go into industry.[13] In the mid-1950s, the grammar schools, 'enjoying in any case the reflected glory of their former esteem', continued to provide 'the chief avenue, within the state system of education, to occupations of the highest social and economic standing'.[14] They remained, in short, 'the goose which lays the golden eggs'.[15] Cyril Norwood's ideals may have failed to take hold, but the tripartite system of secondary education still gave every appearance of being the modern incarnation of Plato's philosophy. The structural divisions involved in the tripartite system were also consistent with existing social inequalities and prejudices.

Yet in spite of all this the grammar schools were insecure in their supremacy. Ministry officials were quickly aware of the fragility of the new system. Sir Robert Wood, in a thoughtful minute to the Minister of Education, in April 1946, pointed out that earlier criticisms of class distinction were now less applicable:

Now that secondary education has been made free – only a very small fee-paying area remains – and admission or allocation is determined by qualification and not by ability to pay, no question of class distinction arises. The case for a variety of schools and the allocation to these schools depend not on class distinctions but on intelligence distinctions or differences – distinctions imposed by Nature and outwith the control of man. We are, indeed, attaining Plato's rule that 'children must be placed not according to their father's conditions, but the faculties of their minds'.

Even so, he maintained, there were potentially important new grounds for criticism, which would be difficult to refute:

even though it may be admitted that class distinctions disappear, we are next confronted with the objection that by having different types of secondary school we should only be replacing social class distinctions by equally objectionable intellectual distinctions – creating an aristocracy of intellect in the Grammar Schools and putting the 'runners-up' in the Secondary (Technical) Schools, and 'the field' in the Modern Schools. It is idle to deny that there is not [sic] some substance both on social and educational grounds in this objection.

He predicted that pressure in favour of multilateral or common schools would increase as a direct result of this.[16] The question of how to develop the system further also caused concern within the Ministry. As Toby Weaver observed in 1955,

If the rate and development of separate technical schools is increased, and if the gamble fails, we shall have entrenched for as long as we can foresee the three-tier system of Plato's Republic that is already hardening – the 'fliers', whether humanists or technologists in academic grammar schools, the technicians and managers in second-creaming technical schools, and the 'pedestrians' in banausic modern schools with little hope of challenge or standard in their courses.[17]

Comprehensive schools in these circumstances offered a simple, attractive and less expensive alternative.

The grammar schools themselves were equally aware of imminent challenge. As early as 1946, the Incorporated Association of Head Masters (IAHM) felt obliged to warn publicly about 'the threat to the grammar schools'. The uncertain prospects of such schools, it alleged, was due to a confusion between the ideas of uniformity and of equality. Forty years before, there had been only about 500 grammar schools, with fewer than 100,000 pupils; now, there were 1,500, with 580,000 pupils, 80 per cent of whom came from state primary schools. The Association claimed credit on behalf of the grammar schools for achieving 'quality in education', through modern advances in curricula and methods of teaching. It emphasised too that the grammar schools remained relevant to contemporary needs. In the Services, for example, 85 per cent of all commissions won had gone to grammar school boys: 'In all the technical branches of the Service grammar school education was found to be essential for a commission. It was boys from these schools who were, almost exclusively, responsible for the development of Radar, jet propulsion and atomic research. They provided the bulk of the RAF air crews.'[18] Now, it concluded, such schools were under threat. These were forebodings that over the following fifteen years or so proved justified as local education authorities began to move towards comprehensive reorganisation and the Labour Party approved comprehensives as official policy.[19]

Thus if the Education Act of 1944 and its associated policy statements represented an attempt to pre-empt radical criticisms of secondary education, as has increasingly been suggested,[20] its success was strictly limited. The future lay with reformers like G.C.T. Giles, Old Etonian and President of the National Union of Teachers, who argued forcefully the urgent need for 'a new outlook – a *New School Tie*'.[21] Giles argued that 'Up to now, we have never had in this country even the pretence of a national or democratic system of education . . . Our system as it exists now is a caste system reflecting the class divisions of our society.'[22] He acknowledged that the 1944 Act was a 'big step forward', a 'great opportunity'. Even so, Giles contended, it was crucial to continue the 'levelling-

up process' against 'the force of reaction and privilege'.[23] At the secondary stage
in particular, the introduction of multilateral education was essential: 'The
advantages of this type of secondary school are obvious. It brings together in
one school a cross-section of the community. It makes possible a wider and
more varied curriculum, while preserving a common core of culture.'[24] It was
to respond to this kind of vision of the future that the adherents of grammar
schools were obliged to reformulate their own rationales.

   In the postwar period, too, there was a noticeable shift in the terms of debate
from those that Norwood and others had employed in the interwar years.
Norwood had emphasised aspects of 'character' at least as much as intellect;
therefore he did not depend upon the idea of 'mental measurement' or
psychometrics in his discussions of 'leadership' or in his rationalisations of
inequality and educational distinctions. He was far from alone in this.
According to Gillian Sutherland, there was a 'patchy and uneven understanding
and reception of mental measurement in England' before 1940.[25] After the war,
on the other hand, the increasing dominance of secular as opposed to moral
concerns and a preoccupation with individual opportunity lent additional
weight to what Sir Robert Wood called 'intelligence distinctions or differences', conceived as 'distinctions imposed by Nature and outwith the control
of man'. Butler noted privately as his Education Bill was being debated in 1943
that political interest had changed its focus during the twentieth century 'from
the soul of man to his economic position'.[26] This was broadly true of
educational debate. It was an important shift that was to shape the character of
the new attempts of the postwar years both to defend the position of the
grammar schools and to revise the notion of education for leadership.

THE IDEOLOGY OF ERIC JAMES

It was within this context that Eric James, High Master of Manchester
Grammar School, tried to defend the values and ideals of the grammar school.
Born in 1909, James had been educated at Taunton School in Southampton and
then at Queen's College, Oxford. He spent twelve years as an assistant master at
Winchester College, from 1933 until 1945, before being appointed to
Manchester Grammar School where he remained until 1962. With this
platform he asserted a strong role by attempting to redefine the established
notion of education for leadership to appeal to postwar society. Arguably his
view harked back to the aspirations of the grammar schools of the early
seventeenth century, in contrast with those of nineteenth-century public
schools. Above all else, though, he tried to convey the relevance and
importance, for the twentieth century, of enlightened social and political
leadership. In this he was strongly influenced by his reading of Plato's Republic,
which he had won as a prize at school and which was to become his 'Bible'.[27] His
experience at Winchester in the 1930s under the headmaster Spencer Leeson

also had an important effect upon his outlook. Leeson had previously been Head of Merchant Taylors' School, and was later to become chairman of the Headmasters' Conference during the war years and Bishop of Peterborough from 1949 until his death in 1956. He has been described as 'a lover of tradition, even though his views on education were in many respects liberal and modern'.[28] Himself a keen student of Plato,[29] Leeson was anxious to see the qualities cultivated by the public schools extended to 'boys from homes of every kind'.[30] This was to become James's avowed aim at Manchester. As he later remarked, 'My ambition was to give pupils from every walk in life . . . the same kind of intellectual and cultural advantages that my pupils at Winchester had.'[31] Like Norwood, but a generation later, he took it upon himself to try to apply what he perceived as the essential 'advantages' of the public schools to the wider population of the 'new secondary education'.

Much of James's anxiety and general position was clearly evident in an article he wrote for the *Times Educational Supplement* in February 1947, under the heading 'The challenge to the grammar schools: attack upon standards and values'. He argued that 'Among the most disturbing features of the present educational scene is a feeling of despondency among those teaching in grammar schools, and a fear lest these schools may be unable to maintain their standards in the face of certain contemporary tendencies.' There was a general lack of appreciation for grammar schools, he alleged, despite their outstanding successes in the twentieth century. In a strong echo of the IAHM's earlier warning, James continued:

The grammar schools have created in the past 45 years the means on which alone we may solve our problems of expert manpower by seeking to ensure that the more intellectually gifted children of every class may make their fullest contribution to the national life, yet they see this great achievement, that they know to be still imperfect but which is developing fast, in danger of replacement by new types of school open to the gravest objections on every ground. And for what end? To realise a social homogeneity which it is the proudest and not unfounded boast of the grammar schools that they themselves have already largely achieved.

The comprehensive schools represented an attack on academic values and a threat to the national culture itself. Academic standards, he concluded, were far from irrelevant to the real world, but helped to nurture ability in 'practical affairs': 'the Classical Sixth are not necessarily inhabitants of an ivory tower. It has not been an accident nor a misfortune that so many of our most gifted administrators have been forced to answer the fundamental questions of political theory by reading Greats at Oxford.' Here were the early signs of what was to become James's key theme. But his dominant note at this stage was in terms of academic 'standards': 'any lowering of the standards of what can be done in grammar schools will close the door to studies such as these to many of those capable of pursuing them – the door which for 40 years and more these schools have been fighting not unsuccessfully to open.'[32] The *TES* made a direct reply to James's arguments in its leading article in the same issue, arguing in favour of comprehensive schools.[33] Over succeeding weeks there was a flurry of correspondence on this topic, and also a strong attack upon James's notion of culture by Joan Simon who argued that his argument was essentially class-based: 'The common man [*sic*], as he comes into his own, will not be content passively to absorb the traditional culture which the grammar school now so generously offers to all classes.'[34] The terms of debate were generally set by this early date. The defenders of the grammar schools were now equating their achievements with the heritage of an endangered traditional culture, in much the same way that advocates of the public school ethos between the wars had tended to see that ethos in terms of an 'English tradition'. In both cases critics challenged the right of such schools to define what was best or most authentic in English culture. James thus appeared to be championing middle-class culture as distinct from more broadly based or distinctively working-class forms. As had been the case before the second world war also, therefore, arguments in favour of 'education for leadership' tended to be associated with middle-class aspirations of taste, social influence and – potentially – control.

James returned to the fray in 1949 with a more elaborate explanation of his viewpoint. He emphasised the historic achievements first of Thomas Arnold, and then of Sir Robert Morant. Arnold, he suggested, 'believed in the classics as an instrument in the hands of men full of a sense of the schoolmaster's pastoral function, by which a sense of moral purpose could be infused into English education'.[35] Such efforts raised the prestige of the public schools: 'By raising their prestige, the schools were enabled to take advantage of a changed social environment and become the schools of the upper classes, and thus Arnold and his followers associated the classical curriculum more definitely than before with education for leadership.'[36] However, by concentrating almost wholly on the classical curriculum, they had also given the impression that it was not 'useful' as such but simply part of the education of a 'gentleman'. The Education Act of 1902 had transformed the situation, making possible a national system of secondary education:

The insight of Sir Robert Morant, an insight that has still received far too little recognition, appreciated that a vast expansion and a radical reform of the grammar schools was necessary if England was to maintain her economic position, if schemes of social reform, not least in education itself, were to be carried through, and if democracy was to be a stable form of government producing its own educated leadership.[37]

In the new state grammar schools, unlike the public schools, there was fierce competition among rival subjects for time in the curriculum. They were also responsible for educating a twentieth-century democracy, which meant that 'The content of this education has to provide the intellectual and moral equipment for men and women confronted with the problems of revolutionary changes in social, economic, and spiritual life.'[38] They also provided the potential leaders of society, and here James explicitly associated Morant with Plato's notion of the 'philosopher-king':

In one sense Plato and Morant were equalitarian, for they emphasised the need for recruiting the intellectual leaders of society from any class in which they could be found. The 1902 Act was a step towards this equality of opportunity in the prospect which it revealed of an efficient higher education open to the able minority of every class. It was a Platonic conception, a movement towards the view that the kind of education a person receives should depend only on his talents.[39]

Thus James formulated his revisionist case for 'education for leadership', seeking to adapt the curricula and ideals of the nineteenth century to new needs and demands, specifically the 'revolutionary changes in social, economic, and spiritual life'.

In 1951 James attempted to explain this theme in more detail in his best-known work, *Education and Leadership*. Central to his fully developed thesis was the need for a modern society to be able to recognise and develop the characteristics of leadership. A recognisable and distinct elite was an essential requirement of society, now as in the past. Education, he argued, now provided the means to create an elite that was fair and enlightened:

Leadership could never again be the unquestioned dominance of an illiterate population by birth or wealth; it must be of a kind that should secure the adherence of a more or less educated nation – educated enough, to put it at its lowest, to be vulnerable to the demagogy of the new penny press, and increasingly conscious of its power and its rights.[40]

He insisted that education should be directed towards this end.

The social and political elite thus produced would be based neither on birth nor on wealth, but on talent or 'merit'. Such, indeed, was the historic task of the grammar schools, 'the spearhead of a social revolution no less real for being unspectacular'.[41] According to James, 'One of the most significant aspects of the educational and social history of the past fifty years has been the way in which national leadership in almost every sphere has been increasingly recruited from the products of the ordinary grammar schools.' Thus,

Every child from Bricktown Secondary School who secures a commission, or a position in the administrative civil service, or a controlling place in industry or commerce, is a portent of an immense social change, the slow creation of an elite of merit, a transfer of power to those whose qualification for wielding it is neither birth nor wealth, but talent.[42]

Because of this change, the grammar schools could increasingly ensure not only that 'no potential leaders are overlooked in our processes of selection', but also that 'the leadership we produce is indeed enlightened'.[43] In particular, James suggested, this enlightened elite should possess 'integrity, courage, judgement, stability, tact, and perseverance'.[44] This was in addition to high intelligence, which James saw as a prerequisite for enlightened social and political leadership. Even so, he clearly stressed the importance of developing appropriate skills and sense of responsibility in this future elite. It was the role of the grammar schools, as he saw it, to nurture this combination of qualities.

James also took every opportunity to stress the democratic quality of this process: 'education is the greatest safeguard that leadership shall be not only wise but democratic'.[45] He stoutly defended Plato on this point: 'It must be recognised, too, how profoundly democratic was his conception. No writer has ever emphasised more persistently that potential leaders should be recruited from every class; no equalitarian could surpass the ruthlessness with which he rejects the hereditary principle and demands the rejection of the children of guardians if they are themselves unsuitable.'[46] James indeed echoed R.C. Lodge's view of Plato's theory of 'education for leadership', first published in 1947, supporting different education for different types of people. According to Lodge, Plato attacked the abuses of democracy, while promoting physical, moral and intellectual excellence: 'Science, wisdom, philosophy: these are the *desiderata* for leadership, and these are the fruits of education bestowed upon persons of ability.'[47] Lodge argued that rigorous testing could determine the selection of candidates and thus permit equality of opportunity. But this necessarily meant that there should be different kinds of education for different types of people: 'In fact, education for leadership can be given wisely only to students who have demonstrated that they possess the capacity for leadership. This is recognised as true in our time; and it is only reasonable to recognise it as equally true in Plato's time.'[48] Yet both Lodge and James were in fact setting themselves against contemporary opinion about the implications of Plato's thought.

James was thus in some respects at least an unrepentant Victorian. His perspective defended an emphasis upon classical studies, supported the established role of 'boarding-schools', stressed the importance of moral character and public service, and made very little mention of the possibility of women leaders. Nevertheless, his thesis was essentially revisionist in that it argued strongly for social mobility through academic selection, and sought to appeal to secular, twentieth-century sensibilities and aims. The reception given to his views would test the popularity of both novel and received invocations of 'education for leadership'.

THE RISE OF THE MERITOCRACY

James proved to be isolated politically no less than philosophically. His defence of the grammar schools, while commanding respect even from leading adversaries, was insufficient to prevent a continued movement of opinion in favour of comprehensives. At a conference organised by the IAHM in October

1954, three Labour Party MPs were invited to hear views of grammar school supporters. James seized the opportunity to argue his point. He suggested that 'The new social mobility created by the grammar schools should have made them the pride and hope of the Labour Party; their accessibility made them solvents of class privilege. What the Labour Party had to ask themselves was whether the comprehensive school was more likely than the grammar school to contribute to the social ends which they held.'[49] One participant, the future Labour leader Hugh Gaitskell, was particularly impressed with James's

telling points, the most important of which I thought (and it came up several times during the weekend), was the fact that in some areas to start a comprehensive school, instead of the present division between secondary modern and grammar schools, would in fact lead to more not less class division. You would get a residential area on the one side, where there was a comprehensive school and all the people there would be drawn from the middle or lower middle class. On the other hand, you would have a working class area, and equally there all the children would come from working class parents. This would be in contrast with the present situation, whereby in the grammar school itself, owing to the fact that the places were free and that entry was on merit, there was now a complete mixing up.[50]

Nevertheless, Gaitskell and his delegation pressed the case for the comprehensives, pointing out that 'in the main the segregation at 11 did lead to a class structure, whereas what we wanted was more social cohesion'.[51]

Several prominent advocates of the comprehensives criticised James's view on the grounds that its notion of leadership was outdated. Anthony Crosland, for example, pointed out that modern societies had new requirements for their leaders:

We cannot, I think, yet be at all sure what system of education is most likely to generate the type of leadership which we require; indeed it is not altogether clear, in our rapidly changing society, what type of leadership we do require. But *prima facie* judgements, and a consideration of the experience of other countries, certainly do not point unequivocally to a Platonic elite.[52]

Robin Pedley, Director of the University of Exeter Institute of Education, and the sociologist Raymond Williams similarly dismissed James's idea of leadership in emphatic style.[53] James's argument was therefore vulnerable to criticism on the grounds that other forms of education and government were more appropriate to the late twentieth century.

Equally it invited analysis of the kind of society that would eventuate were the grammar schools to triumph. It was this latter theme that Michael Young investigated most thoroughly in his influential satire *The Rise of the Meritocracy*, first published in 1958. Born in 1915, and educated at Dartington Hall, the experimental school in Devon, Young had been secretary of the research department in the Labour Party before taking up sociology at the London School of Economics in the 1950s. His term 'meritocracy' quickly became a widely recognised description of 'Government by persons selected on the basis of merit in a competitive educational system; a society so governed; a ruling or influential class of educated people.'[54] As such, it might well be used to explain Eric James's view of 'education for leadership'. Yet it was at the same time a thinly veiled attack upon this kind of viewpoint, seeking to demonstrate its possible divisive consequences.

Young's was a work of no little imagination. First, he projected himself forward to the year 2034 to write an account of the history of education in Britain. Second, he wrote as if the efforts of people such as James on behalf of the grammar schools had succeeded. His vision of the future showed the pressure for comprehensive schools to be a storm that soon passed: 'The vandals were vanquished and the city stood.'[55] In due course, 'The 1944 Education Act began to tell, and our country has continued to forge ahead ever since. From being first with the Industrial Revolution of the nineteenth century, Britain became first in the intellectual revolution of the twentieth. The workshop of the world became the grammar school of the world.'[56] The narrator of Young's invented history identifies himself with this transformation, putting across a view of the relationship between education and society very similar to that which Eric James had proposed, and addressing himself to fellow members of the elite. James indeed is quoted by the narrator on several occasions as a major authority on the 'meritocracy', and it is difficult to resist the view that Young was responding directly to James's work. Young even notes in his introduction that 'I will illustrate my essay with reference to the period between 1914 and 1963, on which I specialised at the Manchester Grammar School.'[57] He echoes James in his emphasis upon the importance of the talented few: 'Civilisation does not depend upon the stolid mass, the *homme moyen sensuel*, but upon the creative minority, the innovator who with one stroke can save the labour of 10,000, the brilliant few who cannot look without wonder, the restless elite who have made mutation a social, as well as a biological, fact.'[58] Young, like James, envisaged an elite selected 'according to brains and educated according to deserts', allowing 'rule not so much by the people as by the cleverest people: not an aristocracy of birth, not a plutocracy of wealth, but a true meritocracy of talent'.[59] It is in his history of the refining of the selection processes for the 'cleverest people' that Young goes rather beyond James's notion of education for leadership.

Young documents the rise of the principle of 'selection by merit' in Britain, first in the reforms of the civil service and then in the system of mass education. According to Young, the socialists of the twentieth century promoted equality of opportunity, but then began to support 'sentimental egalitarianism of the modern sort'[60] in the form of comprehensive schools: 'In the name of equality they wantonly sacrificed the few to the many.'[61] But by the 1980s 'our modern notions passed the acid test of productivity'; through 'the scientific management of talent', Britain regained its international supremacy.[62] With general opinion turning against comprehensives, 'it became possible to concentrate

upon the most fundamental of reforms, that is, upon the all-round improvement of grammar schools'.[63] In 1972 a learning wage was approved by the
government; universities began selecting all their entrants on merit properly
tested in the examination-room; grammar school teachers, especially science
teachers, were awarded higher salaries; public schools were thrown open to
talented children. Most importantly, selection methods were improved to
allow accurate testing at all ages. With this accomplished, the principle of
seniority in industry and the professions began to yield to the principle of merit.
Prospective marriage partners were encouraged to consult the intelligence
register; efforts were made to merge the principles of heredity and merit and
thus create a new 'hereditary elite'. Differences between grades were recognised
not by salaries 'but by the payment of such varying expenses as could be justified
by the needs of efficiency'.[64] Ultimately, 'the world beholds for the first time the
spectacle of a brilliant class, the five per cent of the nation who know what five
per cent means . . . In the course of a mere hundred years we have come close to
realising at one stroke the ideal of Plato, Erasmus, and Shaw.'[65] But this process
had also stimulated discontent. Older people were passed over for promotion
by younger colleagues with merit; offspring with lower intelligence than their
parents were doomed to downward mobility. Intelligent women often
preferred 'romance' to science and became the leaders of a new movement: 'For
the only time within living memory a dissident minority from the elite has
struck up an alliance with the lower orders, hitherto so isolated and so docile.'[66]
Young's narrator expresses confidence that this rebellion can be overcome, but
he is himself killed at Peterloo in May 2034. As Young points out in his final
footnote, 'The failings of sociology are as illuminating as its successes.'[67]

By comparing James's vision with that of Young, we can perceive the
potential qualities and flaws of the 'meritocracy'. It was a doctrine that equated
equality of opportunity with the creation of a new social and political elite. It
substantially revised the nineteenth-century conceptions of education for
leadership in favour of the primacy of academic selection. But it fell victim to
distaste for the 'elitist' and 'undemocratic' connotations that it seemed to imply,
and which Young's fantasy magnified so brilliantly. Psychometrics, or the
'unnatural science' of mental testing, had been widely influential in the 1930s,
but although intelligence tests continued to be used in the postwar period their
validity was being increasingly challenged during the 1950s.[68] Even more
alienating in the context of the 1950s was the spectre of eugenics − once a
respectable social-scientific movement but since the rise of fascism in the early
1930s increasingly confined to the extreme right wing.[69] By extending and
distorting James's suggestions, Young did not merely reduce them to the level
of absurdity; he was also representing them in terms designed to make them
appear too dangerous to contemplate.

James was not impressed by Young's argument. He continued to insist that
democracies needed their own kind of leadership no less than did other forms of

government, and was unrepentant in his view that 'the first prerequisite for the creation of the right kind of democratic leadership is to devise an educational system which gives the fullest opportunities to the able child'.[70] He explained to Anthony Sampson in the early 1960s:

One may be worried by the idea of a 'meritocracy' – but what's the alternative? If you want to have equality of opportunity, you inevitably have a meritocracy: but you can mitigate the dangers, by producing essentially *humane* meritocrats. The grammar schools must have their own *noblesse oblige* – but in order to have that, they have to *know* that they are a new kind of aristocracy – as Etonians know it.[71]

He was awarded a life peerage as Lord James of Rusholme, and in 1962 became Vice-Chancellor of York University. There can be little doubt that James's general educational approach was widely seen as discredited, as inappropriate for an egalitarian society, as too narrow in its conception of ability. Yet it was also true that critics of these ideas suggested few tangible alternatives. When the new comprehensive schools failed in their mission to create an equal society, the result tended to be social inequalities without the public spirit or mission that had once helped to mitigate some of their worst effects.

EXCELLENCE OR LEADERSHIP?

James's argument failed to win favour even where it might have been most expected to do so, within a Ministry of Education striving to maintain the position of grammar schools. Sir David Eccles as Minister was a notable sceptic. At a high-level Ministerial meeting on secondary education in February 1955, for example, it was noted that 'As an introduction to the problems of selection, there was a discussion of the aims of secondary education. Were we trying to produce, as in the view of Dr Eric James, a small elite, or were we rather aiming to produce in everyone the virtues hitherto characteristic of the middle classes. The Minister rather favoured the latter view.'[72] Sir Edward Boyle, under-secretary at the Ministry of Education in the late 1950s and later himself Minister of Education, was a keen supporter of Popper's view of Plato, going so far as to remark privately that

Ever since I read K.R. Popper's 'Open Society' as an undergraduate I have always been sympathetic to the view that Plato was a menace, but that Marx was simply in error. Despite all the brutalities perpetrated under Communist regimes, I still feel that Plato's concept of a tiny minority, with Guardians enjoying a uniquely privileged access to Ultimate Truth was a far more disastrous chapter in the history of thought than the confusions in Marxist theory.[73]

Not all of Boyle's colleagues were so learned: Lord Hailsham, another Conservative Minister of Education, had never read Popper.[74] Even so, it is clear that the notion of education for leadership met with some resistance within the Ministry of Education in the 1950s.

The reason for such coolness, beyond the strictly philosophical rationalisations, was probably the pragmatic calculation that this line of thought had
become unpopular and was unlikely to prevail in a democratic, egalitarian
society. As such, it threatened to damage the reputation of the grammar schools
rather than help them. Indeed, it is noticeable that defenders of the grammar
schools increasingly sought to avoid appearing to advocate a 'small elite', and
for this reason effectively discarded James's ideal and rhetoric. An emphasis on
equality of opportunity was likely to be more compatible with the prevailing
theme of social equality while also cultivating a strong role for the maintenance
of individual differences. By the late 1950s, and throughout the 1960s, such
adherents tended to emphasise the 'excellence' characteristic of the grammar
schools much more than their supposed role in producing 'leaders'. This stance
allowed them to present grammar schools as vital, in an immediate sense, for the
whole population, since all who were sufficiently 'able' would have an equal
opportunity to achieve 'excellence'. The debate over grammar schools and
comprehensives revolved more and more around 'standards'. In 1956, Harry
Rée, Headmaster of Watford Grammar School, was prepared to acclaim
James's contribution to the debate. James, he argued, had insisted upon the
importance of the grammar schools and thus helped to raise them 'in their own
esteem and in the eyes of the public'.[75] But he was careful to modify James's
claims for leadership:

> The Grammar Schools do not set out consciously to produce leaders. It is, of course, a
> fact that many Grammar School boys, because of certain exceptional qualities of brains
> and character, resulting in a measure of self-confidence, develop into natural leaders, and
> for these experience as members of a Prefects' Room is invaluable. There are, however,
> many others who qualify for a Grammar School education but who – because of some
> strain of natural modesty, or perhaps honesty – will never become leaders. It is quite
> right that they should be in the Grammar Schools, and when they leave and become
> clerks and poets, research workers or farmers they may well make a more valuable
> contribution to the community than many a 'successful leader'.[76]

Rée chose to emphasise instead of this the cultivation of excellence of all kinds.
By 1965, the Conservative case for grammar schools was conducted entirely in
these terms. In the major House of Commons debate on comprehensive schools
on 21 January 1965, Quintin Hogg's Conservative motion emphasised 'the need
to raise educational standards at all levels', and therefore the necessity to retain
'grammar schools and other existing schools of proved efficiency and value'.[77]
James's distinctive rhetoric was conspicuous by its absence. Similarly, a strong
defence of grammar schools published by Robin Davis in 1967 made little
mention of 'leadership' but stressed repeatedly the academic traditions of
grammar schools.[78] The same was true of the early 'Black Papers'.[79]

Labour won the political struggle: comprehensives spread rapidly from the
1960s. But it might be said that Conservative arguments had a strong influence
on the character and orientation of such schools. Obliged to defend themselves

in terms of 'standards', most comprehensive schools tended to emphasise academic subjects and examinations. The debate between critics and advocates of the comprehensives hinged largely on the issue of academic achievement, usually as measured by public examinations. In 1970, Caroline Benn and Brian Simon noted that 'schools intensify their traditional aspects during the transitional phase, the more so in areas where the problem of "selling" the comprehensive is most urgent'. Thus, they suggested, 'In matters of uniform, speech days, and stress on GCE academic attainment to the exclusion of other forms of excellence, it is almost as if comprehensive schools are saying: "We can easily beat selective schools at their own game."'[80] This proved to be not simply a 'transitional' phenomenon; indeed, the debate over academic achievement continued long after the majority of secondary schools had became comprehensives. The 'Great Debate' launched by prime minister James Callaghan in the autumn of 1976 was in part an attempt to answer or pacify Conservative accusations of declining educational standards.[81] The question remained contested and unresolved. But while this battle raged, questions about the social purposes of secondary education tended to be neglected. Curriculum initiatives designed to encourage discussion of such issues not only met with uneasiness based on suspicion of 'indoctrination' and 'social engineering', but were also often confined to non-academic or lower-attainment pupils. Thus as Geoff Whitty has pointed out,

While overt education for citizenship has continued to exist in the lower streams of the comprehensive schools, it has generally been considered a low status activity among teachers when compared with academic history and geography teaching, and teachers of these latter subjects have consistently distanced themselves from those concerned with social studies, social education and citizenship.[82]

In such ways were the forms and structures of the academic curriculum of the grammar schools maintained within the comprehensive schools at the same time that their moral curriculum withered away. Social class inequalities triumphantly survived the transition to the new form of institution. And yet the spread of the comprehensives also consolidated and confirmed the defeat not only of Eric James's more narrow notion of leadership training but also of broader and more egalitarian attempts to encourage education for citizenship.

Thus Eric James's contribution is chiefly significant for the lack of support that it attracted, as an indication of the decay and dispersal of a once potent educational ideology. Education for leadership, celebrated in the late nineteenth century and even in the interwar period as a quintessentially English tradition, was in the 1950s unpopular and unfashionable in spite of James's energetic attempts to refashion it for a new audience. The nineteenth-century system of middle-class values and schools had effectively disintegrated. As one socialist critic, Margaret Cole, correctly observed, 'Dr James's plea for segregated education for selected "brilliant" children sounds a very different note from

Arnold's sermons to Christian gentlemen.'[83] James's ideas were as much a measure of this disintegration as they were an attempt to revive the key characteristics of education for leadership. In the 1940s and 1950s, while there were those who persisted in seeking to redefine this ideal for a new age, the social, cultural and political context effectively ensured their failure. In the aftermath of the second major war in a generation, and as the sun finally set on the British Empire, the middle classes had lost the confidence that had marked the products of the public schools only fifty years before. They had also lost the unity and coherence of the Victorian governing elite, and with it the ability to impose a particular set of values upon the rest of society. In their place there grew not social equality as such, for all the hopes and plans of the wartime and immediate postwar period. There was instead a growing emphasis upon competitive individualism through academic examinations, both in grammar schools and comprehensive schools, which avoided the qualities and characteristics that James had attempted to cultivate. This pointed towards the 'affluent society' of the late 1950s, towards the competition of the market place in which when times were hard only the fittest survived; potentially towards social inequality bereft of social conscience or remorse. If James's vision was indeed a 'meritocracy', this was surely not what he had in mind.

6

THE TECHNOCRATS

Despite his failure to prevent the demise of the grammar schools, and the general unpopularity of the notion of education for leadership in the 1950s, Eric James enjoyed considerable success and influence in one area: science education. Several initiatives of the time sought to promote the formation of an industrial, social and political elite, based on the public and grammar schools; novel only in the sense that it was to be grounded in science and technology, suitably adapted to this purpose, rather than simply in the classics. At the same time that James's general approach was in decline, a potent technocratic vision of English society visibly gained ground.

SCIENCE AND EDUCATION

The lack of interest exhibited by most public schools in science education had long been cause for reproach. The Clarendon report of 1864 complained that 'Natural science . . . is practically excluded from the education of the higher classes in England.' Indeed, it continued, 'Education with us is, in this respect, narrower than it was three centuries ago, whilst science has prodigiously extended her empire, has explored immense tracts, divided them into provinces, introduced into them order and method, and made them accessible to all. This exclusion is, in our view, a plain defect and a great practical evil.'[1] While this situation existed, the claims on behalf of the public schools that they produced appropriate leaders of society were highly vulnerable. As Martin Wiener remarks, the 'virtual absence of science of any sort from their curricula' seemed to exemplify their 'detachment from the modern world'.[2] According to Peter Gordon and Denis Lawton,

Science and technology should have become a major part of the public school curriculum in order to give the ruling classes some kind of justification for their continued power and influence. But only a few decision-makers saw this, one of them being Robert Lowe who argued that masters should know more about the new knowledge than their men.[3]

It was, however, to become a major source of contention during the twentieth century. By the 1950s, indeed, a new scientific and technological middle class was seeking to promote its own 'power and influence' by redefining the notion of education for leadership to match up with rapid scientific change.

The first world war in particular stimulated widespread complaint about the lack of scientific knowledge and technological awareness exhibited by those who had supposedly been educated to lead. Some critics took this to mean that the public schools should abandon their leadership pretensions. Others sought to reform the curriculum of the public schools to allow their pupils greater access to scientific knowledge. The Thomson committee, established to inquire into the position of natural science in the education system, recommended that public schools should recognise more readily the claims of science for a larger role in the curriculum:

while the great majority of these schools offer adequate opportunities for the study of Science to those boys whose parents desire it, there has in the Public Schools as a whole been no general recognition of the principle that Science should form an essential part of secondary education. If this principle were recognised, all boys would receive a reasonable amount of instruction in Science, extending over a substantial part of the school course. They do not now.[4]

Lord Sydenham of Combe, president of the British Science Guild, was quick to derive an appropriate moral: 'We are not producing trained leadership sufficient for our needs, and the diffusion of knowledge is pitifully inadequate to the requirements of a modern State.' This deficiency led naturally, he argued, to mistakes and inertia in the direction of public policy and in administration. He concluded: 'The power of reasoning from facts and of "rapid and accurate generalisation", combined with the habit of "method and arrangement", is the best possible qualification for Cabinet Ministers as well as for leadership in lower places; and the British Science Guild has persistently urged that science should take a prominent place in the education of our public servants.'[5] The key theme, then, was the perceived need to equip the future elite with scientific and even technological knowledge and skills which would fit them for leading posts in the twentieth century, rather than the unalloyed classical training that had been deemed appropriate for their Victorian predecessors. This concern raised another central problem: how to teach science and technology for such pupils in a way that incorporated the public school ethos. For these purposes, science education had to be reinterpreted in terms of culture, morality and citizenship, in search of a blend of 'humanism' and 'science' that would be appropriate preparation for the likely leaders of society in the late twentieth century.

The onset of a second major war in 1939, and the increasing prominence of scientific interests, served to renew such agitation. This was generally distinct from the criticisms of such as T.C. Worsley; it sought to revise the curriculum of the public schools to sustain their established purposes in a changing society, rather than to abolish them. It also differed from the ideas of Cyril Norwood, being principally concerned with curriculum change to promote science and technology as well as with the 'morality' associated with the classic 'English tradition'. And among the most interesting and influential leaders of this kind of agitation was Eric James. While still an assistant master at Winchester, James complained in his earliest sustained work *Science and Education*, written jointly with S.R. Humby and published in 1942, that 'the introduction of science into the curriculum has been too slow and halting to keep pace with the demands of our society, and the science introduced has suffered under the stigma of being a purely "technical" study which has never been correlated with "cultural" education'.[6] This meant, they suggested, that

The modern civil servant has had to face the administration of industry, of transport, of public health and of labour in a world created by forces that his education did nothing to lead him to understand. He has found it necessary to improvise methods in which his education gave him no training. It is remarkable that in fact he has succeeded at all.

They emphasised that the public schools were 'still largely responsible for the education of our governing classes': 'Whether we regard it as right or wrong, the position still is that the recruits for the higher ranks of the professions, the civil service and politics are still largely drawn from a fairly small group of schools, represented on the Headmasters' Conference.' In many such schools, 'a man can still boast that he is completely ignorant of science, yet he would regard a similar ignorance of Latin quantities or of the pronunciation of Greek names with pity not untouched with scorn'.[7] In this situation, they argued, science education of a kind that would fit the future elite for their public and social responsibilities should be introduced. They concluded that 'Ignorance of science and lack of a scientific outlook are widespread among the leaders and administrators of the present generation', and that to address this problem meant 'blending a scientific attitude with what is best in our traditional education'.[8] In the postwar period considerable attention was devoted to discovering the best way of achieving this. While it was based upon the same basic assumptions as that of the more general elitist argument on behalf of the grammar schools, it attracted little of the controversy associated with the 'meritocratic' debate.

As has already been seen, by the 1950s James was a highly prominent advocate of adapting the education of the elite to new social and political needs. His work was greeted with particular warmth in scientific circles. The science periodical *Nature*, for example, described *Education and Leadership* as a 'tract for the times', and emphasised 'the implications for to-day of the Platonic conception of education'.[9] In 1955, addressing the Science Masters' Association, James pursued this theme further, arguing that scientists should be able to use their gifts in administration and government:

Unless many of those now being trained in the sciences rise to the positions in administration that have hitherto been held by arts men a grave impoverishment of the intellectual resources of government will follow. Plato envisaged his philosopher kings as having been trained in the mathematics and science of his day. We must see that his vision is realised.

This, he considered, thrust great responsibility upon science teachers, for if 'an increasing proportion of able men are inevitably going to be educated as scientists of one kind or another, we must be sure that the education they receive fits them to be citizens and statesmen'.[10]

Such demands matched both a growing need for more qualified scientific personnel, and continuing uncertainty about the role of established curricula and institutions in preparing future administrators, managers and other leaders. They also appealed to middle-class scientists and technologists seeking greater recognition for the social importance of their work, and more influence and involvement in the direction of society. In the early 1950s, the *Times Educational Supplement* became strident in its demands for a particular kind of school science reform. A leading article that appeared in February 1952, entitled 'Technocracy', contrasted contemporary requirements with those for which the public schools had catered at the turn of the century:

Fifty years ago he would have read Greats and managed a tract of India; to-day he reads engineering and will manage a shop in an aircraft plant. It is difficult to judge which of the two roles ranks as more important, but one can say that education for the first was performed more successfully than education for the second. Nourished on Plato and Aristotle we have been more successful in producing rulers than manufacturers and merchants.

It was important to reform such attitudes as quickly as possible, the *TES* averred, in the interests of economic and industrial growth: 'Arnold and the others met the need of their times by populating the world with men educated to lead. Heads to-day would do well to consider the present need for manufacturers and merchants of the highest capacity.'[11] As the *TES* insisted, such a reformed approach would still constitute education for leadership, albeit in a novel form: 'It is fantastic to suppose that the government of a territory is somehow more dignified, more humane, than the government of 2,000 fellow citizens in a factory. Handling men, directing their effort, maintaining justice among them – the task is the same and calls for qualities equally high.'[12] Several initiatives and publicists promoted school science education for such pupils in this same spirit over the following decade, advocating a more 'humanistic' and 'liberal' approach while also defending the unique qualities of the public and grammar schools for the purposes of this kind of preparation.

CAPTAINS OF INDUSTRY

These attitudes appear to have had an important influence with regard to the creation of the 'Industrial Fund', established in 1955 to finance the equipment of science laboratories in public schools. This scheme developed from an idea of

A.H. Wilson, a director of Courtaulds, who was interested in increasing contacts between industry and schools.[13] Wilson discussed the possibility of such a scheme with Anthony Part of the Ministry of Education,[14] following which the Ministry sought advice. Eric James was a key adviser on the kind of scheme that should be created. He was concerned that any fund should be highly selective, and therefore suggested that applications should not be invited indiscriminately. He recommended that a high-level committee should be set up to ask 'a number of selected schools' whether they were 'held up in their scientific work for lack of money, either for equipment or capital development'. Replies would then be considered 'and decisions reached having regard to the resources of the school'. He concluded forcefully:

I am strongly of the opinion that the money should be devoted in the first place to those schools who *already* have large science sixth forms and from which large numbers of boys go to the university to read science. I should regard it as a mistake – unless the money were unlimited – for an attempt to be made to build up science in dim schools with dim staffs and no scientific tradition.[15]

Part agreed that 'it would be best to "invest in success"'.[16] After further discussion on the most appropriate criteria,[17] Wilson was invited back to the Ministry. It was decided at this stage that maintained schools should be excluded from the scheme, on the grounds that LEAs were responsible for their accommodation and equipment. Only independent and direct grant schools would therefore benefit from the scheme. Part advised that the Ministry should not be officially represented on the committee of such an enterprise, but could usefully provide relevant information behind the scenes. He noted also that

It would have to be decided whether assistance was to be limited to schools already strong in science (e.g. Manchester Grammar School) or whether some help should also be given to the weaker brethren (e.g. Monkton Combe and, no doubt, many of the girls' schools). In principle, Mr Wilson said that he did not wish to limit help simply to the strongest.[18]

Several potential industrial sponsors were nervous at the possible political implications of this kind of scheme,[19] and these anxieties delayed further negotiations until after the general election of May 1955.[20]

Progress towards the launch of a scheme was rapid from this point, but involved several 'compromises'. It was decided that boys' independent schools should be 'considered first'; then 'when they have been dealt with adequately', direct grant schools; and then girls' independent schools. Wilson noted that 'the general feeling' among the sponsoring firms 'was that the Independent Schools have the greater need', and he was 'prepared to accept that view because otherwise agreement was likely to be impossible'.[21] A charitable trust was to be set up with a target of £2 million, 'for the encouragement of the teaching of science, whether pure or applied in certain schools, by the provision of new or enlarged science buildings and the provision of permanent equipment, and on a selective basis'.[22] It was on this basis that the scheme proceeded. Over the next seven years it awarded about £3 million for science laboratories and equipment in such schools. The schools involved were thus enabled to promote the science education of their pupils, without an excessive capital outlay. The scheme helped to reform the public school curriculum to take greater account of science, with the explicit aim of adapting the preparation of the future leaders of society to a changing environment. As the report of the Industrial Fund's Executive Committee made clear in 1957,

It is not enough to make researchers and technologists of them. At their best the humane studies in the VIth produced first-rate people of great flexibility of mind, who were in the best sense highly educated and cultured people. It is now the business of the science masters to see that their ministrations do not produce narrow specialists, but help the best minds with whom they are in contact to make of science the core of an equally liberal education.[23]

This was a practical expression of Eric James's educational and social vision. The Industrial Fund was, from choice no less than by necessity, a selective scheme based upon the public schools, oriented towards elite groups which might thus be encouraged to take up scientific and industrial careers. But the 'highly educated and cultured people' that the scheme aspired to produce would also have a strong claim to influence government and policy in more general terms.

A similar interest was emphasised by another organised grouping on behalf of industry, the Federation of British Industries (FBI). A key concern here was to attract the future 'captains of industry', principally from the public and grammar schools. The FBI was anxious to recruit more public and grammar school boys for their leadership qualities and broad education, and sought to attract them away from their more usual route to the professions. But it seemed necessary also to reform the curriculum of such schools to prepare potential recruits for executive positions in industry. This meant not direct training or vocational preparation, but a synthesis of the traditional 'humanism' of the grammar and public schools with the relevant ingredients of science.

The FBI's education committee, first established in 1917, was revived after a short hiatus at the end of 1942 in order that the Federation could submit evidence to the Fleming committee on public schools.[24] The memorandum that it prepared for this purpose emphasised the 'character, leadership and team spirit' produced by boarding school education, and suggested that these qualities would be 'of great value in the industrial world'. The curriculum of such schools might need a measure of reform to prepare pupils for industrial careers:

The Committee does not, however, believe in stengthening the vocational element in the school curriculum, nor does it desire to emphasise the mere acquisition of factual knowledge. Indeed, this latter element tends, in their opinion, to be overstressed in education generally. What is needed is a curriculum which will develop mental capacity, the power of expression and a broad scientific and social outlook.[25]

These views were amplified in a report issued by the committee in May 1944 entitled *Industry and Education*. Again it looked to boys with sixth form and university education for the future executive grades, and sought 'the power of self-expression and of understanding and judgment' in such recruits no less than 'detailed knowledge in a particular subject or group of subjects'.[26] Such priorities were maintained in the postwar years. According to Percy Dunsheath, chairman of the FBI's education committee, 'Much thought is being given nowadays to the question of leadership, and nowhere is it a more urgent problem than in the fields of commerce and industry.'[27] It is noteworthy that organised industry showed very little interest in, or awareness of, the secondary technical schools in the 1950s. At a discussion on recruiting policy with the FBI's education committee in June 1947, one keen observer, Sir George Schuster, expressed what was widely seen as the basic problem:

The majority of headmasters of public schools were not really aware of industry's needs or whether it was preferable for a lad to enter industry direct from school or first to graduate from a university. It was vitally necessary today that industry had a fair share of the best talent available, and public school boys should have proper advice before entry as to the various alternatives available and be properly looked after after entry.[28]

A working party on recruitment of secondary school leavers was established in 1952, chiefly to seek ways of recruiting grammar school boys.

These aspirations were clearly evident in an important conference with heads of public and grammar schools (all male) organised by the FBI at Ashorne Hill, Warwickshire, in November 1955. The conference secretary, G. Withers, noted privately that the aim was 'to let headmasters know what industry is trying to do, how it depends on the schools for its potential leaders, and the kind of training it provides for them'.[29] Opening the conference, Sir Reginald Verdon Smith, chairman and managing director of the Bristol Aeroplane Company, emphasised the new needs of postwar industry, and suggested that the 'broad liberal education' of the public and grammar schools was the best foundation for industrial leadership. He looked also towards 'the emergence of a new blend of humanism and science in the education of the next generation', which could only be attained in such schools.[30] A.G. Grant, managing director of Whessoe Ltd and the new chairman of the FBI's education committee, reminded the conference that one half of the nation's working population were in industry – about twelve million people. 'More than three-quarters of the twelve million are of course the actual producers and their jobs and skills are indeed legion. But to plan, organise, and sell their production industry has what I like to think of as its civil service. It is into the civil service of industry that grammar school and public schoolboys should go.' Warming to his theme, he argued that despite a growing need because of advancing techniques and growing complexity for more able men in industry, the 'best brains' were being diverted 'away from industry and to the universities'. Industry, he concluded, should take 'new and positive action' to change this situation.[31] Informal discussions at that conference apparently 'indicated a fairly widespread apprehension that VIth form leavers were not equipped to play an effective part in a world dominated by science – the scientist to use his science fully and the arts man to exercise his abilities and influence'.[32] The conference finally agreed on the need to 'equip boys for life', and that this would involve merging the tradition of the humanities with the teaching of science, 'so that while boys would still incline to one discipline or the other, they would above all develop into civilised human beings equipped to tackle the problems of life in industry'.[33] One Bristol industrialist, J.L. Kimber, was especially enthusiastic about such a prospect, writing to Sir Norman Kipping, director-general of the FBI, after the conference to suggest that two aspects in particular were important for the preparation of 'young men' for general industrial management. On the one hand, he averred, they should be 'reasonably mechanically minded so that when they talk to their technical experts on production matters they can follow them, and perhaps at the same time decide whether they are being led up the garden!'. On the other, they

must obviously have that indefinable quality – leadership – and to this end the Sixth Form boy should I think, wherever possible, be given a chance of taking some responsibility at school, whether it be for discipline such as a prefect, or a secretary and organiser of sports sections, or any other work of that type, in addition to his straightforward education.[34]

Kimber responded with equal enthusiasm:

It seems to me that the greater part of our difficulties spring from the division between the humanities and science which has arisen in the sixth forms of our public and grammar schools. If we could do something about the curricula to remove this division, or at least make it less sharp, we should ultimately have technical and non-technical people who could understand each other.[35]

A strong theme emerged in this and other similar calls, for the new science education in such schools to take on the cultural and personal qualities formerly attached to the classics, in order to achieve the same ultimate ends of service, responsibility and leadership.

Public and grammar schools also had a vested interest in science curriculum reform of this kind. It was hoped that such reform would demonstrate the ability of public and grammar schools to adapt to changing needs and conditions without sacrificing their established traditions. To these ends, they also sought an appropriate blend of humanism and science. This was a key objective of H.P.D. Lee, Head of Winchester College from 1954.[36] F.L. Allan, president of the Incorporated Association of Head Masters (IAHM) and Headmaster of Wallasey Grammar School, stressed a similar theme, arguing that only grammar schools could produce the 'technologists' identified in the White Paper *Technical Education* in 1956.[37] In its evidence to the Crowther committee on the education of boys and girls from fifteen to eighteen years of age, the IAHM made much of the scientific and social relevance of the grammar schools, as 'the focal point of English education', which 'must educate not only the scientists and technologists of the future but the leading figures of all other spheres of life and thought'. It concluded with a stirring appeal for moral standards to be maintained alongside increased scientific output: 'The English-man of 1984 must know much about the physical world, whatever his specialisation or his profession, but he must be governed and inspired by firm moral principles if humanity is to avoid destroying itself by its own cleverness.'[38] The clear implication was that this combination of qualities could be nurtured only in the grammar schools with their unique blend of liberal traditions and scientific appreciation. It is true that this enthusiasm for school science reform was far from being a unanimous desire or preoccupation, whether in the grammar schools or in public schools or in industry. But in the afterglow of the successful conference with the public and grammar schools in November 1955, A.G. Grant of the FBI could pronounce himself satisfied with the prevailing trend: 'It is clear that the Grammar Schools are now vividly aware of what the modern world needs and of the fact that science and industry largely *are* the modern world. The same, I feel, goes for the public schools (via Lee) and for the universities (via [Philip] Morris). The leaven of Vernon Smith's paper is working actively.'[39]

MEN OF AFFAIRS

The aims of the school science initiatives of the Science Masters' Association (SMA) in the late 1950s were strongly influenced by these priorities. Professor Nevill Mott, Cavendish Professor of Experimental Physics at Cambridge, and Professor Alexander Todd, also of Cambridge, emphasised the educational value of science and the potential role of science in a general education for the most able pupils. The SMA took its cue from this approach. Todd, in his presidential address to the SMA in January 1957, argued that the nation was suffering 'from an archaic system of school education which is wrongly based for modern conditions and orients too many of the ablest children towards the arts side'. He continued: 'Our present specialized educational pattern operates especially unfavourably on science because of our clinging to an outworn nineteenth-century set of cultural traditions.' But his concern for changing the balance between the arts and science and technology focused exclusively upon the 'ablest children', especially boys, in the public and grammar schools, with whom he linked in a quite explicit way the future social and political elite: 'I consider it entirely wrong to claim that the education of future administrators and men of affairs is satisfactory, if it gives them no acquaintance with science and the scientific method. No modern man is properly educated if he has no knowledge of science.'[40]

It was very much in this spirit that Henry Boulind, chairman of the SMA's

Science and Education Committee, sought to reform grammar school science syllabuses. He declared in a letter to the *New Scientist* in June 1957 that 'we consider that science is essential to the education of *all* pupils', affirming also that 'Every responsible member of a democracy such as ours should be trained to observe and think scientifically, and to know something of the way in which scientists work, and of the future possibilities and limitations of science.'[41] Even so, he was especially concerned about able grammar school pupils who, as he put it in a private memorandum, 'will subsequently occupy a position of some responsibility, and will be among the "top" 10% or so that Professor Mott [or Todd?] would call "men-of-affairs"'.[42] Thus, as he told his colleagues,

Adequate scientific education is essential for the whole population, and certainly for the 20 per cent of pupils of the 'grammar school type' who will become 'men of affairs' in administration, industry, business, teaching and other professions. It may be that education will in the future be centred upon science just as it has been centred upon classics in the past. The Association should take action, first, by proposing new aims, methods and syllabuses that will extend and revitalise science teaching and, more than anything else, enable this country to take a leading place in the world of the future, and second, by persuading the Ministry and the Examining Boards to accept new syllabuses and new aims.[43]

These were precisely the actions that the Association took over the following five years.

This focus was also that of most leading science publicists and politicians in the 1950s and early 1960s. Thus, for example, the scientist Jacob Bronowski discussed the need for science curriculum reform essentially in terms of the requirements of the governing elite:

We are hamstrung everywhere in public life by a tradition which treats science merely as a technical skill . . . Our public life is full of these mutinous humanists affecting a hollow disdain for the technical fabric of civilisation, who govern what they do not understand . . . When a society is penetrated, as ours is, by technical skills and engines, the decisions of State cannot be taken out of the context of science . . . The foundation for these judgments is knowledge: a knowledge of science as easy and familiar as is the educated man's knowledge of literature and of history. The man who can tell Milton from Kipling, who knows that Pitt and Napoleon were contemporaries but stood on opposing sides, must be equally clear on the contexts of, and the differences between, a mean and a meson.[44]

Again here we see an emphasis on the need to recognise science as an important part of the wider culture, as more than 'merely' a 'technical skill', and a direct connection made between an appropriate science education and influence over the society as a whole. In similar vein Lord Hailsham, appointed as Britain's first Minister for Science in 1959, argued the importance of developing what he called 'scientific judgment' – 'the ability to distinguish between charlatanry and good work, between good and bad arguments in the field of material things, and between the purely hypothetical and the well-confirmed scientific theory'.[45] According to Hailsham, science education had differing aims for different kinds of people. For the 'mass of the people', science was necessary so that they could discharge their functions as consumers and voters. The 'bureaucracy', that is, 'the people who in every modern state have the power of executive decision both in Government and society at large', equally needed science to fulfil its responsibilities, which would entail 'a highly educated and, where necessary, specialized administrative class'. Meanwhile, the 'aristocracy', those 'who by their talents and training have the power of making new scientific discoveries and so of keeping the whole fabric alive', should 'have the training and equipment to enable them to discharge their task'.[46] Such an arrangement, he emphasised, should encourage efficient and rational government. The 'bureaucracy' and the 'aristocracy' would possess the 'scientific judgment' to be able to organise and lead the society and nation; the 'mass of the people' would not.

Such visions reinforced the idea of reforming science education in order to enhance its 'cultural' aspects in terms that grammar and public schools could understand. More radical, though again appealing to this elite audience, was the view that technology, as distinct from pure science, should be encouraged in such schools. Perhaps the most eloquent proponent of this view was Sir Eric Ashby, particularly in his book *Technology and the Academics*. Ashby suggested that in the nineteenth century a 'narrowly pragmatic attitude to science' had meant that 'scientific education tended to be regarded as more suitable for artisans and the lower middle classes than for the governing classes'. He saw technology as a potential means of integrating the 'false antithesis' that had developed between science and humanism: 'Unlike science, technology concerns the applications of science to the needs of man and society. Therefore technology is inseparable from humanism.'[47] Ashby was particularly interested in changing attitudes within universities, although he also hoped 'to get the schools to send their best boys to do engineering' in higher education.[48] Another development in this vein concerned explicitly with grammar and public schools was sponsored by John Dancy, Master of Marlborough College in Wiltshire. Dancy, himself coincidentally a former pupil of Eric James, went so far as to argue in his presidential address to the British Association in 1965, that 'technology and a liberal education, far from being antithetical, are not even complementary to each other: that on the contrary some experience of technology is an essential ingredient *within* a liberal education'. He blamed English interpretations of Plato's thought for contemporary prejudice against technology: 'Plato was social and intellectual snob rolled into one, a combination irresistible to the English. *His* intellectual theory matched and reinforced *our* traditional social practice.'[49] Dancy was most enthusiastic about what he called 'a remarkable and gratifying upsurge of interest in technical studies among boys' selective secondary schools, whether grammar or "public"'.[50] It seems likely that his interest was due at least in part to his anxiety to respond to continuing criticisms of public schools such as his own. Replying directly to Rupert Wilkinson's historical critique of the 'proconsular' type of leader produced by public schools, he emphasised that industry was especially keen to acquire leaders from this source. The old notion of 'leadership', he claimed, had now developed to become the 'key-concept of responsibility', which was vital 'whether in industry or elsewhere'.[51] The promotion of technology in such schools, he no doubt hoped, would equally demonstrate the continuing relevance of public schools to society and close the remaining gap between them and industry. In order to do so, however, it was necessary to square the circle and reconcile 'technology' with 'liberal education'. Here the attempt to adapt the classic nineteenth-century tradition to changing conditions was stretched to its utmost, as Dancy related the Arnoldian vision not to classics and Christianity but to industry and technology. Indeed Dancy and Ashby went well beyond most of their colleagues and the large majority of science teachers in grammar and public schools in their willingness to contemplate a key role for technology. Pure science was one thing, technology quite another. There was little organised or sustained support for any attempt to introduce 'technology' for the elite on a national scale.[52] This suggests an important weakness in the technocratic vision: although the technocrats were generally agreed on their notion of society, they were divided or at least had significant differences of emphasis with regard to the kind of science curriculum that they were prepared to champion. It was a fragile and insecure coalition with little in the way of a mass basis, organisation or agreed principles. And yet it exerted strong educational and political influence in the 1950s and early 1960s, as its general message seemed to coincide with the needs of the nation as a whole. It is therefore important that we should try to understand both the appeal of this technocratic vision in the context of its time, and the reasons for its longer-term failure.

A TECHNOCRATIC VISION

In his powerful work, *Technocracy*, Jean Meynaud points out that the 'technocratic trend' reflects some of the most important aspects of contemporary societies: 'Chief among these is the kind of neo-liberalism which typifies a mixture of social conservatism and a belief in technical progress, with the second of these two elements lending an air of respectability to the first.'[53] These traits were certainly characteristic of the demands for school science reform in the 1950s. They also help to explain how Eric James's views on science education gained greater credence than his more general ideas on the role of the grammar schools. An ideology rooted in the nineteenth-century public school but now adapting to the political, economic and cultural context of the 1950s created a very English vision of technocracy.

The technocratic vision of English society, industry and administration that shone through these varied projects was novel in one sense but hackneyed in another. Novel, in that science education in the public and grammar schools, and in some cases technology also, was designed to produce the captains of industry, the 'men of affairs', the Whitehall mandarins of tomorrow; but far from new in that the initiatives were pervaded by and largely based upon strongly held assumptions about the role of the elite in society, and of the continued role of the public and grammar schools in providing this elite. Whereas their Victorian predecessors had looked to classics and 'Greats' to produce Empire builders, in the 1950s sponsors of science curriculum reform hoped to produce similar leaders suited for late twentieth-century society. According to Charles Day, in France the graduates of the *Ecole polytechnique* were 'men of gold, who needed only to be refined', while those of the *Ecole d'arts et metiers* 'could at best hope to become men of brass, second-level managers and industrialists rather than true leaders of men'.[54] A similar distinction could be made in the English context between the technocratic vision of the public and grammar schools, and the 'men of brass' of secondary technical schools and technical colleges.[55] As Brian Jackson and Dennis Marsden commented in 1965, 'the old purpose of education – the training of a ruling elite – has not collapsed under the new purpose – the training of enough able people to man our technological society. More and more – as Eton builds its science blocks – the two are allies, putting the same people into the same place at the same price.'[56]

The results failed to live up to expectations. The technocratic vision faded as it became evident that 'scientific judgment' was prone to the same problems and mistakes as other kinds of approach to politics and administration, and that it could not prevent industrial decay and social conflict.[57] It was decisively undercut also by the educational reforms of the 1960s in which comprehensive schools took the place of grammar schools. During the 1960s, too, competitive individualism and the motif of 'excellence' superseded the notion of leadership in school science initiatives, especially in the Nuffield Foundation Science Teaching Project. The social and cultural concerns that had been an important dimension of school science reform in the 1950s faded as the new curriculum initiatives became involved in detailed negotiations with examining bodies, and made strenuous efforts to be accepted into the 'educational bloodstream'.[58]

The Nuffield Foundation took over from the SMA's earlier initiative at the end of 1961, and continued to be interested principally in O-level science courses taught mainly in grammar schools. Eric Rogers of Princeton University, director of the Foundation's physics project, emphasised his concern to educate future 'men of affairs',

thinking of our young people at a later stage, not when they are learning science at school, but a dozen years later when they are out in the world, a young man in a bank presently to be a manager, an important person in business or industry, or above all the parents of young children giving the next generation a first view of science.

For such people, he insisted, it was most important to teach science for 'understanding', in part to ensure that 'governors and administrators who learnt science at school confer intelligently with scientists on the vital problems of our age'.[59] But this vision was soon translated into an overriding aim for high academic standards. Even at the beginning of the Nuffield Foundation's involvement, Boulind of the SMA expressed strong suspicion that the focus of the new physics curriculum would drift away from 'physics for the educated citizen' towards 'physics for the future honours physicist',[60] and thus lose interest in its potential social implications. He was assured that 'physics for the educated citizen' would be the 'prime concern' of the initiative.[61] And yet this seemed to be interpreted in an increasingly narrow way as the Nuffield project came to be introduced in the schools. One problem here was that although they had originally been designed for the top 20 per cent of pupils, in the public and grammar schools, by the time the new programmes were ready the grammar schools were giving way to comprehensives. This tended to mean in practice a self-conscious 'watering down' of the new science curriculum for the mass of the school population, but also an emphasis on academic standards manifested in examinations for the most able. At a time of growing anxiety about the position of average and below-average pupils in the new comprehensive schools, Tony Becher of the Nuffield Foundation affirmed in 1972 that 'the most important aim at the moment must be to take into account the continuing needs of these abler pupils who (whether in comprehensive or in grammar schools) will want to take O-level examinations or their equivalent in years to come'.[62] Rogers was especially uneasy about the effects of examinations and the new educational environment upon the original 'spirit' of the Nuffield curriculum, telling Becher that 'Between our easy questions that all Comprehensive School teachers press me for, the new watered down programme that a number of people are offering as substitutes, and now pseudo-Nuffield exams, I think you and I will soon say we have failed except for the present generation of Nuffield teachers in a decreasing set of grammar schools.'[63] The technocratic vision that had helped to inspire the Nuffield curriculum reforms had degenerated to a narrow concern with academic examinations; at its most elevated, indeed, to 'physics for the future honours specialist'. Thus according to Maurice Savory, chairman of the science teachers' research committee and a key figure in the 'Science in Society' project of the late 1970s, Nuffield science had exerted a 'profound influence' on the schools but had failed in one important respect: 'We were very happy looking inwards on our subject; we were concerned with science for the enquiring mind and we failed to show the relevance of it to the world outside the classroom.'[64]

In a way, indeed, this was a symptom of a more general problem. The concern of initiatives such as the Industrial Fund to make science 'the core of an equally liberal education' to that of the old Classical Sixth, and to produce 'highly educated and cultured people' rather than 'narrow specialists', had been in essence a radical variant on the familiar moral curriculum of education for leadership. When it faded, it gave way not to a more democratic and inclusive moral curriculum but to a moral vacuum, a 'culture of individualism'. Structural inequalities remained as divisive and as alienating as ever in the comprehensive schools, but lost their Platonic rationale and social agenda. Difficulties encountered in trying to encourage more attention for the social implications of science in secondary schools in the 1970s and 1980s provided further evidence of remoteness and narrowness. The academic, cognitive-intellectual curriculum inherited from the grammar schools left little room for such initiatives except for those pupils who were deemed to be failures.

In some ways the government initiative in the late 1980s to introduce 'city technology colleges' (CTCs) in selected urban areas echoed the tripartism of the 1940s. It stirred anxiety in some quarters that such institutions would create a new technocratic elite. Local education authorities, struggling to cater for pupils of all abilities and aptitudes, expressed particular concern that the CTCs would substitute 'technological aptitude' for 'academic excellence' in 'defining a new elite'.[66] There was substance to such fears in the sense that the CTCs threatened to divert resources from other local schools and thus to create a fresh source of inequality. But unlike, for example, the Industrial Fund of the 1950s, there appeared to be little in the way of a coherent moral, social or cultural vision motivating the new initiative. Cyril Taylor, chairman of the CTCs Trust, took pains to avoid any impression that the scheme had aims other than that of promoting technology – a stance received with general scepticism but also attracting criticism from observers who argued that pupils should also be equipped to make 'critical judgements' about technology involving 'complex moral and social issues'.[66] It seemed entirely possible that even if the CTCs did create a 'new elite' it would be one unprepared for the problems of leadership that it would encounter.

Thus in hindsight the technocrats of the 1950s did not represent a vigorous new social movement struggling for its birth, despite all appearances. It was on the contrary a distant and ironic echo of an ideology that had attained its zenith in the late nineteenth century. Like the meritocratic approach to which it was closely related, the technocratic vision was more a symptom of the decline, dispersal and disintegration of the classic ideology of education for leadership in new and changing circumstances, much more than a harbinger of the future. Bronowski talked of exorcising 'Dr Arnold's ghost' from the schools; Dancy declared the importance of 'laying the ghost of Plato'. But both they and others were in a real sense merely reviving the essential message of Arnold and Plato, that of 'education for leadership', in new and contemporary form. It had some potency and appeal, chiefly because it wrapped up its essential 'social conservatism' in the 'respectability' of technocratic aspirations. Even so, neither the energetic advocacy of Eric James nor the scientific vocabulary of the technocrats proved capable of reproducing what had been the most outstanding achievement of the Victorian public schools. Despite hopes for a new style of government and leadership, in practice nothing emerged that was anything like as cohesive as the 'identifiable elite' of 'English gentlemen' in the late nineteenth century. The 'English tradition' of education for leadership was still capable of adaptation to changing circumstances. But its manifestation as technocracy must be judged in retrospect not so much as a sign of things to come as an echo of the past, a stage in its further dissolution and dispersal in postwar England.

7

TRIBUNE

Norwood, James and many other twentieth-century adherents of 'education for leadership' saw the Labour Party as a natural enemy of the values and priorities that they cherished. Such hostility tended to be mutual, as Labour's educational policy generally advocated greater equality and the abolition of structures that resisted or restricted this growth. Public schools were subjected to trenchant criticisms, as were the grammar schools after 1945. Less noticed, and certainly less successful, than the dominant Labour emphasis upon equality has been a tendency in socialist thought that has sought effective leadership of the working class based on new kinds of training and education. This latter kind of approach attempted to develop in various ways the 'popular leaders' envisaged by J.A. Hobson.

THE LABOUR TRADITION OF EQUALITY

Throughout the present century, the Labour Party and the organised labour movement in general have usually insisted upon 'equality' and 'democracy' in education. Key figures in this regard were the historian R.H. Tawney, especially in the interwar period, and Anthony Crosland in the 1950s and 1960s. In his major work *Equality*, published in 1931, Tawney fiercely denounced what he called the 'religion of inequality'. He was especially critical of the character and effects of education in England. The public schools, he noted, were 'traditionally connected with the middle and upper classes': 'Drawing their pupils mainly, not from the public primary schools, but from the so-called preparatory schools, and catering for the requirements of the wealthier sections of the community, they form virtually a closed educational system of their own, side by side with the system of public education which has as its foundation the elementary school.'[1] This educational system helped to account for the exclusive character of political leadership. Greater 'practical equality' was now imperative, according to Tawney, for the sake of the community as a whole:

Social well-being does not only depend on intelligent leadership; it also depends upon cohesion and solidarity. It implies the existence, not merely of opportunities to ascend, but of a high level of general culture, and a strong sense of common interests, and the diffusion throughout society of a conviction that civilization is not the business of an elite alone, but a common enterprise which is the concern of all.[2]

This could not develop, however, until the 'hereditary curse' of English education, 'its organisation upon lines of social class',[3] was abolished:

The English educational system will never be one worthy of a civilised society until the children of all classes in the nation attend the same schools . . . The capital fact about English educational policy is that hitherto it has been made, except at brief intervals, by men few, if any, of whom have themselves attended the schools principally affected by it, or would dream of allowing their children to attend them . . . Rightly regarded, the preparation of the young life is obviously the greatest of common interests. As long as the character of educational organisation is determined, not by the requirements of the young, but by the facts of the class system, it is impossible for that truism to receive recognition.[4]

Tawney concluded that educational reform was crucial for the development of a more equal and just society.[5]

Tawney made an important contribution towards this end by drafting the influential pamphlet *Secondary Education for All* for the Labour Party in 1922. He was also to the fore during the second world war with strong demands for social reconstruction 'based on a broad foundation of informed conviction among ordinary men and women'. The 'survival of political democracy', he argued, now depended on 'the creation of a democratic society'; but 'such a society can no more be based on the rule of an intellectual *elite* over an ignorant or apathetic people than on the landed oligarchies of the past or the financial oligarchies of today. Democracy needs experts, representatives and leaders; but it needs them as servants, not as masters.'[6] In this situation he emphasised the need to reconsider the future of the public schools. In general, he declared powerfully, 'We ought to resolve, while democracy and national unity are the words on all lips, to act on our principles, by ending educational inequalities which gravely cripple the first and make a mockery of the second.'[7]

In the postwar period, Crosland was a central figure in the consolidation of Tawney's general approach. His *The Future of Socialism* (1956) also presented education as a key factor in the development of a more equal society. Despite the reforms of the 1940s, he argued, 'The school system in Britain remains the most divisive, unjust, and wasteful of all the aspects of social inequality . . . The 1944 Education Act set out to make secondary education universal; and formally it has done so. Yet opportunities for advancement are still not equal.'[8] Crosland stressed the continuing predominance of the grammar schools in explaining such inequality, and he called for the widespread adoption of comprehensive schools to replace them. But he was also anxious to avoid allowing the public schools to become 'the breeding-ground of a new, superior intellectual elite'.[9] He supported the findings of the Fleming report of 1944, in the hope of achieving 'a gradual integration of these schools into the State system of education'.[10] This in turn might allow the introduction of 'a "comprehensive" system of education, under which all children would ideally share the same broad experience at least up to the official school-leaving age', an arrangement that he regarded as 'a condition of creating an equal and "classless" society'.[11] Within a decade of writing this highly influential work, Crosland found himself in a position to put some of his ideas into practice. As secretary of state for education in Harold Wilson's Labour government from 1965 until 1967, he presided over comprehensive reorganisation and established another committee to consider the role and future of the public schools.[12]

Both Tawney and Crosland rejected the idea of grooming a small elite for leadership and governance, and, as has been seen in an earlier chapter, Crosland was unimpressed with the new arguments put forward by Eric James. The case against Platonic notions of education for leadership was also expressed most cogently by Richard Crossman, Oxford don and future Labour cabinet minister, in his work *Plato Today* (1937). Crossman denounced Plato's philosophy as 'the most savage and the most profound attack upon liberal ideas which history can show'.[13] Plato's ideas on education, Crossman alleged, 'would be most acceptable to Sir Oswald Mosley'.[14] The modern equivalents of Plato were the enemies of progress and democracy: 'Only when Western civilization has shaken off the shackles of the past and created a new social order worthy of the human dignity of the common man, will democracy and religion be once more realised in human society.'[15] It was this general ideal, consistent with the advocacy of working-class interests, that inspired the educational policy of the Labour Party and the Trades Union Congress (TUC). Clive Griggs's work on the TUC's 'struggle for education', and Rodney Barker's important study of the Labour Party, both tend to emphasise the pursuit of equality.[16] According to Barker, this pursuit was not as hectic as it might have been: 'The language which was always familiar within the party often gave the impression that a new heaven and earth were in the making; but in the field of education there was a tacit assumption that all would be well if only the advantages of the old heaven and the old earth were spread more evenly.'[17] But although there were differences of interpretation among adherents of 'equality of opportunity', it was a slogan that certainly provided some common ground so far as educational reform was concerned. The socialist politics of the early twentieth century was crucial in focusing attention on issues relating to equal opportunity in and through education.[18] This focus on equality and its social implications provides the keynote of policy, opinion and historiographical writing on labour and education in the twentieth century.

A MODERN UTOPIA?

Against this dominant emphasis upon equality and democracy, it is also possible to perceive a concern with educating an effective and authentic working-class leadership, a vanguard of the movement. In part, this has represented a desire to exploit the established channels of elite education, the public schools, in the interests of the working class and of socialism. Many of the leaders of the Labour Party were themselves educated at public school, and it is fair to argue that in large measure they were rejecting the values imparted by their education in becoming involved in labour politics. John Strachey, a marxist in the 1930s and a minister in Clement Attlee's Labour government, was an Old Etonian who had apparently disliked his school and been unpopular there. According to his biographer, 'in after life, Strachey frequently said, as a joke, that he became a socialist, or even a communist, because he had not got into the Eton Cricket XI'.[19] There were, of course, more serious political and ideological reasons for rejecting the conventional paths offered by a public school education. But even among those who experienced alienation from the public school ethos, there was a sense in which that ethos also influenced them in their desire to serve and lead the community with which they identified themselves.

Some recruits to the Labour cause from the public schools clearly saw their own role as one of providing guidance and leadership for this new movement. Hugh Dalton, educated at Eton and King's College, Cambridge, noted after the general election of 1918 that although the Labour Party had made gains, 'It has suffered, for the moment, for keeping most of its brain in its left big toe. What is chiefly needed is (1) improved organisation in the constituencies, (2) an influx of brains and middle-class non-crank membership'.[20] Such figures as Sir Stafford Cripps, Hugh Gaitskell and Richard Crossman, all products of Winchester, sought to apply their public school education to resolve such problems. The families of both Cripps and Gaitskell had a long tradition of public service, in the Army and the Indian civil service. A.F. Thompson suggests that

at Winchester they all learnt to think clearly and master a subject; they absorbed from the school as well as their families a belief in the duty of public service; and they were given to understand that the privileged owed something to the lower orders. If they must be rebels and reformers, it was important to be 'gentlemanly' as well as 'intellectual'. Meritocrats to a man, their approach to the possibility of radical change was physiocratic, *de haut en bas*.[21]

Philip Williams, Gaitskell's biographer, has supported this view, arguing that 'As a young man he repudiated the pressures for external conformity that Winchester imposed, but its basic values had marked his character.'[22] Clement Attlee, Gaitskell's predecessor as Leader of the Labour Party, also came from a public school background. Attlee was highly conscious of the traditions of his *alma mater*, Haileybury College, founded by the East India Company to educate men for service to the Empire. According to Trevor Burridge,

Perhaps what his schooling provided for him best on the social level was not so much a group of friends or an entrée into an old boy network as a personal shorthand of psychology and language. He shared the memories, the sentiments, the jargon and to some extent the nostalgia of the British public-school educated elite. These were political assets later on; even if 'they' were to have difficulty in understanding him, he found it easy to understand and hence to deal with 'them' . . . If he learned one lesson from his first experiences with adversity it was the importance of common and personal loyalties. The effect of his schooldays was to cast him into a psychological mould that would endure to the end of his life. Few things are stranger in the history of the Labour Party than that it should have had as its leader for so long a man who in so many respects was the quintessence of the public school type.[23]

A further irony was his willingness to select other Old Boys of Haileybury as members of his political team in a way that Stanley Baldwin might have approved.

Equally significant, though, were the various attempts during the twentieth century to develop alternative, and more appropriate, sources of education for socialist leadership. These usually emanated from middle-class socialist intellectuals and activists. In a similar sense to their moralist, meritocratic and scientific counterparts they might well be interpreted as trying to rationalise continued middle-class control, or at least a measure of 'enlightened' middle-class influence, in a radically transformed society. The socialist advocates of education for leadership, however, had the especially difficult task of needing to reconcile – to themselves as well as to others – a necessarily elitist view with the tenets of democracy and equality to which the labour and socialist movements aspired.

Such schemes often tended to be visionary in their hopes for a new kind of society and transformed social relationships, as opposed to the more pragmatic ambitions of many in the labour movement for a more equitable and efficient arrangement of the society that already existed. One early example of this utopian viewpoint was the notion of the 'samurai' put forward by the writer and social critic H.G. Wells in his book *A Modern Utopia*. This work, published in 1905, imagined a class of 'voluntary nobleman who have taken the world in hand'.[24] This kind of group was necessary, he argued, because the modern utopia would not be created 'by the chance occasional co-operations of self-indulgent men, by autocratic rulers or by the bawling wisdom of the democratic leaders'.[25] Wells's notion of the *samurai* was based explicitly on the class of guardians in Plato's *Republic*. He distinguished between four main classes of mind: the Poietic, the Kinetic, the Dull and the Base. The education of the people would vary accordingly: 'Education is uniform until differentiation becomes unmistakable, and each man (and woman) must establish his position with regard to the lines of this abstract classification by his own quality, choice, and development.'[26] The poietic and the kinetic were to form the *samurai*, a 'voluntary nobility',[27] 'in whose hands as a class all the real power of the world resides'.[28] Any intelligent and healthy adult over twenty-five could become a *samurai*. It appears that

Practically the whole of the responsible rule of the world is in their hands; all our head teachers and disciplinary heads of colleges, our judges, barristers, employers of labour beyond a certain limit, practising medical men, legislators, must be *samurai*, and all the executive committees, and so forth, that play so large a part in our affairs are drawn by lot exclusively from them.[29]

All of these would be expected to follow the Rule, intended 'to exclude the dull and the base altogether, to discipline the impulses and emotions, to develop a moral habit and sustain a man in periods of stress, fatigue, and temptation, to produce the maximum co-operation of all men of good intent, and, in fact, to keep all the *samurai* in a state of moral and bodily health and efficiency'.[30] Nearly all of the population would qualify for free schooling in a college or upper school from fourteen to eighteen years of age, when examinations would be held. About 10 per cent would fail this examination, and such failures could not become *samurai*, although it would be possible to sit for it again later in life. It would also be necessary to have a satisfactory knowledge of the Canon embodying the idea of the order, and of proscribed behaviour. Wells concluded: 'The tendency is to give a practically permanent tenure to good men.'[31]

Critics were quick to point out parallels with Plato's guardians. One reviewer noted that 'The *Samurai* represent an ingenious device for securing efficient government, which is not quite like anything that has been suggested before.' Even so, he added, 'The *Samurai* are, in fact, the Platonic "guardians", born again into an age of electricity and statistics.'[32] Wells's vision did not fire the enthusiasm of most of his socialist colleagues, even those who usually sympathised with his ideas. David Low strongly disapproved of the notion, as he later recalled:

I didn't believe in his scientific Samurai . . . – the technical *elite* that, according to him, were to take over the future of the world. I can remember only my own disapproval, 'I should have to be very careful indeed of your damned supermen with their damned oil-cans H.G., arranging everything for us boobs whether we like it or not,' I said. 'I have use for socialism only so far as it helps us all to grow to our full stature mentally as well as physically, and I might have to stand Samurai, too, up to a point. But by God I would keep an eye on them . . .' I could never repose the sublime trust he did in scientists, who seemed to me a remarkably simple-minded set of people apart from their specialities.[33]

Such suspicion of the elitist and authoritarian connotations of the *samurai* was an orthodox and pragmatic reaction. There was what would today be called a strong meritocratic dimension in the classifying of this 'voluntary nobility'. Certainly Wells's ideas did not result in any practical scheme of reform. But his utopian notion of 'education for leadership' was to be echoed in various forms by other socialist intellectuals in the twentieth century.

Much more influential in a tangible or practical sense were Wells's fellow Fabians, Sidney and Beatrice Webb. They shared Wells's aspirations for a governing elite, though with significant differences. In the 1890s, Sidney Webb had been a key architect of the new London School of Economics and Political

H.G. Wells, the frontispiece to *A Modern Utopia* (1905) – 'the Platonic "guardians",
born again into an age of electricity and statistics'

Science, hoping thus to provide facilities for training experts in economics to organise society on rational, scientific lines.[34] They were keen admirers of Sir Robert Morant, and supported his Education Act against fierce and wide-ranging opposition in 1902. Wells's *Anticipations of the Reaction of Mechanical and Scientific Progress upon Human Life and Thought*, which were his first thoughts on the character of the future elite, met with the Webbs' general approval. On the other hand, they felt that Wells placed too much emphasis on 'engineers and chemists' in the 'dominant class of the future'. Along with these, Sidney Webb insisted, there would be 'the trained administrator, the expert in organising men – equipped with an Economics or a Sociology which will be as scientific, and as respected by his colleagues of other professions, as Chemistry or Mechanics'.[35] Beatrice Webb also criticised Wells's ideal of a 'world run by the physical-science-man straight from his laboratory'.[36] The relationship between Wells and the Webbs was often strained amid the political and social discords of the Fabian Society,[37] but despite their differences they clearly had much in common in terms of their respective visions of the future. More broadly, such ideas reflected an emerging tendency in early twentieth-century Fabianism towards an emphasis on government by 'experts', somewhat at odds with the democratic tenets of Fabians in the late nineteenth century.[38] Middle-class meritocrats no less than they were socialists, their notion of the most appropriate education for the leaders of the new world coincided with their vision of themselves, as enlightened and efficient intellectuals unconstrained by the dogmas of the past.

In the 1930s, Beatrice Webb was able to relate this earlier notion of the 'vocation of leadership' to a new-found utopia, the Soviet Union. The Communist Party of the Soviet Union seemed to her, in her old age, to provide the 'discipline' and 'metaphysic' that previous political elites had lacked.[39] The Webbs' conversion to the 'new civilisation' of the Soviet Union indicates a point of contact between the utopian socialist hopes and a more strictly marxist rationale for 'education for leadership'. In the latter conception, the revolution-ary vanguard of the working class and the need to train this advanced section would be emphasised. Marxist–Leninist political theory depicted the Commu-nist Party as the source and guardian of proper interpretations of the needs of the working class.[40] In the Soviet Union, the increase in selectivity for various types of school after the age of fifteen that characterised the reforms of 1958 has been held 'to envisage a docile majority led or at least activated by an expert *elite* of politicians, scientists, and production men and women'.[41] In England, there was a strong autodidactic tradition in the early decades of the century in which self-taught worker-intellectuals pursued knowledge and, through this means, power. Unlike the Workers' Educational Association, which encouraged the 'proletarian intellectual' to transcend or ignore social class barriers,[42] such groups aspired to develop a working-class vanguard or revolutionary leader-ship through marxist political education. J.P.M. Millar, formerly general secretary of the National Council of Labour Colleges and editor of *Plebs*, has recalled that whereas 'The great majority of Labour party supporters believed that satisfactory progress could be achieved through a combination of liberal middle-class and working-class leadership', the Plebs League believed that reform could be achieved 'only if the working-class acted independently in both the industrial and political spheres and controlled their own educational arrangements and so achieve political power'.[43] The 'proletarian philosophers' such as T.A. Jackson made an important contribution to socialist debate in the early twentieth century.[44] This marxist strain of thought and practice, together with the utopianism of Wells and his kind, meant that 'education for leadership' was at least a legitimate topic for debate within the labour and socialist movements.

Other socialist proposals in this vein were designed to resist the general trend towards examination-oriented, competitive individualism in favour of a renewed emphasis upon community spirit. Thus they were influenced less by meritocratic or materialistic considerations than by romantic and moralistic attitudes. Henry Morris, chief education officer of Cambridgeshire from 1922 to 1954, exemplified this kind of approach with his ideal of the 'village college'. Not himself a product of a public school, according to his biographer Harry Rée he made up for this during the first world war in the Royal Army Service Corps: 'As an officer in the R.A.S.C. he learned how to deal effectively with administrative responsibilities, and also, perhaps more important, to exercise responsibility, according to the accepted English mode of leadership.'[45] These features were important influences, as were his friendships with Sidney and Beatrice Webb and G.D.H. Cole, his binding loyalty to local government, and 'an active and almost Victorian social conscience'.[46] His vision of the village college aspired to a revitalisation of the village community, with the college at the centre. Morris's famous memorandum to the Cambridgeshire County Council, 'The Village College', in 1925, argued forcefully that 'The village college would change the whole face of the problem of rural education. At the community centre of the neighbourhood it would provide for the whole man, and abolish the duality of education and ordinary life.'[47] With the disappearance of the old land owning class, he continued, 'The responsibilities of leadership and the maintenance of liberal and humane traditions in our squireless villages (which are the rule not the exception in Cambridgeshire) will fall on a larger number of shoulders – they will fall on the whole community.' Thus, 'The village college will be the seat and guardian of humane public traditions in the countryside, the training ground of a rural democracy realising its social and political duties.' If this did not eventuate, he warned, 'The alternative would be a countryside like that in some continental countries, prosperous perhaps, but narrow and materialistic, without native distinction and charm, and with no instinct for even the popular arts.' On the other hand, 'The village college would provide the chance for creating for the countryside a new type of village leader and teacher with a new status and a wide function embracing human welfare in its biggest sense – spiritual, physical, social and economic.'[48] Morris had some local success for his plans, with the opening of new village colleges such as Sawston in 1930 and Impington in 1939. He also enjoyed a wider influence. The prominent Fabian intellectual G.D.H. Cole, for example, felt that Morris's ideas might offer a clue to how to replace the public schools. Cole explained to R.A. Butler in May 1942 that 'He looked to the adult colleges linked with the continuation school for the training of leaders of the community. He considered that Morris of Cambridgeshire had given us the example and the Cambridge Rural Colleges should be copied in the towns.'[49] Like the earlier Labour Colleges, too, Morris's village colleges sought to refashion social leadership through *adult* education, rather than depending on state secondary schools which in many cases seemed merely to imitate the attitudes of the public schools.

In some ways similar to Morris, certainly in their search for a community ethic in education, were some of the advocates of comprehensive education in the 1950s. These, of course, unanimously rejected the older models of education for leadership embodied in the public schools, and the 'leadership' rationale of the grammar schools offered by Eric James. On the other hand, they were willing to suggest that the new comprehensive schools should promote the development of democratic leaders of the community. Anthony Crosland, while denouncing James's notions, recognised that modern leadership required 'good judgment in public affairs', which 'does not obviously demand an intensive academic education'.[50] Another key quality was technical efficiency, which Crosland saw as most likely to arise not from selective education of the most able children, but from an improvement in average technical ability lower down the scale. Also, he argued, leadership demanded a 'democratic quality', which meant in his view that children should share broadly the same education. Robin Pedley also envisaged a new and more democratic version of leadership emerging from the comprehensives:

The principal need of modern democracy is not that we should pick or train a class of leaders whom the rest can follow with unquestioning loyalty, but that we should spread responsibility much more widely and encourage intelligent discussion and active participation in councils and committees by everyone. Enlargement must replace selection, socially as well as in the curriculum.[51]

Similarly the sociologist Raymond Williams felt able to propose a comprehensive school curriculum that included 'Extensive practice in democratic procedures, including meetings, negotiations, and the selection and conduct of leaders in democratic organisations. Extensive practice in the use of libraries, newspapers and magazines, radio and television programmes, and other sources of information, opinion and influence.'[52] This democratic conception of education for leadership thus suggested the active preparation of all future citizens to participate and lead in community activities. In practice, however, it tended to take second place to the need to establish and consolidate the comprehensives.

A technocratic strain of socialist thinking on the potential role of education is also evident, especially in the 1950s and 1960s. C.P. Snow's influential work on the 'two cultures' and on science and government sought both a less specialised curriculum and a greater role for the scientists thus produced in the affairs of state. As he expressed the problem, 'Most of the decisions of absolutely major importance all over the world in the next 20 years are going to have a large scientific content. If these decisions are taken by people without scientific insight, without any scientific experience, then the likelihood is they are going to be unwise and unimaginative decisions.'[53] Snow was closely allied to the Labour Party and Harold Wilson's plans for exploiting the 'scientific revolution'. These concerns were also well expressed by Richard Crossman in his article 'Scientists in Whitehall', shortly before Wilson's general election victory in 1964. Industrial nations, Crossman argued, must adapt to changing circumstances – 'And this means that our British Establishment must become "science-based". Throughout this century, it has been not only unscientific in its outlook and in its education, but actively hostile to science and technology.' Top class administrative positions were usually taken by 'the Whitehall Mandarin – the pure professional administrator without specialist knowledge or specialist interest'. By contrast, Crossman claimed, 'In the technological revolution to which we are now committed, we shall be in a state of permanent emergency in which we shall permanently need the marriage of established Civil Service and outside expertise that we developed as a temporary expedient in World War I and perfected in World War II.'[54] Such thinking again reflected a reaction against the classics-based elitism of the nineteenth-century public schools, but sought to substitute for it a new kind of elite founded upon scientific knowledge.

A number of these initiatives and notions for a socialist version of education for leadership emanated from intellectuals, marxists and utopians on the fringes of the organised labour movement. Others were prompted by antipathy to existing forms of educational institution: that is to say, their inspiration was primarily negative or oppositional. At various times, though, they were of some influence and retain social and political significance. Probably the most significant and influential socialist experiment in education for leadership to be attempted in the present century was based upon a unique combination of these utopian, marxist and oppositional aspects. This experiment was the Left Book Club of the 1930s and 1940s; its creator, Victor Gollancz.

THE LEFT BOOK CLUB

The Left Book Club would at first sight appear to have little in common with public schools. Firmly committed to socialist ideology and radical politics, it is unlikely that the LBC would have attracted Cyril Norwood or Eric James to its cause. Yet they were inspired in equal measure by a belief in the need to promote enlightened leadership, through the right kind of education, in twentieth-century society. They also shared the hope that contemporary developments offered a vital opportunity to do so. According to Victor Gollancz, the socialist publisher and chief promoter of the LBC from its birth in 1936 until its demise twelve years later, the LBC was above all else an educational agency. He insisted that the Club had 'set out as an *educational* body', and that it 'must at all costs retain its educational character'.[55] This educational function was at the heart of its political and social purpose: 'it is education for the concrete end of establishing a social order in which there is international peace and an equal share in the gain as well as in the toil of living'.[56] To this end, it sought to create a politically educated elite, a twentieth-century version of the clerisy.

Born into a strict Jewish family in April 1893, Gollancz soon rebelled against the authority imposed by his father. He later recalled that 'my father's orthodoxy made me dislike and distrust all orthodoxies as such'.[57] He was an autocratic figure, impatient and impulsive, and rarely content to follow an orthodox party line. After becoming a socialist during the first world war, he was soon attracted to the idealism and militancy of the guild socialist movement. His socialist zeal was essentially religious in character: 'A socialist must have his nose in blue books. His brain must be wrestling with economic theory. But his heart must be longing for the City of God.'[58] He was prominent in Labour Party circles, but disliked what he saw as Labour's 'materialistic' approach to politics and its failure to provide moral leadership. Following Labour's victory in the general election of 1945, Gollancz became increasingly critical of the party's performance in office and general political approach, calling for a 'return to Christian socialist ideals' with which he associated the early 'pioneers' of the Independent Labour Party.[59] His disappointed ideals and aspirations are vividly reflected in his view that the Labour Party 'had a priceless opportunity, in 1945, to be the body of priests that the Church has failed to be: they could have, in word and deed, proclaimed the ethical road as the road to salvation, and the materialistic road as the road to damnation. Their failure to do this has been, in my view, a supreme betrayal.'[60] The Left Book Club may be interpreted in terms of Gollancz's ambition to create, through education, 'the body of priests that the Church has failed to be'.

Gollancz's early educational experiences probably also influenced his later ambitions. He was educated at St Paul's School in London and as a scholar of New College, Oxford, where he won the Chancellor's Latin essay prize in 1913 and gained a first in honour moderations the following year. It was his experience as a teacher at Repton, a public school, during the first world war that shaped his determination to use the medium of publishing as an educational force. This early episode highlights Gollancz's socialist idealism, and also the essentially elitist character of his approach to education in general. It led him towards a socialist conception of 'education for leadership', rooted in Platonist,

Renaissance and public school values but with important novel aspects to meet the changing social and political scene. His central ambition was to use political education to create enlightened social leadership and spread the message of socialism. This aim is evident in his efforts both at Repton and in the LBC.

Gollancz was seconded to Repton from the army in 1916 to help the school's Officers' Training Corps, but was soon involved in teaching classics and other subjects. He found that, although the boys were basically 'good' as individuals, they were also in general 'intolerant, class-ridden, narrow, self-righteous, smug, superior, ignorant; grotesquely ignorant, in particular, of conditions on their own doorstep and in the world outside'.[61] But this did not lead him to support the abolition of public schools, or even their 'dilution' through scholarships for working-class pupils. Rather, he insisted that they should remain 'a class preserve', but be transformed into 'engines of political progress' by changing the nature of the education that they bestowed upon the future social and political elite.[62] He saw the public schools as strongholds of liberal values, which needed to be preserved and strengthened, but he also argued that radical changes to their curricula could transform the political attitudes of their pupils, with beneficial results for society as a whole. So it was that at Repton Gollancz engaged in 'the experiment in "political education" that was to make me a publisher'.[63]

A fervent admirer of the classical ideals of the Renaissance, Gollancz defended the traditions of the public schools on the grounds that they were based upon those 'liberal and humane' ideals. In his view, the virtue of the old classical curriculum was that it had attempted 'to impart a genuine love of letters, and an entirely disinterested knowledge of the nobility of two great civilisations'.[64] However, that civilisation had often been too narrow and unsuitable for many pupils, and during the nineteenth century had degenerated into 'the minute reading of traditional texts, selected for style more than matter . . . the cult of composition, and the perfunctory study of superficial history crowded into a spare hour'.[65] Thus he hoped 'not to abolish these strongholds, but to save what was left of their liberalism from the decay that was destroying it and even converting it into its opposite, and so to release the original impulse for a fruitful expression in modern conditions'.[66] This, he suggested, might be achieved by introducing 'political education' into the curriculum of the public schools. Political education, including the study of history and a consideration of the meaning of liberty, discipline and Christianity, would remedy the 'ignorance' and 'prejudice' of public school boys, and help to 'substitute the spirit of enquiry for the spirit of acquiescence'.[67] The end product, according to Gollancz, would be true 'citizens' – 'not mere citizens of their country but citizens of the world: and not mere citizens of the world either, but citizens, over and above that, of God'.[68]

Gollancz's educational views may be taken as an example of the argument, often voiced in early twentieth-century Britain, that educational reform could change the nature of society. Public schools, he insisted, could become 'instruments by means of which a genuine and complete democracy may be achieved'.[69] This was akin to Tawney's view of what 'secondary education for all' might achieve. However, Gollancz was critical of several aspects of contemporary left-wing thinking on education. First, he dissented from those who wished to abolish public schools completely: 'To revolutionise the Public Schools is one of the crying needs of the age; to destroy them would be fatal.'[70] Moreover, he argued, the idea of throwing these schools open to all social classes through local scholarships 'could only be made by reformers completely ignorant of the real nature of the difficulties involved'. Such policies usually resulted in 'hideous failure', or at best created an 'inevitably unreal and superficial democracy'.[71] But his most hostile comments were reserved for contemporary calls, stimulated by the war, for more 'practical' education in schools. This, he declared, would lead to 'not education at all, but simply a rule and thumb training in the arts of "efficiency" and "success"'.[72] He hoped to help individuality and independent thought flourish, and feared that these qualities might be destroyed by 'a steady pressure towards short-hand and book-keeping'.[73] As he later recalled, he wanted to encourage public schools to become 'more liberal, not more commercial or militarist'.[74] Political education, then, might revive the essentially liberal aspects of the public schools, producing 'men who are splendidly free in mind and spirit'.[75] His central aim was 'to produce a man capable of independent thought, and of applying that thought to political and social questions'.[76] On the wider scale, his ideal was 'a race of men who, equipped with knowledge, imagination, and constructive skill, will be able to build a new national and international order of which the foundation is reverence for personality and the keystone brotherhood'.[77] This was exactly the same rationale as was to motivate the Left Book Club. Both at Repton and through the LBC, Gollancz placed his faith in educating an elite group in the ideals that he held to be crucial for the leadership of a modern society. These ideals were essentially moral and religious in character, and emphasised the qualities of western culture that seemed to be endangered through the commercialism and militarism of the twentieth century.

Gollancz's educational ideas soon proved too much for Repton and, after a brief period in which classes in political education were begun and a new school magazine was launched, he was dismissed in 1918. He was nevertheless quite unrepentant. He continued to insist upon the importance of creating an 'army' of 'missionaries of thought about the great problems of life and society, fashioned out of those who are of the people and understand and sympathise with their emotions'.[78] He turned to publishing in order to continue, rather than abandon, his educational work. The extravagant hopes invested in the Left Book Club may be explained by the crucial role that propaganda through the new media of communications was thought to play in the forming of public opinion. Gollancz sought to exploit this supposed influence by forming his own publishing company in 1928, and using it to disseminate the political, social, intellectual and religious ideals that he had championed at Repton. He saw a sinister new force at work in the modern publishing house; he also saw that it could be exploited equally well to serve the ideals that he held dear. Like Franklin Roosevelt's radio 'fireside chats' of the 1930s and J.B. Priestley's 'Postscript' talks of 1940, Gollancz's Left Book Club may be seen as an effort to use the new methods of communication to educate and 'enlighten' the public, and thereby to influence their political behaviour. In another way, he could be likened to Henry Morris in the way that he conceived adult education as the most likely way to preserve the humane ideals once associated with the public schools, and attempted to use it to contruct an alternative kind of 'education for leadership'. Thus the channels of mass education that were being constructed and developed in the new century were to be adapted first to preserve traditional values, and thence to usher in a new age of equality and idealism. But surely the most surprising, and the most revealing, comparison is between Gollancz and Cyril Norwood. On opposite sides of the conventional political divide, Gollancz and Norwood were both active in spreading the ethos of the public schools that had once been confined to a small social elite to a larger audience, through the modern technology and state apparatus that was now available to them. Both too interpreted this task in a highly moral way, equating the liberal values of a western culture that was now endangered with Christianity, and setting these values against the contemporary threats of materialism and individualism. Certainly their views of the Great War were very different, and no doubt their ideas of the social relationships that would exist in their ideal society did not entirely coincide. And yet the similarities in their outlooks were at least as profound as their differences, joined as they were through the middle-class tradition of social conscience and morality.

The LBC attracted progressives who were becoming alarmed at the rise of fascism, were disillusioned by the National Government, but were impatient with the Labour Party as a vehicle of protest. It was intended to provide political education on a large scale, to 'enlighten' the public as to the benefits of socialism and the dangers inherent in capitalism and fascism. It also sought to unite all progressives behind a dynamic and well-informed socialist leadership, thereby creating the ideological and mass basis for a British 'popular front' that might defeat the National Government and avert war. Gollancz saw no contradiction between the educative function and philosophical ideals of the Club and its political objectives; indeed, he saw them as inextricably linked. However, tensions did emerge between the 'educational' and the 'political' aspects of the Club, with the result that Gollancz chose increasingly to emphasise its educational role. The LBC's support for the popular front movement, and the close cooperation with the Communist Party that this entailed, soon led to conflict with the Labour Party.[79] The European crisis of autumn 1938, temporarily resolved by the settlement at Munich, led Gollancz to examine his conscience and change his priorities. He decided henceforth to emphasise the educational and independent nature of the Club above all else.[80]

The LBC's notion of 'education' thus involved independence from any political party, although it was an ideal that was often compromised due to the pressures of the time. Education was also encouraged in terms of 'the giving of *knowledge*' to the public. This implied that there existed a corpus of objective information, or truth, which, if it were given to the public in an impartial and reasoned manner, would enlighten them as to the condition of the contemporary world and lead them to change it. The educational method of the Club would lead to 'the formation of an instructed and enlightened public opinion'.[81] The Club was able to make people politically active, Gollancz suggested, 'because we open their eyes to reality'.[82] This amounted to 'scattering the mists from another mind, so that the other mind may see straight and clear'.[83] The instructors in this process were held to have sole access to the truth about the world, and to constitute an educated elite. The LBC, for Gollancz, was a body of teachers and learners. Even the most 'enlightened' could always continue to learn, since education included '*self*-education too – a really fresh examination of our problems in the light of today, and not a mouthing of stereotyped shibboleths'.[84] They also had a duty to ensure that they passed on their knowledge to those who were less well informed: 'While remaining *learners*, while getting more and more of our citizens to become learners, we must also be *teachers and missionaries* on a grand scale.'[85] In this way, the Club would be an 'instrument of enlightenment', while its active members would become 'missionaries in the greatest of all tasks – that of spreading political knowledge'.[86] The task that the LBC set for itself, as 'a body of politically educated men and women', was 'to think out honestly and clearly the problems that confront us, and, on the basis of that thought, to provide *democratic leadership* in every constituency throughout the country'.[87] But the leadership thus created was more obvious than the democracy it bestowed.

Furthermore, it was suggested, such education could promote not only knowledge but also the values of 'civilisation'. Gollancz stressed the need for the LBC to defend liberty, including 'intellectual freedom'. He returned to this theme repeatedly after the beginning of the war, using it to support the maintenance of civil liberties, and also increasingly to criticise the inflexibility of Communist Party discipline. The society that emerged from the war must be 'a society in which every man and woman is at least encouraged to think for himself, and to form an independent judgment on the basis of all the facts'.[88] Another aspect of civilisation, according to Gollancz, was responsibility. It was particularly important, he argued, 'to build up a body of men and women who are thinking out for themselves, in a steady continuous way, the problem of modern civilisation, and so can form the *basis* of a real democracy'. The members of the LBC would be 'professional citizens'.[89] He noted that the Greek word for a man who did not vote at elections or take part in the political life of the city was *idiotes*, from which the word 'idiot' is derived. As the Spens report on secondary education in 1938 also recognised, the threat of fascism highlighted the need to 'educate for citizenship'.

These aims and values underlay the various educational activities of the LBC. As well as the monthly books, and the issue of *Left News* and several pamphlets, the LBC sponsored many developments which were intended to spread knowledge. It also encouraged the development of a hierarchy comprising 'a highly educated rank and file and also cadres of leaders capable of guiding us to victory'. Gollancz announced that members of the Club who made use of its facilities for political education 'will become, if I may put it so, the *elite*, the shock troops, of our movement'.[90] There were also efforts to create links with other agencies of adult education like the Workers' Educational Association and the Central Labour College, 'fostering a growing unity of purpose'.[91] These educational activities had the same basic aims as Gollancz's earlier work at Repton: to build up a politically educated elite to defend 'civilisation' against capitalism and war.

Gollancz saw this elite group as a vanguard, going so far as to compare it with the leaders of the Russian Revolution who had been able 'to give direction to the needs and desires of the masses'.[92] Gollancz, like Plato, hoped to breed a group of 'philosopher-kings'. But events dictated otherwise. Labour's victory in 1945 consolidated the ascendancy of the party machine and the established leadership, and forced idealists of the stamp of Gollancz into an unhappy choice between acquiescence and futility.[93] Gollancz's scheme to create an educated, dissenting elite or clerisy was in the tradition of Samuel Coleridge and John Stuart Mill. Both at Repton and through the LBC, he was inspired by Plato's classical ideal to seek to create an enlightened social elite. His socialism may have been close to that of R.H. Tawney or A.S. Neill, but his educational ideas were more akin to Thomas Arnold or, in his own generation, Cyril Norwood. He was essentially interested in 'education for leadership', in 'teachers and missionaries', in discovering 'cadres of leaders capable of guiding us to victory'. He also tended to place greater emphasis on male rather than female leadership. And he continued to assert the basic importance of a classical curriculum. On the other hand, his own experiences encouraged him to go beyond the facilities provided by the public schools, and to make full use of the new media of the twentieth century. Hence the paradox of an agency committed to profound social and political change, but rooted in neo-classical views on knowledge, reason and enlightened elites. The guiding lights of the LBC were Plato and Shelley. It is indeed a prime example of a revisionist approach to education for leadership.

EDUCATION AND THE WORKING CLASS

The experiences of the Left Book Club have been discussed in some detail partly because they exemplify so many of the classic properties of 'education for

leadership' in twentieth-century England, but also because they reveal much
about the characteristics and weaknesses of the socialist species of the genre. A
unique mixture of utopian, marxist and oppositional tendencies, the LBC was
probably the most important and influential initiative of its type. That it still
failed to achieve its long-term goals gives rise to the issue of why the 'leadership'
strain of socialist thought remained marginal and relatively weak within the
labour movement and Labour Party.

One important reason for this seems to have been an increasing suspicion of
the role of education in alienating 'successful' working-class children from their
political and cultural roots. In the early decades of the century, it had been
possible to assume that educated working-class children would become 'leaders'
of their class. By the 1950s this notion was almost discredited: the processes of
education, even of the new state secondary education, seemed instead to
promote individual social mobility for this 'talented' minority at the expense of
class consciousness. As was seen in an earlier chapter, the Minister of Education,
Sir David Eccles, was aware of the significance of this tendency, preferring to
'produce in everyone the virtues hitherto characteristic of the middle classes'
rather than seek to cultivate a 'small elite'.[94] Richard Hoggart's *The Uses of
Literacy*, published in 1957, vividly depicted the sense of loss of the 'scholarship
boy': 'With them the sense of loss is increased precisely because they are
emotionally uprooted from their class, often under the stimulus of a stronger
critical intelligence or imagination, qualities which can lead them into an
unusual self-consciousness before their own situation.'[95] Such pupils tended to
become 'declassed', solitary and uncomfortable: 'He loses something of the
gamin's resilience and carelessness, of his readiness to take a chance of his
perkiness and boldness, and he does not acquire the unconscious confidence of
many a public-school-trained child of the middle-classes. He has been trained
like a circus-horse, for scholarship winning.'[96]

Brian Jackson and Dennis Marsden also discussed the ways in which such
education developed through a study of eighty-eight working-class children in
a northern industrial city, published in 1962 under the title *Education and the
Working Class*. They noted that most working-class children failed to compete
successfully at school, either in reaching grammar school or in reaching the
sixth form, but that 'The working-class child who does win entry to the
grammar school must accommodate himself to the prevailing middle-class
values, or rub up against them.' Indeed,

There is something infinitely pathetic in these former working-class children who lost
their roots young, and who now with their rigid middle-class accent preserve 'the
stability of all our institutions, temporal and spiritual' by avariciously reading the lives of
Top People, or covet the public schools and glancing back at the society from which
they came see no more there than 'the dim', or the 'specimens'.[97]

Such successes became, through these rigorous educational processes, 'middle-
class citizens'.[98] In this context, the hope of enhancing the quality and strength

of working-class leaders through the extension of secondary education to all was bound to diminish.

An indication of this fading hope, even by the 1930s, was perhaps the increasingly sharp division within the labour movement between 'trade unionists' and 'intellectuals'. Ernest Bevin of the Transport and General Workers' Union, for instance, became impatient at the unreliable and often disloyal tendencies of the intelligentsia. His biographer, Alan Bullock, emphasises the difference between him and Sir Stafford Cripps, a leader of the intellectual Left in the 1930s: 'Cripps slender and ascetic, the passionate doctrinaire to whom ideas were more real than human beings, Bevin thick-set and earthy with a critical power of judgment tempered by long experience of men.' Cripps had been educated at Winchester, did not join the Labour Party until he was forty years old, and was a successful and wealthy barrister. As Bullock points out, 'He had little experience of politics or men and none at all of working-class life . . . To Bevin he appeared the embodiment of all that most exasperated him in middle-class intellectuals telling the trade unions and "the workers" what they ought to do.'[99] The historian E.H. Carr shrewdly observed in 1939 that while the 'trade unionist tends to regard the intellectual as a utopian theorist lacking experience in the practical problems of the movement', the 'intellectual condemns the trade union leader as a bureaucrat'.[100] This reflected not merely personal antipathy but an increasingly sharp division between the working-class labour movement centred in the trade unions, and middle-class socialist intellectuals who had their own priorities and ideals. By the 1930s, education represented not a bridge between these factions but a symbol of what divided them, the instrument of alienation by which the most likely leaders of the working class were lost forever to an alien culture. In a political movement suspicious of middle-class control and hostile to middle-class aspirations for leadership, the role of middle-class intellectuals was tolerated only insofar as they stuck to ideas and avoided delusions of grandeur. Thus Clement Attlee was prepared to encourage the Left Book Club in relation to its 'function of making socialists and providing a forum for discussion by and education of socialists'. But he warned Gollancz that 'if it combines with this definite political activities affecting organisation and policy, it will be in danger of losing its utility'.[101] If they were to be philosophers, they could not be kings; and vice versa. The dominant impression of the 'educated' henceforward was not of potential leaders but of marginal, even disreputable, almost irrelevant thinkers.

A further factor that tended to reduce the appeal of education for working-class leadership was the 'betrayal' of the labour movement by several of its leaders in the early 1930s. In their very different ways, Ramsay MacDonald and Oswald Mosley both seemed to exemplify the dangers involved in depending upon strong leaders. MacDonald, a working-class boy who had risen to become Labour's first prime minister, abandoned his party in 1931 to form a National Government, thus precipitating Labour's electoral collapse in the general election of that year from 181 to 54 Parliamentary seats.[102] Thereafter he symbolised the danger of Labour leaders losing touch with their working-class roots and succumbing to the temptations of the Establishment. Sir Oswald Mosley, aristocrat and officer, educated at Winchester and Sandhurst, became a Labour Party member in 1924. He immediately became a champion of the rank and file, a dynamic leader of the working-class movement with impeccable Establishment credentials, the 'dandy of the revolution'.[103] It was an adventure that ended when Mosley resigned from the Labour government in 1930, then formed his own party, and finally became the most prominent fascist leader in the country. MacDonald and Mosley, discredited but still active, were stark reminders of the fallibility of leaders even before the rise and fall of the Continental dictators.

The trauma of these defections encouraged additional emphasis in the labour movement upon the values of solidarity and equality. Attlee was himself strongly influenced by these events, and owed much of his success to their pervasive effects. The lesson that he derived from the loss of MacDonald and others was to trust in the general membership of the party: 'During all my years in the movement, what has impressed me most is that its strength depends, not on the brilliance of individuals, but on the quality of the rank and file.'[104] Attlee's leadership was the antithesis of MacDonald's. As he told the socialist intellectual Harold Laski in 1944: 'I am sorry that you suggest that I am verging towards MacDonaldism. As you have so well pointed out I have neither the personality nor the distinction to tempt me to think that I should have any value apart from the Party which I serve.'[106] Thus by the 1940s both 'education' and 'leadership' were tainted commodities within the labour movement. The combination was unacceptable: inspiring, highly educated leaders became objects of suspicion. Bevin was admired for his leadership qualities because he was relatively uneducated; Attlee was forgiven his education because of his ostentatious modesty.

On the other hand Cripps and, later, the Bevanites attracted regular comparisons with Mosley and Hitler.[107] Such suspicion was directed at Aneurin Bevan, in spite of his working-class and mining roots, partly because of his association with Mosley, Cripps, John Strachey and other 'aristocratic' rebels. It also arose perhaps from his training at the Central Labour College in London from 1919 until 1921. This experience gave him a theoretical grounding in marxism, and in particular an admiration for the ideas of the Uruguayan philosopher José Enrique Rodo. The latter encouraged Bevan to foster an image of himself as a member of a cultivated elite, very different from the average run of trade unionists or miner MPs.[108] Although Bevan himself was very far removed from either a public school background or fascist sympathies, his intellectual friends and the Platonic connotations of his ideas and cultural aspirations were enough to encourage resentment and hostility within Labour ranks. At the same time it could be said that despite the general consolidation of the tradition of equality in the Labour Party in the 1930s and 1940s, something of the spirit of earlier socialist initiatives to promote education for leadership was kept alive through Bevan. In particular we may point to the radical journal founded by Cripps in 1937 as reflecting to some extent this oppositional tradition, and even to the significant title of that journal: *Tribune*.

Thus the conflicts in Labour politics in the 1930s combined with the more general reaction against old and new ideals of education for leadership, to consolidate the Labour emphasis upon equality in and through education. The utopian, marxist and oppositional strains, always marginal, were almost excluded from consideration in the struggle to establish comprehensive schools. There is little sign of their revival despite a recent willingness to seek fresh approaches in Labour thinking on education. Yet despite all this our examination of education for leadership in twentieth-century England would have been incomplete without showing its manifestation as socialism. Again it illustrates the pervasive character of this ideal in modern society and the continuing attempts to recast and revitalise the tradition, in this instance for radical social purposes on behalf of the working class. The ideal of the 'tribune' evoked by J.A. Hobson at the beginning of the century remains a ghost in the machine.

8

OUR MODERN GUARDIANS

Such have been the continuing, and the changing, characteristics of education for leadership in twentieth-century education. Plato has been much more influential than Marx in English secondary education. Attempts to revise what was still often described as the 'English tradition' had an important bearing on the character and direction of educational change. Assertions of the values of community, character, morality and citizenship with which they were associated, represented significant responses to contemporary problems. There is no doubt, though, that the efforts of the revisionists met most commonly with failure and disappointment. With the overall decline of the classic nineteenth-century ideology, and the general failure of attempts to revive and revitalise it during this century, we need now to ask whether we have lost anything in this gradual process, and how to explain the character of our modern 'guardians'.

POLITICS AND CULTURE

Decline and dispersal have been central themes in this book. The public school ideology, at the peak of its authority in the late nineteenth century, has been undermined by changing political, social and cultural expectations. Even though it retained much of its former influence, and the public schools themselves by and large survived these changes, their rationale as the exclusive source of future leaders was contested and effectively lost. By the 1960s it was a role to which only the critics of the public schools referred. Attempts to transfer their ideals and traditions to the new state system of secondary education and the mass of the population were largely frustrated. It is arguable that the decline in fortunes of the Platonic ideal of education for leadership was due in large measure to a strong reaction against the classic attributes of late nineteenth-century public schools. Their manifest inequalities and snobberies came widely to be seen as unattractive and divisive. Increasingly, too, they were perceived to be essentially static and old-fashioned, even obsolete. The appearance of shared values and unchanging ideals and traditions was a key source of the authority of the public schools in the late nineteenth century. But it also gave later generations an easy target for criticism. Often the outward appearance was misleading: the classical curriculum, for example, was a dynamic and complex subject coalition whose form, content and aims were under constant debate.[1] Yet such nuances, and the variety and change that they implied in terms of school practice, were seen as less significant than the general values that the public schools had in common.

Criticism of such values was all the stronger because of twentieth-century problems for which the public schools could be held responsible. First, the major wars of 1914–18 and 1939–45 seemed in retrospect to demonstrate the fatal consequences of public school leadership. Worsley's barb, directed at the 'ruling class' of public school products in 1941, found its mark: 'They were trained to lead, and they have led us up the garden.'[2] Thus Peter Parker links the sacrifices and lives lost in the Great War directly to the influence of the 'public school ethos', both among members of those schools and among a wider public.[3] Second, the ethos of the public schools, their resistance to science and technology and indifference to industry, could be blamed for the relative economic and industrial decline of Britain during the twentieth century. On this theme Martin Wiener has been especially persuasive, and Correlli Barnett most forthright.[4] On both fronts, military and economic, the public schools, once so authoritative, have been reduced to the level of scapegoats. It seems equally possible to blame the 'public policy choices' of a small 'meritocratic' elite for Britain's relative decline.[5] On the other hand, the evidence here is ambiguous since, as we have seen, for much of the twentieth century the future leaders of the nation continued to be inculcated with variants of the classic public school ethos. It seems likely that the hardened barriers of social class were more directly responsible for Britain's twentieth-century problems, and that the public schools and doctrines of leadership may be conceived at least in one sense as symptoms of this general problem. And yet when these symptoms faded away the 'disease' was not cured, in spite of all the hopes expressed after the second world war, but found new ways of manifesting itself.

Just as the classic ethos of the public schools became démodé during the twentieth century, so their most devout admirers, especially those who refused to compromise on the qualities that they associated with the public schools, suffered a decline in their own reputations. A good example here is Sir Richard Livingstone: an influential voice in the 1920s and 1930s, increasingly isolated thereafter. Livingstone insisted upon the value of classical studies as being 'as suitable to the future civil servant, lawyer, minister and business man, as to the scholar and schoolmaster'.[6] He continued to argue that Plato should guide the values of education, that rulers must be educated to govern wisely and well.[7] And he persisted in his claim that the public schools could best provide such an education through their residential character, their traditions, and their emphasis on cultivating social responsibility:

To feel yourself part of a community which you have a share and a responsibility in making, whose successes are somehow your successes and whose failures cast their shadow on you, to be able to obey and to live and co-operate with other members of the community, this is the essence of citizenship, and this the boy at a good residential school learns unconsciously every day of his life, not by being taught it, but by practising it.[8]

Even more than the views of Cyril Norwood, these ideas seemed anachronistic in the context of a postwar society in which the public schools themselves had lost the confidence to make such claims.

The watershed in the debate over education for leadership seems to have been the period of the second world war. Before that time, the public schools remained at the centre of attention, and the role of the classics, of games and of religion were the key matters for discussion. After the war, the terms of debate shifted: the focus widened to include grammar schools as well as public schools, and the tone changed to one that emphasised science and the meritocracy. Among adherents of the Platonic ideal, this shift in the terms of debate was clearly expressed in the differences between Cyril Norwood and Eric James. Both attempted to address changing concerns and interests while remaining faithful to the notion of education for leadership. Norwood was sensitive to the moral and military concerns of the interwar years, while James appealed to the secular, scientific and socially mobile middle classes of the 1950s. This important shift also draws attention to the contested and changing character of the 'grammar school curriculum' during the twentieth century. The grammar school curriculum was by no means a static or a timeless entity. Like the curriculum of the public schools, it did respond in various ways to internal and external pressures. This was certainly the case with regard to the 'moral curriculum' of the schools, in relation to which we still need more research of the kind that has hitherto been centred on school subjects.[9] The ways in which social or collective norms such as character, responsibility and morality were transmitted within and through the schools were less tangible but no less important than the schools' role in inculcating individual achievement. It appears that in the years after 1945 the individualistic imperatives of examinations increasingly superseded the aspirations and ideals of the Chapel, the sports field and the Officers' Training Corps.

The important differences between ideals, policies and practices in education have also figured prominently in this book. They are seen most clearly, perhaps, in the case of the Norwood report of 1943. Norwood's ideals were translated into specific policy recommendations through a combination of zeal, opportunity and compromise; they were then watered down, neglected or rigidified beyond recognition in subsequent negotiations among interested parties. The Fleming report of the following year attempted to reconcile competing ideals, but ultimately failed, in practice, to satisfy the demands either of 'leadership' or of 'equality'. The tendency of 'education for leadership' to justify or rationalise educational inequalities is a further example of the distance between ideals and practices. The ideal focused on the value accruing to the community from wise and efficient leadership; in practice it brought out the social and political problems arising from inequality. It has become commonplace to stress the importance of 'psychometrics' or mental testing in reinforcing structural inequalities within the education system.[10] Yet this was far from being the only influence that tended in practice to maintain and reconstruct inequalities in educational provision. The theme of education for leadership, in its changing forms, also lent itself toward this end. There is no doubt that at least in some cases this was a conscious aim of adherents of this ideal.

It is possible to interpret these essays in revisionism, at least on one level, as manipulations on the part of an elite group determined to retain power and privilege in the face of the new demands of a mass democracy. Thus the earlier claims for boarding schools, religion, moral character, and even the classics were jettisoned in the interests of their overriding aim, leadership, and the control and authority that this bestowed. And yet there was no single, united elite group, but rather a succession of overlapping, sectional campaigns. Their efforts were only partially successful: inequalities remained, but their claims to leadership were denied them. Often these claims were those of middle-class people – Christian, scientific, managerial, socialist, and others – who felt that their education gave them and their kind a right to influence the direction of society as a whole. Separately and together, they did enough to foster new forms of inequality that endured long after their own idealism and social vision had dimmed.

As well, the leadership theme encouraged other inequalities in an almost careless or incidental way. Inequalities based on gender, for example, were more or less taken for granted. Despite the far-reaching concessions and adjustments in the debate on education for leadership during the twentieth century, male domination was continuously assumed. The ideal remained essentially gender-specific. This was true as much of Eric James and his generation as of the earlier initiatives of Norwood, or even of Wells and Gollancz. Such assumptions about the importance of male leadership, although rarely stated or debated in the open, had clear and practical repercussions. They meant not only that established traditions favoured a focus on the problems and potential of education for boys, but also that new ventures such as Bryanston in the 1930s and the Industrial Fund in the 1950s continued to concentrate attention and resources in the same direction. Secondary education for girls had divided aims, caught between 'domestic' priorities and 'professional' aspirations. But even those who emphasised the need to establish equality of opportunity in employment for women rarely seem to have gone on to suggest that their education should prepare them to become social and political leaders in the same way as men.[11] Certainly there are some women who went on to confound the expectations imposed upon them, Margaret Thatcher being an obvious recent example. And yet such cases also betray the latent prejudice and resistance that have existed against the possibility of female leadership. Images of the philosopher-*king* and the English *gentleman* remained, implicit but enduring.

Thus the ideal of 'education for leadership' had a continuing social and political significance during the twentieth century. It also retained potent cultural connotations, embodying as it did the defence of values and qualities such as community, morality, stability, authority and cohesion in a rapidly changing society and an often threatening world. This was not a purely defensive aspect; its adherents sought to adapt to contemporary change while attempting positively to promote, often widely and aggressively, values hitherto associated with the public schools. Victor Gollancz's activities provided an especially interesting example of this kind of aspiration in action. There was no contradiction, so far as Gollancz was concerned, between the finest traditions of the public schools and his own socialist commitment. The former informed and inspired the latter. After the second world war there was a more defensive note in such appeals, which tended to become nostalgic and elegiac in quality. Thus in 1948 T.S. Eliot warned in vain of the dangers involved in losing continuity in transmitting the culture of a society. He predicted that the rise of equality of opportunity for all would lead not to social equality but to a new form of inequality in which the elites would be ill-equipped to lead:

The elites, in consequence, will consist solely of individuals whose only common bond will be their professional interest: with no social cohesion, with no social continuity. They will be united only by a part, and that the most conscious part, of their personalities; they will meet like committees. The greater part of their 'culture' will be only what they share with all the other individuals comprising their nation.[12]

The educational philosopher and historian G.H. Bantock pursued this theme energetically in following decades, mourning the 'demise' of 'ideals of chivalry assimilated to the traditional notion of a gentleman', and the disintegration of earlier notions of the cultural elite.[13]

Ultimately, the ideal of education for leadership collapsed only partly due to its own contradictions and failures. It fell victim to the dual challenge posed by two ascendant ideals of twentieth-century society and the increasingly powerful interests that they reflected. Competitive *individualism*, a classic bourgeois notion, implied the existence of individual differences and inequalities, but favoured social mobility rather than enlightened elites. Eric James's attempt to reconcile these competing ideals, leadership and individualism, was unsuccessful. Again it seems relevant to cite Sir David Eccles, Conservative Minister of Education in the 1950s, and his preference to try to 'produce in everyone the virtues hitherto characteristic of the middle classes' rather than attempt to cultivate James's 'small elite'.[14] In practice this meant an emphasis on individual achievement measured through academic examinations, and active support for what was deemed to be 'excellence' rather than for 'leadership'. At the same time, social *equality*, as championed by the labour movement, made a frontal assault on the ideals of education for leadership. Margaret Cole, in the early 1950s, argued for a democratic socialist education that would be 'equalitarian, not in the sense of uniformity, but in the sense of "parity of esteem" for every child in the country', and that would also be 'socially equalising, in that it must not aim at producing any separated class or caste'.[15] Michael Young's *Rise of the Meritocracy* was a rebuttal of the ideals of Wells and Webb – the latter a founder of the LSE and a guiding light of the Labour Party, to both of which Young himself was attached – just as much as of James.[16] The ideals of individualism and equality often made uneasy allies, and the tensions between them became apparent in the comprehensive schools. Together, though, they had triumphed in supplanting their more aristocratic rival.

NEW FRONTIERS

This study has, of course, focused mainly upon English secondary education. The theme of leadership in relation to sectors like higher education and former British colonies in the twentieth century deserves further detailed research. Perhaps it is fair to suggest tentatively, even so, that there is a similar story to tell in these other areas. Higher education has provided intellectual authority and the finishing school of a future professional elite throughout our period, while secondary education has lost its former elite basis and become open to all. In the nineteenth century the role of the universities as 'seminaries for statesmen' was assiduously cultivated. At the University of Oxford, in particular, the Union Society, Benjamin Jowett of Balliol College, and areas of the curriculum such as History and 'Greats' exemplified such purposes.[17] In the early part of the twentieth century there seem to have been several attempts to maintain this position and adapt it in a changing context. The proposals for 'Modern Greats', or a new School of Politics, Philosophy and Economics, and the abortive discussions about a 'Science Greats', both at Oxford, represented one such. The initiatives of A.D. Lindsay, first as Master of Balliol and then as founder of the University College of North Staffordshire, were another.[18] In the 1930s, and again in the 1960s, the universities provided an important forum for debate and controversy about the pressing national issues of the day. And yet the institutions of higher education seemed overall to shrink from the implications of social and political leadership during the twentieth century. As in the secondary schools, the values of community service and moral character declined in potency in favour of an increasing dependence on individual achievement measured by competitive examinations. The embarrassment and difficulties created by the public debates of the 1930s and disturbances of the 1960s probably encouraged this tendency to retreat into the 'ivory towers'.[19] The confidence of Jowett of Balliol, who in the late nineteenth century had aspired to 'govern the world through my pupils',[20] had dissipated into narrow academicism.

So far as British colonies are concerned, we already have the benefit of J.A. Mangan's important research centring on the ideals of athleticism. According to Mangan and Walvin, 'After its inception in the mid and late nineteenth-century English public schools, a neo-Spartan ideal of masculinity was diffused throughout the English speaking world with the unreflecting and ethnocentric confidence of an imperial race.'[21] Mangan's earlier research has similarly emphasised the 'imperial diffusion' of English traditions, and the crucial role played by the 'public school administrator, missionary and educationist spread throughout the imperial world, more often than not imbued with a sense of moral commitment and muscular enthusiasm'.[22] In developing such work further, we need perhaps to take greater account of the contested character of this process, the purposes for which it was used in different national contexts, and the ways in which it was interpreted, adapted and even exploited by settlers, colonial elites and indigenous peoples.[23] International schemes such as the Rhodes scholarships, founded in 1903 in accordance with Cecil Rhodes's will to help the endeavours of 'those who have shown during school days that they have instincts to lead and take an interest in their schoolmates which attributes will be likely in after life to guide them to esteem the performance of public duties as their highest aim',[24] should be examined to discover the extent to which they have retained in practice no less than in theory their original purposes. The socio-political and cultural uses made of such ideals in former colonies such as India, New Zealand and Australia are another important focus for research.[25] It may well be that in some cases geographical distance and differing social and political needs have made it easier to reinterpret the ideal of 'education for leadership' than in England, where the shadow of the public schools was longest and their defects and consequences were more evident. Even so, the competing ideals and interests of the twentieth century have probably tended to muffle and distort the original ideology in most instances.

FIRST AMONG EQUALS?

What, finally, has replaced the former emphasis on education for leadership? And what new problems has this left us with? Rupert Wilkinson's study, published in 1964, indicated an important dilemma: 'Especially in the case of democracy, in systems where popularity is exalted as a political asset, rational leadership can only be given by men [sic] who are brave as well as intelligent, men ready to take an unpopular step when they think public interest demands it. Democracy has still not solved the problem, "Who shall govern?"'[26] Changing priorities in secondary education have done little to answer this question. Fear of 'indoctrination' and political bias often inhibited initiatives to transmit social values of ideological causes. Besides this, the academic orientation of the curriculum discouraged such active social concerns, as in the case of attempts to promote 'education for citizenship', or to renew interest in 'science in society'.[27] In this situation, leadership was effectively assumed by the academically successful, with no necessary reference either to the 'public service' values of Norwood, or the 'democratic quality' sought by Crosland. The loss of the tradition of leadership created a vacuum that encouraged an atomistic, opportunist, individualistic notion of leadership very different from that of the earlier sponsors of comprehensive schools, or indeed of the grammar and public schools before them.

Thus it does not seem too fanciful to point to an emerging tension between secondary education and leadership over the past thirty years. In one sense, a gulf has developed between the goals of secondary schools and the cultivation of social and political leadership, similar to that which has often been perceived between education and industry. The qualities encouraged in the comprehensive school tended not to relate to the skills of political leadership, attributes needed for community participation, or the acquisition of a sense of social responsibility. In another way, the 'culture of individualism' promoted by comprehensives[28] might be said to prefigure relationships in society as whole. In adopting the traditions of the grammar schools, the comprehensives discarded their notion of 'leadership' without developing a new approach, more appropriate to schools for all abilities and aptitudes. In spite of a growing and potentially unhealthy preoccupation with individual leadership in political parties, trade unions, business, the media and other public organisations, secondary education had learned to avoid the subject almost entirely.

Nevertheless, there remained a strong possibility that 'education for leadership' would eventually be revived in some new guise. At the end of his critical account of the English 'ruling class', written in 1932, Harold Laski struck a strong note of pessimism about what would arise to take the place of the 'gentleman':

The leader of the future seems not unlikely to be the remorseless one-idea'd man, who governs us by hewing his way to his goal. He has no time for the open mind. He takes clemency for weakness and difference of opinion for crime. He has a horror of a various civilisation and he means by freedom only a stronger kind of chain. Where we would be peaceful, he calls us to the affirmation of power. For the music of idle dreams he offers us the relentless hum of giant machines. The majesty of the forest is, for him, the volume of a timber supply, the rush of waters in the river, the source of electric power. The gentleman scourged us with whips. We must beware lest our new masters drive us to our toil with scorpions.[29]

This was a vision of individualistic leadership committed to economic and industrial efficiency. Arguably it anticipated the individualism and the materialism that were to play an important part in undermining earlier notions of education for leadership. It also highlighted the fact that these tendencies would, if they were allowed to do so, reconstruct the inequalities and social divisions of the past in new and even more rigid ways. Since the 1960s, the business schools have made a strong claim to be 'preparing the business leaders of tomorrow', and have apparently become 'potentially key institutions in the reproduction of the business elite'.[30] If the education system as a whole were geared towards such ends, Laski's vision of the future might be on the way to fulfilment.

The educational reforms of Conservative governments under Margaret Thatcher after 1979 seemed to many critics to point in this direction. These reforms, culminating in the Education Reform Act of 1988, were based solidly on the principle of individual choice. They provided for greater parental choice of schools, for 'independent state schools' outside the control of local education authorities, and for a 'new choice of school' in the form of city technology colleges. They emphasised the role of examinations in assessing standards and individual achievement, taking this principle to the extent of advocating tests for all children at the ages of seven, eleven, fourteen and sixteen. They also encouraged closer attention to the needs of industry and the economy, especially through the Technical and Vocational Education Initiative and a number of other reforms of the school curriculum. It is possible to interpret the broad thrust of these reforms as being the most decisive manifestation of the ideology of competitive individualism. They had no place for older notions of education for leadership, but they excluded egalitarian ideas just as rigorously. They seemed calculated to undermine the LEAs and the comprehensive schools, identified somewhat dubiously as being committed to social equality. A reconstruction of the postwar 'tripartite' system appeared a likely consequence of the reforms. No consideration of the character of the new elite that would be nurtured in this way was evident in the debates that preceded the passing of the Act. Even so, it seemed likely to herald an ironic twist in the career of what Cyril Norwood had once called the 'English tradition'.[31]

In this situation, those looking for alternatives to the Conservative policies of the 1980s might do worse than consider their historical context. Egalitarians, outflanked by their former allies, could seek redress by adapting and assimilating the values associated with education for leadership. In many ways such a development might seem unacceptable. The Platonic influence created a strongly elitist tendency; the shadow of authoritarianism was never far away. But advocates of education for leadership were also associated with values that might if reasserted help to correct some of the most disturbing tendencies of education and society in contemporary England. These values would include active commitment to a 'collective ethic' – the community, public service, citizenship and political and social participation – which might mitigate the current emphasis upon academic, examination-oriented individualism. David Hargreaves has suggested reforms in the curriculum of comprehensive schools designed to cultivate social and cultural qualities:

An increasing number of pupils will continue to be prepared for higher education, but we must also prepare pupils for the new elite positions, such as trade union officials, local councillors and community leaders. We need men and women who will take greater responsibility for the vitality of the various communities, including the local residential communities of which they will become members. These communities need to become more self-determining, more self-reliant and more democratically controlled.[32]

But such reforms, if they were to overcome the problems and handicaps faced by the curriculum initiatives of the last twenty years, would need also to contend with the 'academic curriculum' itself, against the apparatus of established subjects and examinations. It might well be necessary to reduce the influence of examinations, and to find alternative curriculum structures to those embodied in the dominant school subjects. Only in such a way, it seems, would it be possible both to assert the role of the moral curriculum in the schools and to reconstruct it to relate in an appropriate way to the society of the future, and to changes in industry, science and technology. And yet this would entail a major shift in attitudes and expectations, as well as in structures and relationships in the schools, of a kind that curriculum reform has rarely succeeded in attaining on a national scale.

Such a goal could also draw upon the ideals of Henry Morris and G.D.H. Cole, and upon the hopes of the Association for Education in Citizenship 'to fit the pupil for the public duties of citizenship in a democratic state'. Again, it would be necessary here to overcome the suspicion that has developed in the last forty years against 'social engineering' and political bias in the schools. But the kind of emphasis on democratic citizenship that the struggle against fascism in the 1930s and 1940s tended to encourage might still be capable of being tapped, given suitable social and political circumstances.

A reconciliation of the traditions of 'equality' and of 'leadership' would clearly need to involve a much more inclusive and democratic ideal than has been the case in the past, with a place for all social classes regardless of race and gender. This kind of ideal has attracted little attention, except for the tentative notions of early theorists of the comprehensive school such as Worsley, Crosland and Pedley. It may well be that the time has now come to explore the implications of these notions in a more systematic way, to draw a clear distinction between leadership and elitism. A recovery of the original ideals of the comprehensive schools seems overdue in any case, and this will surely involve a more active role for their moral curriculum. This was rarely spelled out in any detail, but seemed to consist in spreading responsibility across the community, and in encouraging a social conscience in those who would have authority in their particular fields. Such themes could provide an attractive keynote for critics of educational policies that have promoted competitive individualism above all else, and might even find themselves closer to an authentic 'English tradition'.

Any such developments should not be expected to have an immediate or even a readily predictable impact on society and government; educational reforms rarely do. And yet there seems good reason at least to give closer attention to the past, present and potential future contributions of secondary schooling in this area. It was Tawney, the prophet of equality, who voiced what might be taken as the most important criterion for judging both past and present initiatives: 'Democracy needs experts, representatives and leaders; but it needs them as servants, not as masters.'[33] The loss of the nineteenth-century tradition of education for leadership did not mean an end to social inequality, but left a moral vacuum that has still to be filled. If education for leadership is to be reconstructed in the future it should be designed to create experts, representatives and leaders as servants of a democratic society rather than as masters. Jackson and Marsden foresaw the danger of education creating a new type of ruling elite, 'as Eton builds its science blocks . . ., putting the same people into the same place at the same price'. Michael Young's nightmare vision of 'rule not so much by the people as by the cleverest people' could just as easily become reality. It may be that to forestall such prospects educators will need to foster positive and coherent alternatives rather than seek to avoid discussion of the subject. In the twenty-first century the 'English tradition' of education for leadership may yet be as keenly contested as it has been over the past one hundred years.

NOTES

I INTRODUCTION

1 Plato, *The Republic* (1976 edn, translated by A.D. Lindsay), III. 414.
2 See especially Rupert Wilkinson, *The Prefects: British Leadership and the Public School Tradition* (1964); J.A. Mangan, *The Games Ethic and Imperialism: Aspects of the Diffusion of an Ideal* (New York, 1986); J.A. Mangan and James Walvin (eds.), *Manliness and Morality: Middle-Class Masculinity in Britain and America, 1800–1940* (Manchester, 1987); and Mark Girouard, *The Return to Camelot: Chivalry and the English Gentleman* (1981).
3 E.g. Geoffrey Walford (ed.), *British Public Schools: Policy and Practice* (1984); Brian Salter and Ted Tapper (eds.), *Power and Policy in Education: The Case of Independent Schooling* (1985).
4 Brian Simon, *The Politics of Educational Reform, 1920–1940* (1974), 248–9.
5 *Ibid.*, 294.
6 A recent discussion of this period is in Michael Sanderson, *Educational Opportunity and Social Change in England* (1987), Ch. 2.
7 See Olive Banks, *Parity and Prestige in English Secondary Education: A Study in Educational Sociology* (1955); Reese Edwards, *The Secondary Technical School* (1960); Gary McCulloch, *The Secondary Technical School: A Usable Past?* (1989); William Taylor, *The Secondary Modern School* (1963).
8 Stephen Ball, 'Introduction: comprehensives in crisis?', in Stephen Ball (ed.), *Comprehensive Schooling: A Reader* (1984), 3.
9 See also Stephen Ball, *Beachside Comprehensive: A Case-Study of Secondary Schooling* (Cambridge, 1981).
10 Ivor Goodson, 'Defining a subject for the comprehensive school: a case-study', in Ball (ed.), *Comprehensive Schooling*, 198. See also Peter Gordon, '"A unity of purpose": some reflections on the school curriculum, 1945–70', in W.E. Marsden (ed.), *Post-War Curriculum Development: An Historical Appraisal* (Leicester, 1979), 6.
11 David Hargreaves, *The Challenge for the Comprehensive School: Culture, Curriculum and Community* (1982), 87.
12 *Ibid.*, 93.
13 *Ibid.*, 51.
14 Raymond Williams, 'Education and British society', in his *The Long Revolution* (1961).
15 Richard Jenkyns, *The Victorians and Ancient Greece* (Oxford, 1980), 245.
16 Wilkinson, *The Prefects*; Peter Parker, *The Old Lie: The Great War and the Public School Ethos* (1987).
17 Correlli Barnett, *The Audit of War: The Illusion and Reality of Britain as a Great Nation* (1986); also, e.g., Martin J. Wiener, *English Culture and the Decline of the Industrial Spirit, 1850–1980* (Cambridge, 1981).

18 Useful works that go some way towards these ends include Richard Symonds, *Oxford and Empire: The Last Lost Cause?* (1986); and Geoffrey Sherington *et al.*, *Learning to Lead: A History of Girls' and Boys' Corporate Secondary Schools in Australia* (Sydney, 1987).
19 McCulloch, *The Secondary Technical School.*

2 AN ENGLISH TRADITION

1   Sir Ernest Barker, 'The education of the English gentleman in the sixteenth century', in his *Traditions of Civility: Eight Essays* (Cambridge, 1948), 124.
2   Joel Spring, *The American School, 1642–1985* (New York, 1986), 32.
3   Henry Steele Commager, 'Leadership in eighteenth-century America and today', *Daedalus*, 90/4 (Fall 1961), 670.
4   See esp. Peter W. Cookson, Jr, and Caroline Hodges Persell, *Preparing for Power: America's Elite Boarding Schools* (1985); and Edward N. Sareth, 'Education of an elite', *History of Education Quarterly*, 28/3 (1988), 367–86.
5   Allen Potter, 'The American governing class', *British Journal of Sociology*, 13 (1962), 309–19.
6   Michalina Vaughan, 'The *Grandes Ecoles*', in Rupert Wilkinson (ed.), *Governing Elites: Studies in Training and Selection* (New York, 1969), 74.
7   Cited in John E. Talbott, *The Politics of Educational Reform in France, 1918–1940* (1969), 17.
8   See William B. Cohen, *Rulers of Empire: The French Colonial Service in Africa* (1971).
9   E.g. Richard J. Wolff, '"Fascistizing" Italian youth: the limits of Mussolini's educational system', *History of Education*, 13/4 (1984), 287–98. Earlier, vivid accounts include L. Minio-Paluello, *Education in Fascist Italy* (1946); George Frederick Kneller, *The Educational Philosophy of National Socialism* (New Haven, 1941); Gregor Ziemer, *Education for Death: The Making of the Nazi* (1941); and Erika Mann, *School for Barbarians: Education under the Nazis* (1939).
10 Plato, *The Republic*, III, 416.
11 *Ibid.*, VII. 540.
12 *Ibid.*, V. 473.
13 R.C. Lodge, *Plato's Theory of Education* (New York, 1947; reissued 1970), 247, 282.
14 E.g. Richard Crossman, *Plato Today* (1937).
15 James Bowen, *A History of Western Education*, vol. II (1975), 81.
16 John M. Major, *Sir Thomas Elyot and Renaissance Humanism* (Lincoln, Nebraska, 1964), 3.
17 Geoffrey Bantock, *Studies in the History of Educational Theory*, vol. I (1980), 102.
18 Quentin Skinner, *The Foundations of Modern Political Thought*, vol. I (1978), 242. Barker also emphasises this: 'The revolution of the sixteenth century consists in the junction and interfusion of these two types.' ('Education of the English gentleman', in *Traditions of Civility*, 132.)
19 See esp. J.H. Hexter, 'The education of the aristocracy in the Renaissance', *Journal of Modern History*, 22/1 (1950), 1–20; Lawrence Stone, *The Crisis of the Aristocracy, 1558–1641* (1965); Joan Simon, *Education and Society in Tudor England* (Cambridge, 1966).
20 Skinner, *The Foundations of Modern Political Thought*, 236.
21 George C. Brauer, Jr, *The Education of a Gentleman: Theories of Gentlemanly Education in England, 1660–1775* (1959).
22 W.A.L. Vincent, *The Grammar Schools: Their Continuing Tradition, 1660–1714* (1969).
23 John Cannon, *Aristocratic Century: The Peerage of Eighteenth Century England* (Cambridge, 1984), 34–5.
24 William Reid and Jane Filby, *The Sixth: An Essay in Education and Democracy* (1982), 2.
25 J.R. de S. Honey, *Tom Brown's Universe: The Development of the English Public School in the Nineteenth Century* (1977), 10.
26 Public Schools Commission, *Report* (Clarendon report, 1864), I, 56 (Parliamentary Papers, 1864, 20).

27 Sheldon Rothblatt, *The Revolution of the Dons: Cambridge and Society in Victorian England* (1968), 51. See also T.W. Bamford, *Rise of the Public Schools: A Study of Boys' Boarding Schools in England and Wales from 1837 to the Present Day* (1967).

28 Donald Leinster-Mackay, *The Rise of the English Prep School* (1984). Also his 'The evolution of t'other schools: an examination of the nineteenth century development of the private preparatory school', *History of Education*, 5/3 (1976), 241–9: 'by the early twentieth century these two types of school, with their differing origins, were complementary parts of an integrated whole'.

29 Honey, *Tom Brown's Universe*. See also, for example, Brian Simon and Ian Bradley (eds.), *The Victorian Public School: Studies in the Development of an Educational Institution* (1975); David Newsome, *Godliness and Good Learning: Four Studies of a Victorian Ideal* (1961): John Chandos, *Boys Together: English Public Schools, 1800–1864* (1984), esp. Ch. 12.

30 Christopher Dilke, *Dr Moberly's Mint-Mark: A Study of Winchester College* (1965), 2.

31 Rupert Wilkinson, *The Prefects: British Leadership and the Public School Tradition* (1964), viii.

32 *Ibid.*, 98.

33 *Ibid.*, 90–1.

34 Martin J. Wiener, *English Culture and the Decline of the Industrial Spirit, 1850–1980* (Cambridge, 1981), 17.

35 *Ibid.*, 21.

36 See, e.g. Correlli Barnett, *The Audit of War: The Illusion and Reality of Britain as a Great Nation* (1986), esp. Ch. 11, 'Education for industrial decline'.

37 Eric Hobsbawm, 'Introduction: inventing traditions', in Eric Hobsbawm and Terence Ranger (eds.), *The Invention of Tradition* (Cambridge, 1983), 1.

38 John Roach, *A History of Secondary Education in England, 1800–1870* (1986), 264–5.

39 Philip Dodd, 'Englishness and the national culture', in Robert Colls and Philip Dodd (eds.), *Englishness: Politics and Culture, 1880–1920* (1986), 21.

40 Barker, 'Education of the English gentleman', in *Traditions of Civility*, 140–1.

41 Harold Laski, 'The danger of being a gentleman: reflections on the ruling class in England' (1932), in his *The Danger of Being a Gentleman, and Other Essays* (1939), 17.

42 Ben Knights, *The Idea of the Clerisy in the Nineteenth Century* (Cambridge, 1978), 13–14.

43 Geoffrey Bantock, *Studies in the History of Educational Theory*, vol. II (1984), 111.

44 F.W. Garforth, *Educative Democracy: John Stuart Mill on Education in Society* (Oxford, 1980), 45.

45 Matthew Arnold, *Culture and Anarchy* (1869; ed. J. Dover Wilson, Cambridge, 1946).

46 Gillian Sutherland (ed.), *Arnold on Education* (1973), 15. See also W.F. Connell, *The Educational Thought and Influence of Matthew Arnold* (1950).

47 See Carl Kaestle, '"Between the Scylla of brutal ignorance and the Charybdis of a literary education"; elite attitudes towards mass education in early industrial England and America', in Lawrence Stone (ed.), *Schooling And Society: Studies in the History of Education* (Princeton, 1976), 177–91; also Brian Simon, *The Two Nations and the Educational Structure, 1780–1870* (1960).

48 Harold Silver, 'Ideology and the factory child: attitudes to half-time education', in his *Education as History: Interpreting Nineteenth- and Twentieth-Century Education* (1983).

49 Robert Lowe, 'Primary and classical education' (1867), in David Reeder (ed.), *Educating our Masters* (Leicester, 1980), 125–6. See also James Winter, *Robert Lowe* (Toronto, 1976); and D.W. Sylvester, *Robert Lowe and Education* (Cambridge, 1974).

50 See Eric Eaglesham, 'The centenary of Sir Robert Morant', *British Journal of Educational Studies*, 12/1 (1963), 5–18, and 'Planning the Education Bill of 1902', *British Journal of Educational Studies*, 9/1 (1960), 3–24.

51 Peter Gordon and Denis Lawton, *Curriculum Change in the Nineteenth and Twentieth Centuries* (1978), 22. See also Eric Eaglesham, 'Implementing the Education Act of 1902', *British Journal of Educational Studies*, 10/2 (1961), 153.

52 Gail Savage, 'Social class and social policy: the civil service and secondary education in England during the interwar period', *Journal of Contemporary History*, 18 (1983), 275–6.

53 Harold Perkin, 'The pattern of social transformation in England', in Konrad H. Jarausch (ed.), *The Transformation of Higher Learning, 1860–1930* (Chicago, 1983), 207.

54 Fritz Ringer, *The Decline of the German Mandarins: The German Academic Community, 1890–1933* (Cambridge, Mass., 1969), 5–6.

55 Rothblatt, *The Revolution of the Dons*, 257.

56 Christopher Harvie, *The Lights of Liberalism: University Liberals and the Challenge of Democracy, 1860–86* (1976).

57 See, e.g., John Springhall, 'Building character in the British boy: the attempt to extend Christian manliness to working-class adolescents, 1880–1914', and Allen Warren, 'Popular manliness: Baden-Powell, scouting, and the development of manly character', both in J.A. Mangan and James Walvin (eds.), *Manliness and Morality: Middle-Class Masculinity in Britain and America, 1800–1940* (Manchester, 1987), 52–74 and 199–219.

58 Lord Aberdare, 'Leadership for youth', *The Fortnightly*, January 1943, 24–9.

59 *Times Educational Supplement*, 3 November 1928, leading article, 'Leaders for social service'.

60 *TES*, 3 November 1928, feature, 'Welfare of youth: the Duke of York's appeal'.

61 Raymond Williams, *The Long Revolution* (1961), 170. See also Richard D. Altick, *The English Common Reader: A Short History of the Mass Reading Public, 1800–1900* (Chicago, 1957).

62 Gary D. Stark, *Entrepreneurs of Ideology: Neoconservative Publishers in Germany, 1890–1933* (Chapel Hill, North Carolina, 1981).

63 E.g. S. Lowery and M.L. de Fleur, *Milestones in Mass Communications Research: Media Effects* (1983), Ch. 1.

64 J.A. Hobson, *The Crisis of Liberalism: New Issues of Democracy* (1909; ed. Peter Clarke, 1974), 109.

65 *Ibid.*, 112.

66 Alfred Zimmern, *Learning and Leadership: A Study of the Needs and Possibilities of International Intellectual Cooperation* (1928), 109.

67 *Ibid.*, 26.

68 Leonard Woolf, *Barbarians at the Gate* (1939).

69 Lord Lloyd, *Leadership in Democracy* (1939), 21. See also John Charmley, *Lord Lloyd and the Decline of the British Empire* (1987).

70 E.g. E.R. Norman, *Church and Society in England, 1770–1970: A Historical Study* (Oxford, 1976); J.F. Glaser, 'English Nonconformity and the decline of Liberalism', *American Historical Review*, 63/2 (1958), 352–63; Stephen Koss, *Nonconformity in Modern British Politics* (1975), Ch. 9.

71 See, e.g., W.H.G. Armytage, *The Rise of the Technocrats: A Social History* (1965); David Caute, *The Fellow-Travellers: A Postscript to the Enlightenment* (1973).

72 E.g. Arthur Marwick, 'Middle opinion in the thirties: planning, progress and political "agreement"', *English Historical Review*, 79/2 (1964), 285–98.

73 Sir Walter Moberly, *Plato's Conception of Education and its Meaning for Today* (1944), 6.

74 *Ibid.*, 28.

75 *Ibid.*, 26–7.

76 Sir Richard Livingstone, 'Education for a world adrift' (1943), in his *On Education* (Cambridge, 1956), 145.

3 THE END OF THE OLD SCHOOL TIE?

1 Mark Girouard, *The Return to Camelot: Chivalry and the English Gentleman* (1981), preface.

2 *Ibid.*, 290.

3 J.A. Mangan, *Athleticism in the Victorian and Edwardian Public School* (Cambridge, 1981), 207.

4   Correlli Barnett, *The Audit of War: The Illusion and Reality of Britain as a Great Nation* (1986); Paul Addison, *The Road to 1945: British Politics in the Second World War* (1975).

5   Bernard Darwin, *The English Public School* (1929), 22–3.

6   Rev. Spencer Leeson, *The Public Schools Question, and Other Essays Connected with Secondary Education* (1948), 9.

7   Robert Skidelsky, *English Progressive Schools* (1969), esp. Part 2; W.A.C. Stewart, *Progressives and Radicals in English Education, 1750–1970* (1972), esp. Chs. 8, 20.

8   Skidelsky, *English Progressive Schools*, Part 4; Stewart, *Progressives and Radicals*, Ch. 17.

9   Richard Ollard, *An English Education: A Perspective of Eton* (1982), 184.

10 *Ibid.*, 2.

11 Harold Laski, 'The danger of being a gentleman: reflections on the ruling class in England' (1932), in his *The Danger of Being a Gentleman, and Other Essays* (1939), 22, 26.

12 David Low, *Low's Autobiography* (1956), 120.

13 Robert Birley to Sir Edward Boyle, n.d. [January 1957] (Boyle papers, 660/3977).

14 J.B. Firth, 'Hitler's revolution in Germany's school system: Nazi education's supreme object – a race of Fuehrers', *Daily Telegraph*, 9 August 1940.

15 T.C. Worsley, *Barbarians and Philistines: Democracy and the Public Schools* (1940), 7.

16 *Ibid.*, 9.

17 *Ibid.*, 15.

18 *Ibid.*, 260.

19 *Ibid.*, 266.

20 T.C. Worsley, *The End of the 'Old School Tie'* (1941), 11.

21 *Ibid.*, 12.

22 T.C. Worsley, *Flannelled Fool: A Slice of Life in the Thirties* (1967), 191–2.

23 Edward C. Mack, *Public Schools and British Opinion since 1860: The Relationship between Contemporary Ideas and the Evolution of an English Institution* (New York, 1941), 458.

24 *Ibid.*, 462.

25 *TES*, 9 March 1940, leading article, 'Public schools'.

26 *TES*, 11 May 1940, leading article, 'The public schools'.

27 *TES*, 10 May 1941, leading article, 'Public and other schools'. For a recent discussion of the changing role of the *TES* during the war, see Joan Simon, 'Promoting educational reform on the home front: *The TES* and *The Times* 1940–1944', *History of Education*, 18/3 (1989), 195–211.

28 Cyril Norwood, 'Harrow School', *Morning Post*, 5 May 1928.

29 Cyril Norwood, 'Public schools', in *Encyclopaedia Britannica*, 13th edn (1926), supplementary volume III, 262.

30 Cyril Norwood, 'The boys' boarding school', in J. Dover Wilson (ed.), *The Schools Of England: A Study in Renaissance* (1928), 136.

31 Cyril Norwood to F.R.G. Duckworth, 19 October 1938 (Board of Education papers, ED. 136/129).

32 Note of interview with Cyril Norwood, 24 October 1938 (Board of Education papers, ED. 136/129).

33 Cyril Norwood to G.G. Williams, 3 December 1939 (Board of Education papers, ED. 12/518).

34 Cyril Norwood, 'The crisis in education – I', *The Spectator*, 9 February 1940.

35 Cyril Norwood, 'The crisis in education – II', *The Spectator*, 16 February 1940.

36 Worsley, *Barbarians and Philistines*, 252.

37 Lord Hugh Cecil to Lord de la Warr, 21 March 1940 (Board of Education papers, ED. 136/129).

38 Lord de la Warr to Lord Hugh Cecil, 29 March 1940 (Board of Education papers, ED. 136/129).

39 R.A. Butler, 'The common school', 23 January 1942 (Board of Education papers, ED. 136/294).

40 Sir Maurice Holmes, note, 26 January 1942 (Board of Education papers, ED. 136/294).

41 Brian Simon, 'The 1944 Education Act – a Conservative measure?', *History of Education*, 15/1 (1986), 31–43.

42 R.A. Butler, note on discussion with Cyril Norwood, 27 November 1941 (Board of Education papers, ED. 12/478).

43 R.A. Butler, note of interview with G.D.H. Cole, 12 May 1942 (Board of Education papers, ED. 136/599).

44 Association of Governing Bodies of Public Schools, memo to Fleming committee, n.d. [1942] (Cole papers, B. 3/4/C).

45 Independent Schools Association, memo to Fleming committee, n.d. [1942] (Cole papers, B. 3/4/C).

46 Workers' Educational Association, memo to Fleming committee, n.d. [1942] (Cole papers, B. 3/4/C).

47 Standing Joint Committee of Working Women's Organisations, memo to Fleming committee, March 1943 (Cole papers, B. 3/4/C).

48 Trades Union Congress, memo to Fleming committee, n.d. [1942] (Cole papers, B. 3/4/C).

49 *TES*, 29 July 1944, leading article, 'The Fleming report'.

50 Board of Education, *The Public Schools and the General Educational System* (Fleming report, 1944), 4.

51 *Ibid.*

52 *Ibid.*, 40–1.

53 *Ibid.*, 41.

54 *Ibid.*, 44.

55 *Ibid.*, 45.

56 *Ibid.*, 47.

57 *Ibid.*, 48.

58 G.D.H. Cole, draft for BBC broadcast on the Fleming report, 22 August 1944 (Cole papers, B. 3/3/E Box 4).

59 The Public Schools Commission, *First Report* (Newsom report, 1968), vol. I, 19.

60 W.L. Guttsman, *The British Political Elite* (1963); David Boyd, *Elites and their Education* (Windsor, 1973).

61 W.D. Rubinstein, 'Education and the social origins of British elites 1880–1970', *Past and Present*, 112 (1986), 163–207; and Harold Perkin, 'The recruitment of elites in British society since 1800', *Journal of Social History*, 12/2 (1978), 222–34.

62 Geoffrey Walford, 'Introduction: British public schools', in Geoffrey Walford (ed.), *British Public Schools: Policy and Practice* (1984).

63 Clive Griggs, *Private Education in Britain* (1985), 46.

64 Anthony Sampson, *The Changing Anatomy of Britain* (1983), 142–4.

65 Shirley Williams, 'Extending educational opportunity', *Secondary Education Journal*, 10/3 (1980), quoted in Griggs, *Private Education in Britain*, 145.

66 John Dancy, *The Public Schools and the Future* (1963), 96.

67 The Public Schools Commission, *First Report*, vol. II, Appendix 7.

68 Jonathan Gathorne-Hardy, *The Public School Phenomenon, 597–1977* (1977), 377–8.

69 Parliamentary Debates, House of Commons, 20 May 1938, vol. 337, cols. 786–7.

4   THE IDEOLOGY OF SIR CYRIL NORWOOD

1 See C.P. Hill, *The History of Bristol Grammar School* (1951), esp. 190.

2 *Dictionary of National Biography, 1951–1960*, entry on Sir Cyril Norwood (1875–1956), 775.

3   Cyril Norwood and Arthur H. Hope (eds.), *The Higher Education of Boys in England* (1909), 'Conclusion', 558–9.

4   *Ibid.*, 561.

5   J.A. Mangan, 'Imitating their betters and disassociating from their inferiors: grammar schools and the games ethic in the late nineteenth and early twentieth centuries', in Nicholas Parry and David McNair (eds.), *The Fitness of the Nation: Physical and Health Education in the Nineteenth and Twentieth Centuries* (Leicester, 1983), 1–45.

6   Cyril Norwood to Stanley Booker, 8 August 1914 (Bosanko papers).

7   Stanley Booker to Cyril Norwood, n.d. [1916] (Norwood papers).

8   Cyril Norwood to Walter Booker, 16 October 1916 (Bosanko papers).

9   Cyril Norwood to Walter Booker, 29 December 1933 (Bosanko papers). On the 'Lost Generation' and its influence, see Jay Winter, *The Great War and the British People* (1986), esp. Ch. 3.

10   Cyril Norwood, 'Education: the next steps' (presidential address to Educational Science section, British Association for the Advancement of Science, Glasgow, September 1928), 212.

11   Cyril Norwood, *The English Tradition of Education* (1929), 4–5.

12   *Ibid.*, 5–6.

13   *Ibid.*, 6–7.

14   *Ibid.*, 8.

15   *Ibid.*, 20.

16   *Ibid.*, 109.

17   *Ibid.*, 120.

18   *Ibid.*, 243.

19   *Morning Post*, 2 October 1929, leading article, 'English education'.

20   Cyril Norwood, sermon at Harrow, 9 May 1926 (Norwood papers).

21   Cyril Norwood, 'Girls should *not* be educated like boys', interview in *Daily Mail*, 9 October 1928.

22   Norwood, *English Tradition of Education*, v.

23   Cyril Norwood, 'Careers for sons. New avenues of employment: leaders needed. Clearing house wanted for public schools', *Morning Post*, 1 February 1926.

24   Cyril Norwood, 'Unity and purpose in education', in T.F. Coade (ed.), *Harrow lectures on Education* (Cambridge, 1931), 7.

25   *Yorkshire Evening News*, 9 January 1926, 'Compulsory education to 16. More schools, Headmaster of Harrow calls for enterprise'.

26   *Ibid.*

27   Norwood, 'Education: the next steps', 203.

28   *Ibid.*

29   Cyril Norwood, 'The education and outlook of English youth', address to Canadian Club of Montreal, 11 April 1930 (Norwood papers).

30   Cyril Norwood, 'Sons of the poor and schools of the rich', *The Nineteenth Century and After*, June 1935, 698.

31   Cyril Norwood, 'English', in Norwood and Hope (eds.), *Higher Education of Boys*, 330.

32   Cyril Norwood, memorandum to consultative committee, n.d. [1933] (Board of Education papers, ED. 10/151).

33   Cyril Norwood, oral evidence to consultative committee, 24 November 1933 (Board of Education papers, ED. 10/151).

34   Cyril Norwood, *Religion and Education* (1932), 7.

35   John Roach, 'Examinations and the secondary schools, 1900–1945', *History of Education*, 8/1 (1979), 46.

36   Norwood, 'Education: the next steps', 210.

37   *Ibid.*, 211.

38 *Times*, 12 September 1928, leading article, "'Common entrance'".

39 Cyril Norwood, letter to *Times Educational Supplement*, 22 September 1928.

40 See Peter Gordon and John White, *Philosophers as Educational Reformers: The Influence of Idealism on British Educational Thought and Practice* (1979), although no mention of Norwood is made in this book.

41 Coade, 'Introduction', in Coade (ed.), *Harrow Lectures on Education*, ix.

42 T.F. Coade, 'Confessio fidei' (n.d.), in *The Burning Bow: T.F. Coade of Bryanston. A Selection of his Papers* (1966), 32.

43 *Ibid.*, 96.

44 For further details of Bryanston, see W.A.C. Stewart, *Progressives and Radicals in English Education, 1750–1970* (1972), Ch. 16.

45 Ronald Gurner, *I Chose Teaching* (1937), 28.

46 *Ibid.*, 18.

47 *Ibid.*, 53.

48 *Ibid.*, 58.

49 *Ibid.*, 129.

50 Ronald Gurner, *Day Schools of England* (1930), 14.

51 *Ibid.*, 15.

52 *Ibid.*, 16.

53 *Ibid.*, 25.

54 *Ibid.*, 29.

55 *Ibid.*, 73.

56 *Ibid.*, 113.

57 *Ibid.*, 116–17.

58 Eva M. Hubback and E.D. Simon, *Education For Citizenship* (1934), 5.

59 F.C. Happold, *Citizens in the Making* (1935), 8.

60 *Ibid.*, 29.

61 *Ibid.*, 137–8.

62 *Ibid.*, 139–40.

63 F.C. Happold, *Towards a New Aristocracy: A Contribution to Educational Planning* (1943), 92.

64 F.C. Happold, 'The School Company of Honour and Service', in F.C. Happold *et al.*, *Experiments in Practical Training for Citizenship* (1937), 5.

65 Happold, *Towards a New Aristocracy*, 69.

66 Sir Ernest Simon to Oliver Stanley, 15 January 1937 (Board of Education papers, ED. 136/2).

67 Sir Ernest Simon to M.G. Holmes, 18 February 1938 (Board of Education papers, ED. 136/2).

68 Maurice Holmes, note, 24 February 1938 (Board of Education papers, ED. 136/2).

69 Sir Will Spens to M.G. Holmes, 28 February 1938 (Board of Education papers, ED. 136/2).

70 Board of Education, *Secondary Education* (Spens report, 1938), xxxvi.

71 *Ibid.*

72 Cyril Norwood, *Scylla and Charybdis, or Laissez-Faire and Paternal Government* (9th Shaftesbury lecture, 2 May 1932), 10.

73 Norwood, 'Education: the next steps', 211.

74 Cyril Norwood, 'The crisis in education – I', *The Spectator*, 9 February 1940.

75 Cyril Norwood to G.G. Williams, 3 December 1939 (Board of Education papers, ED. 12/518).

76 Cyril Norwood, 'The crisis in education – I', *The Spectator*, 9 February 1940.

77 Cyril Norwood, 'The crisis in education – II', *The Spectator*, 16 February 1940.

78 Cyril Norwood, 'Some aspects of educational reconstruction', *The Fortnightly*, February 1941, p. 107.

79 *Ibid.*, 108.

80 *Ibid.*

81 *Ibid.*, 109.

82 Herbert Ramsbotham to Sir Cyril Norwood, 3 January 1941; Norwood to Ramsbotham, 8 January 1941 (Board of Education papers, ED. 12/478).

83 R.A. Butler, note, 31 July 1941 (Board of Education papers, ED. 12/478); Norwood committee, 1st meeting, 18 October 1941, minute 2 (ED. 136/681).

84 R.A. Butler, note of talk with Sir Will Spens, 20 March 1942 (Board of Education papers, ED. 136/131).

85 G.G. Williams to Sir Cyril Norwood, 26 November 1941 (Board of Education papers, ED. 136/681).

86 G.G Williams, note of talk with Sir Cyril Norwood, 23 December 1941 (Board of Education papers, ED. 12/478).

87 M.G. Holmes to Sir Cyril Norwood, 10 July 1941 (Norwood papers).

88 Sir Cyril Norwood to G.G. Williams, 13 August 1941 (Board of Education papers, ED. 12/478).

89 R.A. Butler, note of interview with Sir Will Spens, 20 March 1942 (Board of Education papers, ED. 136/131).

90 R.A. Butler, note, 14 January 1942 (Board of Education papers, ED. 136/681).

91 Agenda for Norwood committee meeting, 5–8 January 1942, topics for discussion, II(a) (Board of Education papers, ED. 12/478); minutes of 3rd meeting of the Norwood committee, 5–8 January 1942 (ED. 12/479).

92 R.A. Butler, note, 28 May 1942 (Board of Education papers, ED. 136/681).

93 'Provisional summary of proposals', n.d. [1942] (Board of Education papers, ED. 136/681).

94 Board of Education, *Curriculum and Examinations in Secondary Schools: Report of the Committee of the SSEC Appointed by the President of the Board of Education in 1941* (Norwood report, 1943), 20.

95 *Ibid.*, 20–1.

96 *Ibid.*, 21.

97 1st meeting of Norwood committee, 18 October 1941, minutes 2, 3(v) (Board of Education papers, ED. 136/681).

98 R.A. Butler, note, 28 May 1942 (Board of Education papers, ED. 136/681).

99 10th meeting of Norwood committee, 2–3 October 1942 (Board of Education papers, ED. 12/479).

100 Sir Cyril Norwood to R.A. Butler, 23 June 1943 (Board of Education papers, ED. 136/681).

101 Norwood report, recommendation 9, p. 140.

102 *Ibid.*, 140.

103 *Ibid.*

104 *Ibid.*, 45.

105 *Ibid.*, 46.

106 *Ibid.*, 48.

107 *Ibid.*, 17.

108 Norwood committee, 1st meeting, 18 October 1941, minute 2 (Board of Education papers, ED. 136/681).

109 'A note on the grammar school', n.d. [January 1942] (Board of Education papers, ED. 136/681).

110 Norwood committee, 10th meeting, 2–3 October 1942, minute (c) (Board of Education papers, ED. 136/681).

111 Norwood committee, 1st meeting, 18 October 1941, minute 2 (Board of Education papers, ED. 136/681).

112 'Provisional summary of proposals', n.d. [1942] (Board of Education papers, ED. 136/681).

113 *Ibid.*

114 R.A. Butler, note of interview with Sir Cyril Norwood, 21 May 1943 (Board of Education papers, ED. 136/681).

115 Norwood report, 7.
116 *Ibid.*, 66.
117 *Ibid.*, 67.
118 Sir Cyril Norwood to G.G. Williams, 10 June 1943 (Board of Education papers, ED. 12/478).
119 'Final minutes of the Norwood Committee' (unofficial), 23 June 1943 (Board of Education papers, ED. 12/479).
120 R.A. Butler, note, 6 June 1943 (Board of Education papers, ED. 136/681).
121 *Times Educational Supplement*, Comment, 16 March 1956.
122 Jonathan Gathorne-Hardy, *The Public School Phenomenon, 597–1977* (1977), 302, 298.
123 Correlli Barnett, *The Audit of War: The Illusion and Reality of Britain as a Great Nation* (1986), 299, 301.
124 Brian Simon, 'The 1944 Education Act: a Conservative measure?', *History of Education*, 15/1 (1986), 38.
125 *Ibid.*, 39.
126 *Ibid.*, 43.
127 E.g. Stephen Ball (ed.), *Comprehensive Schooling: A Reader* (1984), 2–3.
128 Sir Cyril Norwood to G.G. Williams, 10 November 1943 (Board of Education papers, ED. 12/480).
129 Sir Cyril Norwood to G.G. Williams, 11 May 1944 (Board of Education papers, ED. 12/480).
130 R.H. Barrow to Sir Cyril Norwood, 22 December 1947 (Norwood papers).
131 R.H. Barrow to Sir Cyril Norwood, 4 February [1948?] (Norwood papers).
132 Cyril Norwood, 'Christian Modernism and education', *The Modern Churchman*, September 1948, pp. 231–2.

5   THE RISE AND FALL OF THE MERITOCRACY

1 Otto Neurath, J.A. Lauwerys, 'Nazi text-books and the future – II', *Journal of Education*, 905 (December 1944), 574–6; Otto Neurath, J.A. Lauwerys, 'Plato's "Republic" and German education', *Journal of Education*, 907 (February 1945), 57–8; correspondence and articles in *Journal of Education*, March, April, May, June, July 1945.
2 Karl Popper, *The Open Society and its Enemies*, vol. I (1945), 6.
3 *Ibid.*, 29.
4 *Ibid.*, 52.
5 *Ibid.*, 127.
6 *Ibid.*, 136.
7 Richard Jenkyns, *The Victorians and Ancient Greece* (Oxford, 1980), 227.
8 See Gary McCulloch, *The Secondary Technical School: A Usable Past?* (1989), for further details on the secondary technical schools. Also Reese Edwards, *The Secondary Technical School* (1960).
9 William Taylor, *The Secondary Modern School* (1963).
10 Olive Banks, *Parity and Prestige in English Secondary Education: A Study in Educational Sociology* (1955), 215.
11 Harry Judge, *A Generation of Schooling: English Secondary Schools since 1944* (Oxford, 1984).
12 Board of Education, *Secondary Education* (Spens report, 1938), 101.
13 FBI education committee, 14 July 1943 (FBI papers, MSS 200/F//1/1/116).
14 Banks, *Parity and Prestige in English Secondary Education*, 7.
15 George Whitfield, 'The grammar school through half a century', *British Journal of Educational Studies*, 5/2 (1957), 118.
16 Sir Robert Wood, minute, 15 April 1946 (Ministry of Education papers, ED. 136/787).
17 T.R. Weaver, 'Secondary technical schools', 14 January 1955 (Ministry of Education papers, ED. 147/207).
18 IAHM, *The Threat to the Grammar Schools* (1946), 2.

19 See, e.g., Keith Fenwick, *The Comprehensive School, 1944–1970* (1976).

20 E.g. Brian Simon, 'The 1944 Education Act: a Conservative measure?', *History of Education*, 15/1 (1986), 31–43. Also Frank Musgrove, 'The Black Paper movement', in Roy Lowe (ed.), *The Changing Primary School* (1987), 106–28.

21 G.C.T. Giles, *The New School Tie* (1946), vii.

22 *Ibid.*, 9.

23 *Ibid.*, 25–6.

24 *Ibid.*, 45.

25 Gillian Sutherland, *Ability, Merit and Measurement: Mental Testing and English Education, 1880–1940* (Oxford, 1984), 283.

26 R.A. Butler, diary, 9 September 1943 (Butler papers, G15).

27 Lord James, interview with the author, 10 December 1987.

28 Christopher Dilke, *Dr Moberly's Mint-Mark: A Study of Winchester College* (1965), 135.

29 See his introduction to R.L. Nettleship, *The Theory of Education in Plato's Republic* (Oxford edn, 1935).

30 Rev. Spencer Leeson, *The Public Schools Question, and Other Essays Connected with Secondary Education* (1948), 34.

31 Lord James, interview with the author, 10 December 1987.

32 Eric James, 'The challenge to the grammar schools: attack upon standards and values', *TES*, 1 February 1947.

33 *TES*, 1 February 1947, leading article, 'Learning and liberty'.

34 Joan Simon, 'The conception of culture: needs for new standards and values', *TES*, 15 February 1947.

35 Eric James, *An Essay on the Content of Education* (1949), 27.

36 *Ibid.*

37 *Ibid.*, 35.

38 *Ibid.*, 43.

39 *Ibid.*, 92.

40 Eric James, *Education and Leadership* (1951), 37.

41 *Ibid.*, 38.

42 *Ibid.*, 38.

43 *Ibid.*, 40.

44 *Ibid.*, 26.

45 *Ibid.*, 30.

46 *Ibid.*, 31–2.

47 R.C. Lodge, *Plato's Theory of Education* (New York, 1947; reissued 1970), 241.

48 *Ibid.*, 247.

49 *TES*, 15 October 1954, report, 'New schools for old: headmasters meet Labour MPs'.

50 Philip Williams (ed.), *The Diary of Hugh Gaitskell, 1945–56* (1983), 338–9.

51 *Ibid.*, 339.

52 Anthony Crosland, *The Future of Socialism* (1956), 199.

53 Robin Pedley, *The Comprehensive School* (1963), 181–2; Raymond Williams, *The Long Revolution* (1961), 153–4.

54 *Oxford English Dictionary Supplement.*

55 Michael Young, *The Rise of the Meritocracy, 1870–2033: An Essay on Education and Equality* (1958).

56 *Ibid.*, 46.

57 *Ibid.*, 13.

58 *Ibid.*, 15.

59 *Ibid.*, 21.

60 *Ibid.*, 41.

61 *Ibid.*, 46.
62 *Ibid.*, 46.
63 *Ibid.*, 57.
64 *Ibid.*, 159.
65 *Ibid.*, 103.
66 *Ibid.*, 12.
67 *Ibid.*, 190.
68 Brian Evans and Bernard Waites, *IQ and Mental Testing: An Unnatural Science and its Social History* (1981).
69 G.R. Searle, *Eugenics and Politics in Britain, 1900–1914* (Leyden, 1976); Donald McKenzie, 'Eugenics in Britain', *Social Studies of Science*, 6 (1976), 499–532; Michael Freeden, 'Eugenics and progressive thought', *Historical Journal*, 22 (1979), 645–71.
70 Lord James of Rusholme, *Education and Democratic Leadership* (1961), 8.
71 Anthony Sampson, *Anatomy of Britain* (1962), 190.
72 Ministerial meeting on secondary education, 23 February 1955 (Ministry of Education papers, Ed. 147.206).
73 Sir Edward Boyle to Robert Neild, 5 January 1960 (Boyle papers, 660/4585/1).
74 Lord Hailsham to Sir Edward Boyle, 12 September 1963 (Boyle papers, 660/5524).
75 Harry Rée, *The Essential Grammar School* (1956), 18.
76 *Ibid.*, 39.
77 House of Commons debates – Education (Comprehensive System or Grammar Schools), 21 January 1965, col. 413.
78 Robin Davis, *The Grammar School* (1967).
79 C.B. Cox and A.E. Dyson (eds.), *Fight for Education* (1969); C.B. Cox and A.E. Dyson (eds.), *The Crisis in Education* (1970).
80 Caroline Benn and Brian Simon (eds.), *Half-Way There* (1970), 65–6.
81 *TES*, 15 October 1976, 'What the PM said'.
82 Geoff Whitty, 'Social studies and political education in England since 1945', in Ivor Goodson (ed.), *Social Histories of the Secondary Curriculum: Subjects for Study* (1985), 270.
83 Margaret Cole, 'Education and social democracy', in Richard Crossman (ed.), *New Fabian Essays* (1953), 101.

6 THE TECHNOCRATS

1 Public Schools Commission, *Report* (Clarendon report, 1864), 32.
2 Martin J. Wiener, *English Culture and the Decline of the Industrial Spirit, 1850–1980* (Cambridge, 1981), 21.
3 Peter Gordon, Denis Lawton, *Curriculum Change in the Nineteenth and Twentieth Centuries* (1978), 3.
4 Committee to enquire into the position of natural science in the education system of Great Britain, *Report* (Thomson report, 1918), 11.
5 Lord Sydenham of Combe, *Education, Science and Leadership* (1918), 12.
6 Eric James and S.R. Humby, *Science and Education* (1942), 30, 39–40.
7 *Ibid.*, 42–3, 46.
8 *Ibid.*, 134.
9 *Nature*, 3 November 1951, leading article, 'Leadership, education and technology'.
10 Eric James, 'Science and citizenship', *School Science Review*, 130 (June 1955), 324–6.
11 *Times Educational Supplement*, 15 February 1952, leading article, 'Technocracy'.
12 *TES*, 30 May 1952, leading article, 'Industry's leaders'.
13 A.A. Part to R.A.R. Tricker, 22 July 1954 (Ministry of Education papers, ED. 147/211).

14   A.A. Part, note of interview with A.H. Wilson, 28 July 1954 (Ministry of Education papers, ED. 147/211).

15   Eric James to A.A. Part, 6 December 1954 (Ministry of Education papers, ED. 147/211).

16   A.A. Part to Eric James, 8 December 1954 (Ministry of Education papers, ED. 147/211).

17   J.F. Embling, note, 17 December 1954 (Ministry of Education papers, ED. 147/211).

18   A.A. Part, note of interview with A.H. Wilson, 13 January 1955 (Ministry of Education papers, ED. 147/211).

19   A.A. Part, interview with A.H. Wilson, 8 February 1955 (Ministry of Education papers, ED. 147/211).

20   A.A. Part to A.H. Wilson, 20 June 1955 (Ministry of Education papers, ED. 147/211).

21   A.H. Wilson to A.A. Part, 28 September 1955 (Ministry of Education papers, ED. 147/211).

22   Report on meeting on 'the Industrial Scheme for the Encouragement of Science Teaching in Schools', 27 September 1955, minute 2 (Ministry of Education papers, ED. 147/211).

23   Industrial Fund Executive Committee, *Report* (1957). See also *Nature* 20 July 1957, leading article, 'Science buildings for schools'.

24   FBI education committee, 5 January 1943 (FBI papers, MSS 200/F/3/T2/1/1).

25   FBI, memo to Fleming committee, January 1943 (FBI papers, MSS 200/F/3/T2/1/1).

26   FBI education committee, *Industry and Education* (May 1944) (FBI papers, MSS 200/F/3/T2/1/4).

27   Percy Dunsheath, introduction to G. Copeman, *Leaders of British Industry* (1955). See also Percy Dunsheath, *The Graduate in Industry* (1948).

28   FBI education committee, 26 June 1947, minute 3 (FBI papers, MSS 200/F/1/1/116).

29   G. Withers to J.D. Cairns (Head, Ayr Academy), 3 March 1955 (FBI papers, MSS 200/F/3/T1/327).

30   FBI, *Industry and the Public and Grammar Schools* (1955), 7, 9.

31   A.G. Grant, 'From school to industry, direct and through the university', *ibid.*, 25, 32.

32   FBI education committee, 6 December 1955 (FBI papers, MSS 200/F/1/1/116).

33   FBI, *Industry and the Public and Grammar Schools*, iv.

34   J.L. Kimber to Sir Norman Kipping, 14 November 1955 (FBI papers, MSS 200/F/3/T2/8/12).

35   Sir Norman Kipping to J.L. Kimber, 15 November 1955 (FBI papers, MSS 200/F/3/T2/8/12).

36   See H.D.P. Lee, *Sixth Form Studies* (NUT, 1962).

37   F.L. Allan, 'Grammar schools and the supply of technologists' (1956) (FBI papers, MSS 200/F/3/T2/1/17).

38   IAHM memo to Crowther committee, December 1957 (FBI papers, MSS 200/F/3/T2/1/7).

39   A.G. Grant to F.J.C. Perry, 16 April 1956 (FBI papers, MSS 200/F/3/T2/1/7).

40   Alexander Todd, 'The scientist – supply and demand', *School Science Review*, 135 (March 1957), 160–7.

41   Henry Boulind, letter in *New Scientist*, 20 June 1957.

42   Henry Boulind, circular on '4th panel', 20 January 1958 (SMA papers).

43   Henry Boulind, memorandum, March 1957; quoted in David Layton, *Interpreters of Science: A History of the Association for Science Education* (1984), 232.

44   Jacob Bronowski, 'Science for modern life', *Observer*, 7 and 14 October 1956.

45   Lord Hailsham, *Science and Politics* (1963), 39.

46   *Ibid.*, 40–1.

47   Sir Eric Ashby, *Technology and the Academics: An Essay on Universities and the Scientific Revolution* (1958), 31, 82.

48   Sir Eric Ashby to Sir Harold Hartley, 8 March 1963 (Hartley papers, Box 211).

49   John Dancy, 'Technology in a liberal education', *Advancement Of Science*, October 1965, 379, 382.

50   John Dancy, 'Technical studies in grammar schools', December 1965 (Willis Jackson papers, D9).

51 John Dancy, *The Public Schools and the Future* (1963), 96.

52 See Gary McCulloch et al., *Technological Revolution? The Politics of School Science and Technology in England and Wales since 1945* (1985).

53 Jean Meynaud, *Technocracy* (1968), 193.

54 Charles R. Day, *Education for the Industrial World: The Ecoles d'Arts et Metiers and the Rise of French Industrial Engineering* (1987), 11.

55 On the latter, see, e.g., Gary McCulloch, 'Views of the alternative road: the Crowther concept', in David Layton (ed.), *The Alternative Road: The Rehabilitation of the Practical* (Leeds, 1984), 57-73.

56 Brian Jackson and Dennis Marsden, 'Conclusion 1965', in their *Education and the Working Class* (1962; revised edn, 1966), 250.

57 Margaret Gowing, 'An old and intimate relationship', in Vernon Bogdanor (ed.), *Science and Politics* (Oxford, 1984), is an interesting discussion of this emerging reality.

58 B. Young to G. van Praagh, 9 June 1966 (Nuffield Foundation papers, EDU/52).

59 Eric Rogers, 'The aims of science teaching. Teaching science for understanding', paper delivered at Commonwealth Conference on the teaching of science in schools, December 1965 (Nuffield Foundation papers, EDU/53).

60 H.F. Boulind to Tony Becher, 19 February 1962 (Association for Science Education papers).

61 Tony Becher to H.F. Boulind, 21 February 1962 (Association for Science Education papers).

62 Tony Becher to Eric Rogers, 21 February 1972 (Nuffield Foundation papers, EDU/53).

63 Eric Rogers to Tony Becher, 16 February 1972 (Nuffield Foundation papers, EDU/53).

64 Maurice J. Savory, 'Science in society', in Charles P. McFadden (ed.), *World Trends in Science Education* (Nova Scotia, Canada, 1980), 179.

65 *TES*, 17 October 1986, report, 'Birth of the Tory urban blueprint'.

66 Cyril Taylor, 'Climbing towards a skilful revolution', *TES*, 22 January 1988; Robert Creighton (International Secretary, United World Colleges), letter to *TES*, 5 February 1988.

7   TRIBUNE

1   R.H. Tawney, *Equality* (1931; 4th edn, 1952), 74.

2   *Ibid.*, 111-12.

3   *Ibid.*, 134.

4   *Ibid.*, 157.

5   See also Ross Terrill, *R.H. Tawney and his Times: Socialism as Fellowship* (1973).

6   R.H. Tawney, *Education: The Task Before Us* (WEA educational pamphlet no. 6, 1943), 4-5.

7   R.H. Tawney, 'Introduction', to Barbara Drake, *Education for Democracy* (1941), 6-7.

8   Anthony Crosland, *The Future of Socialism* (1956), 258.

9   *Ibid.*, 276.

10 *Ibid.*, 263.

11 *Ibid.*, 267-8.

12 See especially Edward Boyle, Anthony Crosland, *The Politics of Education* (1971); Susan Crosland, *Anthony Crosland* (1982); John Vaizey, *In Breach of Promise: Five Men who Shaped a Generation* (1983), Ch. 5.

13 Richard Crossman, *Plato Today* (1937), 92.

14 *Ibid.*, 124.

15 *Ibid.*, 207.

16 Clive Griggs, *The Trades Union Congress and the Struggle for Education, 1868-1925* (1983); Rodney Barker, *Education and Politics, 1900-1951: A Study of the Labour Party* (Oxford, 1972). See also Roy Lowe (ed.), *Labour and Education: Some Early Twentieth Century Studies* (Leicester, 1981).

17 Barker, *Education and Politics*, 138.

18 Harold Silver (ed.), *Equal Opportunity in Education: A Reader in Social Class and Educational Opportunity* (1973), xii.

19 Hugh Thomas, *John Strachey* (1973), 16.

20 Hugh Dalton, diary, 29 December 1918, in Ben Pimlott (ed.), *The Political Diary of Hugh Dalton: 1918–40, 1945–60* (1986), 5.

21 A.F. Thompson, 'Winchester and the Labour Party: three "gentlemanly rebels"', in Roger Custance (ed.), *Winchester College: Sixth-Centenary Essays* (Oxford, 1982), 503.

22 Philip Williams, *Hugh Gaitskell: A Political Biography* (1979), 767.

23 Trevor Burridge, *Clement Attlee: A Political Biography* (1985), 15–16.

24 H.G. Wells, *A Modern Utopia* (1905), 121.

25 *Ibid.*, 172.

26 *Ibid.*, 266.

27 *Ibid.*, 279.

28 *Ibid.*, 277.

29 *Ibid.*, 278.

30 *Ibid.*, 279–80.

31 *Ibid.*, 311.

32 R. Major, review of H.G. Wells's *A Modern Utopia*, in *Independent Review*, October 1905; in Patrick Parrinder (ed.), *H.G. Wells: The Critical Heritage* (1972), 114.

33 David Low, *Low's Autobiography* (1956), 283.

34 See E.J.T. Brennan (ed.), *Education for National Efficiency: The Contribution of Sidney and Beatrice Webb* (1975); also A.V. Judges, 'The educational influence of the Webbs', *British Journal of Educational Studies*, 10 (1961–2), 33–48.

35 Sidney Webb to H.G. Wells, 8 December 1901; in Norman MacKenzie (ed.), *The Letters of Sidney and Beatrice Webb* (3 vols., Cambridge, 1978), vol. II, 144.

36 Beatrice Webb, diary, 28 February 1902; in Norman and Jeanne Mackenzie (eds.), *The Diary of Beatrice Webb* (3 vols., 1983), vol. II, 210.

37 See, e.g., Norman and Jeanne MacKenzie, *The Fabians* (New York, 1977).

38 A.M. McBriar, *Fabian Socialism and English Politics, 1884–1918* (1962), esp. Ch. 3.

39 Beatrice Webb to H.G. Wells, 1 November 1934; in MacKenzie (ed.), *The Letters of Sidney And Beatrice Webb*, vol. III, 404–5.

40 Edmund King, 'The concept of ideology in communist education', in Edmund J. King (ed.), *Communist Education* (1963), 13.

41 *Ibid.*, 16. See also Ronald F. Price, *Marx and Education in Russia and China* (1977), esp. Ch. 6.

42 Stuart Macintyre, *A Proletarian Science: Marxism in Britain, 1917–1933* (Cambridge, 1980), 90.

43 J.P.M. Millar, *The Labour College Movement* (1977), 26–7.

44 See also Jonathan Rée, *Proletarian Philosophers: Problems in Socialist Culture in Britain, 1900–1940* (Oxford, 1980), and Carl Levy (ed.), *Socialism and the Intelligentsia, 1800–1914* (1987), esp. Chs. 5, 6.

45 Harry Rée, *Educator Extraordinary: The Life and Achievement of Henry Morris, 1889–1961* (1973), 10.

46 *Ibid.*, 14.

47 *Ibid.* Appendix.

48 *Ibid.* See also Harry Rée (ed.), *The Henry Morris Collection* (Cambridge, 1984).

49 R.A. Butler, interview note, 12 May 1942 (Board of Education papers, ED. 136/599).

50 Crosland, *The Future of Socialism*, 199.

51 Robin Pedley, *The Comprehensive School* (1963), 181–2.

52 Raymond Williams, *The Long Revolution* (1961), 153–4.

53 C.P. Snow, *Recent Thoughts on the Two Cultures* (1962), 11.

54 Richard Crossman, 'Scientists in Whitehall: thoughts on the eve', *Encounter*, 23/1 (1964), 3–10. See also Philip Gummett, *Scientists in Whitehall* (Manchester, 1980).

55 Victor Gollancz, editorial, 'Thoughts after Munich', *Left News*, 31 (November 1938).

56 Victor Gollancz, Harold Laski and John Strachey, 'The LBC in war time', *Left News*, 41 (September 1939).

57 Victor Gollancz, *My Dear Timothy: An Autobiographical Letter to his Grandson* (1952), 108. See also Ruth Dudley Edwards, *Victor Gollancz* (1987).

58 Gollancz, *My Dear Timothy*, 387.

59 Victor Gollancz to A.J. Irvine, 9 June 1955 (Gollancz papers, MSS 157/3/LP/14). See also Victor Gollancz, *Our Threatened Values* (1946).

60 Victor Gollancz to L. Russell, 2 November 1962 (Gollancz papers, MSS 157/3/LI/CB/1/3).

61 Gollancz, *My Dear Timothy*, 32.

62 Victor Gollancz and David Somervell, *Political Education at a Public School* (1918), 5.

63 Victor Gollancz, *More for Timothy, Being the Second Instalment of an Autobiographical Letter to his Grandson* (1953), 22.

64 Gollancz and Somervell, *Political Education*, 7.

65 *Ibid.*, 27.

66 Gollancz, *More for Timothy*, 152.

67 *Ibid.*, 206.

68 *Ibid.*, 179.

69 Gollancz and Somervell, *Political Education*, 3.

70 *Ibid.*

71 *Ibid.*, 5.

72 *Ibid.*, 7.

73 *Ibid.*, 9–10.

74 Gollancz, *More for Timothy*, 155.

75 Gollancz and Somervell, *Political Education*, 9.

76 *Ibid.*, 82.

77 *Ibid.*, 13.

78 Victor Gollancz and David Somervell, *The School and the World* (1919), 70.

79 See, e.g. Ben Pimlott, *Labour and the Left in the 1930s* (Cambridge, 1977); and James Jupp, *The Radical Left in Britain, 1931–1941* (1982), esp. Ch. 10, 'A Communist-led Left'.

80 See Gary McCulloch, '"Teachers and missionaries": the Left Book Club as an educational agency', *History of Education*, 14/2 (1985), 137–53.

81 Victor Gollancz, 'Left Book Club – or League of Victory and Progress?', *Left News*, 53 (November 1940).

82 Victor Gollancz, editorial, 'The Club shows its mettle', *Left News*, 40 (August 1939).

83 Victor Gollancz, editorial, 'The Left Book Club and the crisis', *Left News*, 24 (April 1938).

84 Victor Gollancz, ' + 2,000', *Left News*, 57 (March 1941).

85 Victor Gollancz, editorial, 'The Left Book Club and the crisis', *Left News*, 24 (April 1938).

86 Victor Gollancz, editorial, 'The Club's duty in the future', *Left News*, 30 (October 1938).

87 Victor Gollancz, editorial, 'Professional citizens', *Left News*, 58 (April 1941).

88 Victor Gollancz, 'What type of society?', *Left News*, 42 (October 1939).

89 Victor Gollancz, 'Professional citizens', *Left News*, 58 (April 1941).

90 Victor Gollancz, 'Political education classes', *Left News*, 22 (February 1938).

91 'Left Book Club "associate members"', *Left News*, 16 (August 1937).

92 Victor Gollancz, editorial, 'The Club shows its mettle', *Left News*, 40 (August 1939).

93 See Gary McCulloch, 'Labour, the Left, and the General Election of 1945', *Journal Of British Studies* 24/4 (1985), 465–89. Also, e.g., Angus Calder, 'The Common Wealth Party, 1942–45' (University of Sussex DPhil thesis, 2 vols., 1968).

94 Ministerial meeting on secondary education, 23 February 1955 (Ministry of Education papers, ED. 147/206).

95 Richard Hoggart, *The Uses of Literacy* (1957), 239.

96 *Ibid.*, 244.
97 Brian Jackson and Dennis Marsden, *Education and the Working Class* (1962; revised edn, 1966), 219.
98 *Ibid.*, 153.
99 Alan Bullock, *The Life and Times of Ernest Bevin*, vol. I (1960), 531. See also Robert Dare, 'Instinct and organisation: intellectuals and British Labour after 1931', *Historical Journal*, 26/3 (1983), 677–97.
100 E.H. Carr, *The Twenty Years' Crisis, 1919–1939: An Introduction to the Study of International Relations* (1939), 23–4.
101 Clement Attlee to Victor Gollancz, 9 November 1937 (Strachey papers).
102 See David Marquand, *Ramsey MacDonald* (1977).
103 Robert Skidelsky, *Oswald Mosley* (1975), Ch. 8.
104 Clement Attlee, *The Labour Party in Perspective* (1937), 13.
105 *Ibid.*, 60.
106 Kingsley Martin, *Harold Laski* (1953), 162.
107 See Pimlott, *Labour And the Left in the 1930s*; and John Campbell, *Nye Bevan and the Mirage of British Socialism* (1987).
108 Campbell, *Nye Bevan*, 67–9.

8 OUR MODERN GUARDIANS

1 See, e.g., Christopher Stray, 'From monopoly to marginality: classics in English education since 1800', in Ivor Goodson (ed.), *Social Histories of the Secondary Curriculum: Subjects for Study* (1985), 19–51; F. Campbell, 'Latin and the elite tradition in education', in P.W. Musgrave (ed.), *Sociology, History and Education: A Reader* (1970), 249–64; Committee to inquire into the position of classics in the educational system of the United Kingdom, *Report* (1921).
2 T.C. Worsley, *The End of the 'Old School Tie'* (1941), 11.
3 Peter Parker, *The Old Lie: The Great War and the Public School Ethos* (1987).
4 Martin J. Wiener, *English Culture and the Decline of the Industrial Spirit, 1850–1980* (Cambridge, 1981); Correlli Barnett, *The Audit Of War: The Illusion and Reality of Britain as a Great Nation* (1986).
5 See W.D. Rubinstein, *Elites and the Wealthy in Modern British History: Essays in Social and Economic History* (1987).
6 Sir Richard Livingstone, 'The position and function of classical studies in English education' (1930), in his *The Rainbow Bridge, and Other Essays on Education* (1959), 70.
7 Sir Richard Livingstone, 'Plato and modern education' (1944), and 'Plato and the training of character' (1958), in *The Rainbow Bridge*.
8 Sir Richard Livingstone, 'Education for a world adrift' (1943), in his *On Education* (Cambridge, 1956), 228–9.
9 On the 'moral curriculum', see P.W. Musgrave, *The Moral Curriculum: A Sociological Analysis* (1978); on the history of school subjects, see Goodson (ed.), *Social Histories of the Secondary Curriculum*.
10 Brian Simon, *The Politics of Educational Reform, 1920–1940* (1974), 250. See also Brian Evans and Bernard Waites, *IQ and Mental Testing: An Unnatural Science and its Social History* (1981), esp. 93–4; and Gillian Sutherland, *Ability, Merit and Measurement: Mental Testing and English Education, 1880–1940* (Oxford, 1984), esp. 290.
11 Recent discussions of the ideology of girls' schooling include Joan Burstyn, *Victorian Education and the Ideal of Womanhood* (1980); Felicity Hunt (ed.), *Lessons for life: The Schooling of Girls and Women, 1850–1950* (Oxford, 1987); and *History of Education*, 17/1 (1988), special issue on women and schooling.
12 T.S. Eliot, *Notes towards the Definition of Culture* (1948), 47.

13 Geoffrey Bantock, '"Schooling in Decline"? The twentieth century', in his *Studies in the History of Educational Theory*, vol. II (1984), 309–45.

14 Ministerial meeting on secondary education, 23 February 1955 (Ministry of Education papers, ED. 147/206).

15 Margaret Cole, 'Education and social democracy', in R.H.S. Crossman (ed.), *New Fabian Essays* (1953), 103.

16 Michael Young, *The Rise of the Meritocracy, 1870–2033: An Essay on Education and Equality* (1958), 38.

17 See, e.g. W.A. Ward, *Victorian Oxford* (1965); Christopher Hollis, *The Oxford Union* (1965); Reba Soffer, 'Nation, duty, character and confidence: History at Oxford, 1850–1914', *Historical Journal*, 30/1 (1987), 77–104; Peter Slee, *Learning and a Liberal Education: The Study of Modern History in the Universities of Oxford, Cambridge and Manchester, 1800–1914* (Manchester, 1986).

18 Drusilla Scott, *A.D. Lindsay: a Biography* (Oxford, 1971), is helpful on these new initiatives.

19 On the 1930s, see, e.g., Martin Ceadel, 'The "king and country" debate, 1933; student politics, pacifism and the dictators', *Historical Journal*, 22/2 (1979), 397–422; and Brian Simon, 'The student movement in England and Wales during the 1930s', *History of Education*, 16/3 (1987), 189–203. The conflicts of the 1960s are discussed sympathetically in, e.g., Tessa Blackstone *et al.*, *Students in Conflict: LSE in 1967* (1970); and Edward P. Thompson (ed.), *Warwick University Ltd.* (1970).

20 Richard Symonds, *Oxford and Empire: The Last Lost Cause?* (1986), 10.

21 J.A. Mangan and James Walvin, 'Introduction', in J.A. Mangan and James Walvin (eds.), *Manliness and Morality: Middle-Class Masculinity in Britain and America, 1800–1940* (Manchester, 1987), 3.

22 J.A. Mangan, *The Games Ethic and Imperialism: Aspects of the Diffusion of an Ideal* (New York, 1986), 69.

23 See esp. Jean Barman, review of Mangan's *Games Ethic and Imperialism*, *History of Education*, 16/4 (1987), 314–16; and Gary McCulloch, 'Imperial and colonial designs: the case of Auckland Grammar School', *History of Education*, 17/4 (1988), 257–67.

24 Frank Aydelotte, *The Vision of Cecil Rhodes* (1946), 18. See also George R. Parkin, *The Rhodes Scholarships* (1913); and Lord Elton (ed.), *The First Fifty Years of the Rhodes Trust and the Rhodes Scholarships, 1903–1953* (Oxford, 1955).

25 Geoffrey Sherington, R.C. Petersen and Ian Brice, *Learning to Lead: A History of Girls' and Boys' Corporate Secondary Schools in Australia* (Sydney, 1987), is an interesting example of this kind of research, though focusing on the received image of the corporate schools themselves.

26 Rupert Wilkinson, *The Prefects: British Leadership and the Public School Tradition* (1964), 229.

27 Geoff Whitty, 'Social studies and political education in England since 1945', in Goodson (ed.), *Social Histories of the Secondary Curriculum*, 269–88.

28 David Hargreaves, *The Challenge for the Comprehensive School: Culture, Curriculum and Community* (1982), 87. See also Stephen Ball, *Beachside Comprehensive: A Case-Study of Secondary Schooling* (Cambridge, 1981).

29 Harold Laski, *The Danger of Being a Gentleman, and Other Essays* (1939), 30–1.

30 Richard Whitley, Alan Thomas and Jean Marceau, *Masters of Business: the Making of a New Elite?* (1981), 5.

31 Useful critiques of the 1988 Education Reform Act and of the new 'national curriculum' include Brian Simon, *Bending the Rules: The Baker 'Reform' of Education* (1988); Julian Haviland (ed.), *Take Care, Mr Baker!* (1988); and Denis Lawton and Clyde Chitty (eds.), *The National Curriculum* (1988).

32 Hargreaves, *Challenge for the Comprehensive School*, 162.

33 R.H. Tawney, *Education: The Task Before Us* (WEA educational pamphlet no. 6, 1943), 4–5.

BIBLIOGRAPHY

I. MANUSCRIPTS AND PRIVATE INFORMATION

Association for Science Education	University of Leeds Special Collections
Board of Education	Public Record Office, Kew
John Bosanko papers	private
Lord (Edward) Boyle	University of Leeds Special Collections
Lord (R.A.) Butler	Trinity College, Cambridge
G.D.H. Cole	Nuffield College, Oxford
Federation of British Industries	University of Warwick Modern Records Centre
Victor Gollancz	University of Warwick Modern Records Centre
Sir Harold Hartley	Churchill College, Cambridge
Lord (Willis) Jackson	Imperial College, London
Lord (Eric) James	interview with the author, 10 December 1987
Ministry of Education	Public Record Office, Kew
Sir Cyril Norwood	private
Nuffield Foundation	c/o Nuffield Foundation
Science Masters' Association	University of Leeds Special Collections
John Strachey	private

2. NEWSPAPERS AND MAGAZINES

Advancement of Science	*Nature*
Daily Mail	*New Scientist*
Daily Telegraph	*The Nineteenth Century and After*
The Fortnightly	*Observer*
Journal of Education	*The Spectator*
Left News	*Times*
The Modern Churchman	*Times Educational Supplement*
Morning Post	*Yorkshire Evening News*

3. BOOKS, REPORTS, THESES AND ARTICLES
(Place of publication of books is London unless otherwise stated.)

Addison, Paul, *The Road to 1945: British Politics in the Second World War* (1975)

Altick, Richard D., *The English Common Reader: A Short History of the Mass Reading Public, 1800–1900* (Chicago, 1957)

Armytage, W.H.G., *The Rise of the Technocrats: A Social History* (1965)

Arnold, Matthew, *Culture and Anarchy* (1869; ed. J. Dover Wilson, Cambridge, 1946)

Ashby, Sir Eric, *Technology and the Academics: An Essay on Universities and the Scientific Revolution* (1958)

Attlee, Clement, *The Labour Party in Perspective* (1937)

Aydelotte, Frank, *The Vision of Cecil Rhodes* (1946)

Ball, Stephen, *Beachside Comprehensive: A Case-Study of Secondary Schooling* (Cambridge, 1981)

(ed.), *Comprehensive Schooling: A Reader* (1984)

Bamford, T.W., *Rise of the Public Schools: A Study of Boys' Boarding Schools in England and Wales from 1837 to the Present Day* (1967)

Banks, Olive, *Parity and Prestige in English Secondary Education: A Study in Educational Sociology* (1955)

Bantock, Geoffrey, *Studies in the History of Educational Theory*, vol. I (1980); vol. II (1984)

Barker, Ernest, *Traditions of Civility: Eight Essays* (Cambridge, 1948)

Barker, Rodney, *Education and Politics, 1900–1951: A Study of the Labour Party* (Oxford, 1972)

Barman, Jean, review of J.A. Mangan's *Games Ethic and Imperialism*, *History of Education*, 16/4 (1987), 314–16

Barnett, Correlli, *The Audit of War: The Illusion and Reality of Britain as a Great Nation* (1986)

Benn, Caroline, and Brian Simon (eds.), *Half-Way There* (1970)

Bishop, T.J.H., with Rupert Wilkinson, *Winchester and the Public School Elite: A Statistical Analysis* (1967)

Blackstone, Tessa, *et al.*, *Students in Conflict: LSE in 1967* (1970)

Board of Education, *Secondary Education* (Spens report, 1938)

Curriculum and Examinations in Secondary Schools: Report of the Committee of the SSEC Appointed by the President of the Board of Education in 1941 (Norwood report, 1943)

The Public Schools and the General Educational System (Fleming report, 1944)

Bowen, James, *A History of Western Education*, vol. II (1975)

Boyd, David, *Elites and their Education* (Windsor, 1973)

Boyle, Edward, and Anthony Crosland, *The Politics of Education* (1971)

Brauer, George C., Jr, *The Education of a Gentleman: Theories of Gentlemanly Education in England, 1660–1775* (1959)

Brennan, E.J.T. (ed.), *Education for National Efficiency: The Contribution of Sidney and Beatrice Webb* (1975)

Bullock, Alan, *The Life and Times of Ernest Bevin* vol. I (1960)

The Burning Bow: T.F. Coade of Bryanston. A Selection of his Papers (1966)

Burridge, Trevor, *Clement Attlee: A Political Biography* (1985)

Burstyn, Joan, *Victorian Education and the Ideal of Womanhood* (1980)

Calder, Angus, 'The Common Wealth Party, 1942–45' (University of Sussex DPhil thesis, 2 vols., 1968)

Campbell, F., 'Latin and the elite tradition in education', in P.W. Musgrave (ed.),
    Sociology, History and Education: A Reader (1970), 249–64
Campbell, John, *Nye Bevan and the Mirage of British Socialism* (1987)
Cannon, John, *Aristocratic Century: The Peerage of Eighteenth Century England* (Cam-
    bridge, 1984)
Carr, E.H., *The Twenty Years' Crisis, 1919–1939: An Introduction to the Study of
    International Relations* (1939)
Caute, David, *The Fellow-Travellers: A Postscript to the Enlightenment* (1973)
Ceadel, Martin, 'The "king and country" debate, 1933: student politics, pacifism and the
    dictators', *Historical Journal*, 22/2 (1979), 379–422
Centre for Contemporary Cultural Studies, *Unpopular Education: Schooling and Social
    Democracy since 1944* (1981)
Chandos, John, *Boys Together: English Public Schools, 1800–1864* (1984)
Charmley, John, *Lord Lloyd and the Decline of the British Empire* (1987)
Coade, T.F. (ed.), *Harrow Lectures on Education* (Cambridge, 1931)
Cohen, William B., *Rulers of Empire: The French Colonial Service in Africa* (1971)
Cole, Margaret, 'Education and social democracy', in R.H.S. Crossman (ed.), *New
    Fabian Essays* (1953), 91–120
Colls, Robert, and Philip Dodd (eds.), *Englishness: Politics and Culture, 1880–1920* (1986)
Commager, Henry Steele, 'Leadership in eighteenth-century America and today',
    Daedalus, 90/4 (Fall 1961), 652–73
Committee to enquire into the position of natural science in the education system of
    Great Britain, *Report* (Thomson report, 1918)
Committee to inquire into the position of classics in the educational system of the United
    Kingdom, *Report* (1921)
Connell, W.F., *The Educational Thought and Influence of Matthew Arnold* (1950)
Cookson, Peter W., Jr, and Caroline Hodges Persell, *Preparing for Power: America's Elite
    Boarding Schools* (1985)
Copeman, G., *Leaders of British Industry* (1955)
Cox, C.B., and A.E. Dyson (eds.), *Fight for Education* (1969)
    The Crisis in Education (1970)
Crosland, Anthony, *The Future of Socialism* (1956)
Crosland, Susan, *Anthony Crosland* (1982)
Crossman, Richard, *Plato Today* (1937)
    'Scientists in Whitehall: thoughts on the eve', *Encounter*, 23/1 (1964), 3–10
    (ed.), *New Fabian Essays* (1953)
Daedalus, 90/4 (Fall 1961), 'Excellence and leadership in a democracy'
Dancy, John, *The Public Schools and the Future* (1963)
    'Technology in a liberal education', *Advancement of Science*, October 1965, 379–87
Dare, Robert, 'Instinct and organisation: intellectuals and British Labour after 1931',
    Historical Journal, 26/3 (1983), 677–97
Darwin, Bernard, *The English Public School* (1929)
Davis, Robin, *The Grammar School* (1967)
Day, Charles R., *Education for the Industrial World: The Ecoles d'Arts et Metiers and the Rise
    of French Industrial Engineering* (1987)
Dictionary of National Biography
Dilke, Christopher, *Dr Moberly's Mint-Mark: A Study of Winchester College* (1965)
Drake, Barbara, *Education for Democracy* (1941)

Dunsheath, Percy, *The Graduate in Industry* (1948)

Dyhouse, Carol, 'Social Darwinistic ideas and the development of women's education in England, 1880–1920', *History of Education*, 5/1 (1976), 41–58

Eaglesham, Eric, 'Planning the Education Bill of 1902', *British Journal of Educational Studies*, 9/1 (1960), 3–24

   'Implementing the Education Act of 1902', *British Journal of Educational Studies*, 10/2

   'The centenary of Sir Robert Morant', *British Journal of Educational Studies*, 12/1 (1963), 5–18

Edwards, Reese, *The Secondary Technical School* (1960)

Edwards, Ruth Dudley, *Victor Gollancz* (1987)

Eliot, T.S., *Notes towards the Definition of Culture* (1948)

Elton, Lord (ed.), *The First Fifty Years of the Rhodes Trust and the Rhodes Scholarships, 1903–1953* (Oxford, 1955)

Encyclopaedia Britannica, 13th edn. (1926)

Evans, Brian and Bernard Waites, *IQ and Mental Testing: An Unnatural Science and its Social History* (1981)

Federation of British Industries, *Industry and Education* (May 1944)

   Industry and the Public and Grammar Schools (1955)

Fenwick, Keith, *The Comprehensive School, 1944–1970: The Politics of Secondary School Reorganisation* (1976)

Freeden, Michael, 'Eugenics and progressive thought', *Historical Journal*, 22 (1979), 645–71

Garforth, F.W., *Educative Democracy: John Stuart Mill on Education in Society* (Oxford, 1980)

Gathorne-Hardy, Jonathan, *The Public School Phenomenon, 597–1977* (1977)

Giles, G.C.T., *The New School Tie* (1946)

Girouard, Mark, *The Return to Camelot: Chivalry and the English Gentleman* (1981)

Glaser, J.F., 'English Nonconformity and the decline of Liberalism', *American Historical Review*, 63/2 (1958), 352–63

Gollancz, Victor, *Our Threatened Values* (1946)

   My Dear Timothy: An Autobiographical Letter to his Grandson (1952)

   More for Timothy, Being the Second Instalment of an Autobiographical Letter to his Grandson (1953)

Gollancz, Victor, and David Somervell, *Political Education at a Public School* (1918)

   The School and the World (1919)

Goodson, Ivor (ed.), *Social Histories of the Secondary Curriculum: Subjects for Study* (1985)

Gordon, Peter, '"A unity of purpose": some reflections on the school curriculum, 1945–70', in W.E. Marsden (ed.), *Post-War Curriculum Development: An Historical Appraisal* (Leicester, 1979), 1–8

Gordon, Peter, and Denis Lawton, *Curriculum Change in The Nineteenth and Twentieth Centuries* (1978)

Gordon, Peter, and John White, *Philosophers as Educational Reformers: The Influence of Idealism on British Educational Thought and Practice* (1979)

Gowing, Margaret, 'An old and intimate relationship', in Vernon Bogdanor (ed.), *Science and Politics* (Oxford, 1984), 52–69

Griggs, Clive, *The Trades Union Congress and the Struggle for Education, 1868–1925* (1983)

   Private Education in Britain (1985)

Gummett, Philip, *Scientists in Whitehall* (Manchester, 1980)

Gurner, Ronald, *Day Schools of England* (1930)
  I Chose Teaching (1937)
Guttsman, W.L., *The British Political Elite* (1963)
Hailsham, Lord, *Science and Politics* (1963)
Happold, F.C., *Citizens in the Making* (1935)
  Towards a New Aristocracy: A Contribution to Educational Planning (1943)
Happold, F.C., et al., *Experiments in Practical Training for Citizenship* (1937)
Hargreaves, David, *The Challenge for the Comprehensive School: Culture, Curriculum and Community* (1982)
Harvie, Christopher, *The Lights of Liberalism: University Liberals and the Challenge of Democracy, 1860–86* (1976)
Haviland, Julian (ed.), *Take Care, Mr Baker!* (1988)
Hexter, J.H., 'The education of the aristocracy in the Renaissance', *Journal of Modern History*, 22/1 (1950), 1–20
Hill, C.P., *The History of Bristol Grammar School* (1951)
History of Education, 17/1 (1988), special issue on women and schooling
Hobsbawm, Eric, and Terence Ranger (eds.), *The Invention of Tradition* (Cambridge, 1983)
Hobson, J.A., *The Crisis of Liberalism: New Issues of Democracy* (1909; ed. Peter Clarke, Hassocks, 1974)
Hoggart, Richard, *The Uses of Literacy* (1957)
Hollis, Christopher, *The Oxford Union* (1965)
Honey, J.R. de S., *Tom Brown's Universe: The Development of the English Public School in the Nineteenth Century* (1977)
Hubback, Eva M., and E.D. Simon, *Education for Citizenship* (1934)
Hunt, Felicity (ed.), *Lessons for Life: The Schooling of Girls and Women, 1850–1950* (Oxford, 1987)
Incorporated Association of Head Masters, *The Threat to the Grammar Schools* (1946)
Industrial Fund Executive Committee, *Report* (1957)
Jackson, Brian and Dennis Marsden, *Education and the Working Class* (1962; revised edn. 1966)
James Eric (Lord James of Rusholme), *An Essay on the Content of Education* (1949)
  Education and Leadership (1951)
  'Science and citizenship', *School Science Review*, 130 (June 1955), 316–27
  Education and Democratic Leadership (1961)
James, Eric, and S.R. Humby, *Science and Education* (1942)
Jarausch, Konrad H. (ed.), *The Transformation of Higher Learning, 1860–1930* (Chicago, 1983)
Jeffereys, Kevin, 'R.A. Butler, the Board of Education and the 1944 Education Act', *History*, 227 (1984), 58–77
Jenkyns, Richard, *The Victorians and Ancient Greece* (Oxford, 1980)
Judge, Harry, *A Generation of Schooling: English Secondary Schools since 1944* (Oxford, 1984)
Judges, A.V., 'The educational influence of the Webbs', *British Journal of Educational Studies*, 10 (1961–2), 33–48
Jupp, James, *The Radical Left in Britain, 1931–1941* (1982)
King, Edmund J. (ed.), *Communist Education* (1963)

Kneller, George Frederick, *The Educational Philosophy of National Socialism* (New Haven, 1941)

Knights, Ben, *The Idea of the Clerisy in the Nineteenth Century* (Cambridge, 1978)

Koss, Stephen, *Nonconformity in Modern British Politics* (1975)

Laski, Harold, *The Danger of Being a Gentleman, and Other Essays* (1939)

Layton, David, *Interpreters of Science: A History of the Association for Science Education* (1984)

(ed.), *The Alternative Road: The Rehabilitation of the Practical* (Leeds, 1984)

Lawton, Denis, and Clyde Chitty (ed.), *The National Curriculum* (1988)

Lee, H.D.P., *Sixth Form Studies* (NUT, 1962)

Leeson, Rev Spencer, *The Public Schools Question, and Other Essays Connected with Secondary Education* (1948)

Leinster-Mackay, Donald, 'The evolution of t'other schools: an examination of the nineteenth century development of the private preparatory school', *History of Education*, 5/3 (1976), 241–9

The Rise of the English Prep School (1984)

Levy, Carl (ed.), *Socialism and the Intelligentsia, 1800–1914* (1987)

Livingstone, Sir Richard, *On Education* (Cambridge, 1956)

The Rainbow Bridge, and Other Essays on Education (1959)

Lloyd, Lord, *Leadership in Democracy* (1939)

Lodge, Paul, and Tessa Blackstone, *Educational Policy and Educational Inequality* (Oxford, 1982)

Lodge, R.C., *Plato's Theory of Education* (New York, 1947; reissued 1970)

Low, David, *Low's Autobiography* (1956)

Lowe, Roy (ed.), *Labour and Education: Some Early Twentieth Century Studies* (Leicester, 1981)

The Changing Primary School (1987)

Lowery, S., and M.L. de Fleur, *Milestones in Mass Communications Research: Media Effects* (1983)

McBriar, A.M., *Fabian Socialism and English Politics, 1884–1918* (1962)

McCulloch, Gary, 'The Politics of the Popular Front, 1935–1945' (University of Cambridge PhD thesis, 1981)

'Views of the alternative road: the Crowther concept', in David Layton (ed.), *The Alternative Road: The Rehabilitation of the Practical* (Leeds, 1984)

'Labour, the Left, and the General Election of 1945', *Journal of British Studies*, 24/4 (1985), 465–89

'Pioneers of an "Alternative Road"? The Association of Heads of Secondary Technical Schools, 1951–64', in Ivor Goodson (ed.), *Social Histories of the Secondary Curriculum: Subjects for Study* (1985), 319–47

'"Teachers and missionaries": the Left Book Club as an educational agency', *History of Education*, 14/2 (1985), 137–53

'Imperial and colonial designs: the case of Auckland Grammar School', *History of Education*, 17/4 (1988), 257–67

'The Norwood report and the secondary school curriculum', *History of Education Review*, 17/2 (1988), 30–45

'Education for leadership in the 1950s: the ideology of Eric James', *Journal of Educational Administration and History*, 21/1 (1989), 43–52

'A technocratic vision: the ideology of school science reform in the 1950s', *Social Studies of Science*, 18/4 (1988), 703–24

The Secondary Technical School: A Usable Past? (1989)

McCulloch, Gary, Edgar Jenkins and David Layton, *Technological revolution? The Politics of School Science and Technology in England and Wales since 1945* (1985)

MacIntyre, Stuart, *A Proletarian Science: Marxism in Britain, 1917–1933* (Cambridge, 1980)

Mack, Edward C., *Public Schools and British Opinion since 1860: The Relationship between Contemporary Ideas and the Evolution of an English Institution* (New York, 1941)

McKenzie, Donald, 'Eugenics in Britain', *Social Studies of Science*, 6 (1976), 499–532

MacKenzie, Norman (ed.), *The Letters of Sidney and Beatrice Webb* (3 vols., Cambridge, 1978)

MacKenzie, Norman and Jeanne, *The Fabians* (New York, 1977)

(eds.), *The Diary of Beatrice Webb* (3 vols., 1983)

Major, John M., *Sir Thomas Elyot and Renaissance Humanism* (Lincoln, Nebraska, 1964)

Mangan, J.A., *Athleticism in the Victorian and Edwardian Public School* (Cambridge, 1981)

'Imitating their betters and disassociating from their inferiors: grammar schools and the games ethic in the late nineteenth and early twentieth centuries', in Nicholas Parry and David McNair (eds.), *The Fitness of the Nation: Physical and Health Education in the Nineteenth and Twentieth Centuries* (Leicester, 1983), 1–45

The Games Ethic and Imperialism: Aspects of the Diffusion of an Ideal (New York, 1986)

Mangan, J.A., and James Walvin (eds.), *Manliness and Morality: Middle-Class Masculinity in Britain and America, 1800–1940* (Manchester, 1987)

Mann, Erika, *School for Barbarians: Education under the Nazis* (1939)

Marquand, David, *Ramsay MacDonald* (1977)

Marsden, W.E. (ed.), *Post-War Curriculum Development: An Historical Appraisal* (Leicester, 1979)

Martin, Kingsley, *Harold Laski* (1953)

Marwick, Arthur, 'Middle opinion in the thirties: planning, progress and political "agreement"', *English Historical Review*, 79/2 (1964), 285–98

Meynaud, Jean, *Technocracy* (1968)

Millar, J.P.M., *The Labour College Movement* (1977)

Minio-Paluello, L., *Education in Fascist Italy* (1946)

Moberly, Sir Walter, *Plato's Conception of Education and its Meaning for Today* (presidential address to Classical Association, 1944)

Musgrave, P.W., *The Moral Curriculum: A Sociological Analysis* (1978)

(ed.), *Sociology, History and Education: A Reader* (1970)

Musgrove, Frank, 'The Black Paper movement', in Roy Lowe (ed.), *The Changing Primary School* (1987), 106–28

Nettleship, R.L., *The Theory of Education in Plato's Republic* (Oxford edn, 1935)

Newsome, David, *Godliness and Good Learning: Four Studies of a Victorian Ideal* (1961)

Norman, E.R., *Church and Society in England, 1770–1970: A Historical Study* (Oxford, 1976)

Norwood, Cyril, *The English Tradition of Education* (1929)

Religion and Education (1932)

Scylla and Charybdis, or Laissez-Faire and Paternal Government (9th Shaftesbury lecture, 2 May 1932)

Norwood, Cyril, and Arthur H. Hope (eds.), *The Higher Education of Boys in England* (1909)

Ollard, Richard, *An English Education: A Perspective of Eton* (1982)

Oxford English Dictionary Supplement

Parker, Peter, *The Old Lie: The Great War and the Public School Ethos* (1987)

Parkin, George R., *The Rhodes Scholarships* (1913)

Parrinder, Patrick (ed.), *H.G. Wells: The Critical Heritage* (1972)

Pedley, Robin, *The Comprehensive School* (1963)

Perkin, Harold, 'The recruitment of elites in British society since 1800', *Journal of Social History*, 12/2 (1978), 222–34

Pimlott, Ben, *Labour and the Left in the 1930s* (Cambridge, 1977)

(ed.), *The Political Diary of Hugh Dalton: 1918–40, 1945–60* (1986)

Plato, *The Republic* (1976 edn, translated by A.D. Lindsay)

Popper, Karl, *The Open Society and its Enemies*, vol. 1 (1945)

Potter, Allen, 'The American governing class', in *British Journal of Sociology*, 13 (1962), 309–19

Price, Ronald F., *Marx and Education in Russia and China* (1977)

Public Schools Commission, *Report* (Clarendon report, 1864)

First Report (Newsom report, 1968)

Rée, Harry, *The Essential Grammar School* (1956)

Educator Extraordinary: The Life and Achievement of Henry Morris, 1889–1961 (1973)

(ed.), *The Henry Morris Collection* (Cambridge, 1984)

Rée, Jonathan, *Proletarian Philosophers: Problems in Socialist Culture in Britain, 1900–1940* (Oxford, 1980)

Reeder, David (ed.), *Educating our Masters* (Leicester, 1980)

Reid, William, and Jane Filby, *The Sixth: An Essay in Education and Democracy* (1982)

Ringer, Fritz, *The Decline of the German Mandarins: The German Academic Community, 1890–1933* (Cambridge, Mass., 1969)

Roach, John, *Public Examinations in England, 1850–1900* (Cambridge, 1971)

'Examinations and the secondary schools, 1900–1945', *History of Education*, 8/1 (1979), 45–58

A History of Secondary Education in England, 1800–1870 (1986)

Rothblatt, Sheldon, *The Revolution of the Dons: Cambridge and Society in Victorian England* (1968)

Rubinstein, W.D., 'Education and the social origins of British elites, 1880–1970', *Past and Present*, 112 (1986), 163–207

Elites and the Wealthy in Modern British History: Essays in Social and Economic History (1987)

Salter, Brian, and Ted Tapper, *Power and Policy in Education: The case of Independent Schooling* (1985)

Sampson, Anthony, *Anatomy of Britain* (1962)

The Changing Anatomy of Britain (1983)

Sanderson, Michael, *Educational Opportunity and Social Change in England* (1987)

Sareth, Edward N., 'Education of an elite', *History of Education Quarterly*, 28/3 (1988), 367–86

Savage, Gail, 'Social class and social policy: the civil service and secondary education in England during the interwar period', *Journal of Contemporary History*, 18 (1983), 261–80

Savory, Maurice J., 'Science in society', in Charles P. McFadden (ed.), *World Trends in Science Education* (Nova Scotia, Canada, 1980)

Scott, Drusilla, *A.D. Lindsay: A Biography* (Oxford, 1971)

Searle, G.R., *Eugenics and Politics in Britain, 1900–1914* (Leyden, 1976)

Sherington, Geoffrey, R.C. Petersen and Ian Brice, *Learning to Lead: A History of Girls' and Boys' Corporate Secondary Schools in Australia* (Sydney, 1987)

Silver, Harold, *Education as History: Interpreting Nineteenth- and Twentieth-Century Education* (1983)

(ed.), *Equal Opportunity in Education: A Reader in Social Class and Educational Opportunity* (1973)

Simon, Brian, *The Two Nations and the Educational Structure, 1780–1870* (1960)

The Politics of Educational Reform, 1920–1940 (1974)

'The 1944 Education Act: a Conservative measure?', in *History Of Education*, 15/1 (1986), 31–43

'The student movement in England and Wales during the 1930s', *History of Education*, 16/3 (1987), 189–203

Bending the Rules: The Baker 'Reform' of Education (1988)

Simon, Brian, and Ian Bradley (eds.), *The Victorian Public School: Studies in the Development of an Educational Institution* (1975)

Simon, Joan, *Education and Society in Tudor England* (Cambridge, 1966)

'Promoting educational reform on the home front: The TES and The Times, 1940–1944', *History of Education*, 18/3 (1989), 195–211

Skidelsky, Robert, *English Progressive Schools* (1969)

Oswald Mosley (1975)

Skinner, Quentin, *The Foundations of Modern Political Thought*, vol. 1 (Cambridge, 1978)

Slee, Peter, *Learning and a Liberal Education: The Study of Modern History in the Universities of Oxford, Cambridge and Manchester, 1800–1914* (Manchester, 1986)

Snow, C.P., *Recent Thoughts on the Two Cultures* (1962)

Soffer, Reba, 'Nation, duty, character and confidence: History at Oxford, 1850–1914', *Historical Journal*, 30/1 (1987), 77–104

Spring, Joel, *The American School, 1642–1985* (New York, 1986)

Stanworth, Philip, and Anthony Giddens (eds.), *Elites and Power in British Society* (Cambridge, 1974)

Stark, Gary D., *Entrepreneurs of Ideology: Neoconservative Publishers in Germany, 1890–1933* (Chapel Hill, North Carolina, 1981)

Stewart, W.A.C., *Progressives and Radicals in English Education, 1750–1970* (1972)

Stone, Lawrence, *The Crisis of the Aristocracy, 1558–1641* (1965)

(ed.), *Schooling and Society: Studies in the History of Education* (Princeton, 1976)

Stray, Christopher, 'From monopoly to marginality: classics in English education since 1800', in Ivor Goodson (ed.), *Social Histories of the Secondary Curriculum: Subjects for Study* (1985), 19–51

Sutherland, Gillian, *Ability, Merit and Measurement: Mental Testing and English Education, 1880–1940* (Oxford, 1984)

(ed.), *Arnold on Education* (1973)

Sydenham, Lord, of Combe, *Education, Science and Leadership* (1918)

Sylvester, D.W., *Robert Lowe and Education* (Cambridge, 1974)

Symonds, Richard, *Oxford and Empire: The Last Lost Cause?* (1986)

Talbott, John E., *The Politics of Educational Reform in France, 1918–1940* (1969)
Tawney, R.H., *Equality* (1931; 4th edn, 1952)
    Education: The Task Before Us (WEA educational pamphlet no. 6, 1943)
Taylor, William, *The Secondary Modern School* (1963)
Terrill, Ross, *R.H. Tawney and his Times: Socialism as Fellowship* (1973)
Thomas, Hugh, *John Strachey* (1973)
Thompson, A.F., 'Winchester and the Labour Party: three "gentlemanly rebels"', in Roger Custance (ed.), *Winchester College: Sixth-Centenary Essays* (Oxford, 1982), 489–503
Thompson, Edward P. (ed.), *Warwick University Ltd.* (1970)
Todd, Alexander, 'The scientist – supply and demand', *School Science Review*, 135 (March 1957), 160–7
Vaizey, John, *In Breach of Promise: Five Men who Shaped a Generation* (1983)
Vincent, W.A.L., *The Grammar Schools: Their Continuing Tradition, 1660–1714* (1969)
Walford, Geoffrey (ed.), *British Public Schools: Policy and Practice* (1984)
Wallace, R.G. 'The origins and authorship of the 1944 Education Act', *History of Education*, 10/4 (1981), 283–90
Ward, W.A., *Victorian Oxford* (1965)
Wells, H.G., *Anticipations of the Reaction of Mechanical and Scientific Progress upon Human Life and Thought* (1901)
    A Modern Utopia (1905)
Whitfield, George, 'The grammar school through half a century', *British Journal of Educational Studies*, 5/2 (1957), 101–18
Whitley, Richard, Alan Thomas and Jean Marceau, *Masters of Business: The Making of a New Elite?* (1981)
Whitty, Geoff, 'Social studies and political education in England since 1945', in Ivor Goodson (ed.), *Social Histories of the Secondary Curriculum: Subjects for Study* (1985), 269–88
Wiener, Martin J., *English Culture and the Decline of the Industrial Spirit, 1850–1980* (Cambridge, 1981)
Wilkinson, Rupert, 'Political leadership and the late Victorian public school', *British Journal of Sociology*, 13 (1962), 320–30
    The Prefects: British Leadership and the Public School Tradition (1964)
    (ed.), *Governing Elites: Studies in Training and Selection* (New York, 1969)
Williams, Philip, *Hugh Gaitskell: A Political Biography* (1979)
    (ed.), *The Diary of Hugh Gaitskell, 1945–56* (1983)
Williams, Raymond, *The Long Revolution* (1961)
Wilson, J. Dover (ed.), *The Schools of England: A Study in Renaissance* (1928)
Winter, James, *Robert Lowe* (Toronto, 1976)
Winter, Jay, *The Great War and the British People* (1986)
Wolff, Richard J., '"Fascistizing" Italian youth: the limits of Mussolini's education system', *History of Education*, 13/4 (1984), 287–98
Woolf, Leonard, *Barbarians at the Gate* (1939)
Worsley, T.C., *Barbarians and Philistines: Democracy and the Public Schools* (1940)
    The End of the 'Old School Tie' (1941)
    Flannelled Fool: A Slice of Life in the Thirties (1967)
Young, Michael, *The Rise of the Meritocracy, 1870–2033: An Essay on Education and Equality* (1958)

Young, M.F.D. (ed.), *Knowledge and Control: New Directions in the Sociology of Education* (1971)
Ziemer, Gregor, *Education for Death: The Making of the Nazi* (1941)
Zimmern, Alfred, *Learning and Leadership: A Study of the Needs and Possibilities of International Intellectual Cooperation* (1928)

INDEX

162

Watford Grammar School, 79
Weaver, Toby, 69
Webb, Beatrice, 103–5, 106
Webb, Sidney, 103–5, 106, 124
welfare state, 6
Wellington College, 24
Wells, H.G., viii, 102–3, 106, 122, 124
Westminster School, 14, 52
Whessoe Ltd, 88
White Paper on educational reconstruction
   (1943), 58, 63
White Paper *Technical Education* (1956), 89
Whitgift School, 52
Whitty, Geoff, 80
Wiener, Martin, 15, 82, 120
Wilkinson, Rupert, 1, 6, 15, 93, 125
Williams, G.G., 57
Williams, Philip, 101
Williams, Raymond, 5 75, 107
Williams, Shirley, 39

Wilson, A.H., 86
Wilson, Harold, 100, 108
Winchester College, 14, 15, 18, 70, 84, 89,
   101, 116, 117; Wykehamists, 39
Withers, G., 88
women, 11, 36, 46–7, 74, 77, 86, 114, 122–3
Wood, Sir Robert, 68, 70
Woolf, Leonard, 21
Workers' Educational Association, 36, 105,
   114
world war: First, 6, 16, 23, 24, 25, 31, 43–4,
   51, 52, 83, 106, 108, 109, 112, 120; second,
   6, 8, 15, 23–4, 27, 28–30, 32–40, 55–7, 81,
   83, 108, 120, 121
Worsley, T.C., 7, 28–30, 33, 40, 83, 120,
   128

Young, Michael, 7, 66, 75–8, 124, 129

Zimmern, Alfred, 21